About Your Guide

This comprehensive guide visits all the sites in this most fascinating area, from the Rhône to the Italian border, including the high ground of Haute Provence. In Arles and Nîmes are some of the finest Roman remains outside of Italy. Close by is the Camargue, its wildlife a link with the African coast just a few hours to the south, the way of life unique. East of Arles are hilltop wine villages, quiet and secluded, each with its own character and, frequently, with restaurants that make you regret the time it has taken to discover them.

Côte d'Azur, between Provence and Italy, shares the same clear light and enthusiasm for wine and food, and the same secret hilltop villages, but with a complete contrast. Beside the turquoise Mediterranean sit colourful and lively resorts. From the youthful zest of St Tropez to the opulence of Monaco and the more sedate charms of Menton, there is something for everyone.

As well as the beauty and tranquillity of Provence and the glitter of the holiday coast, there is also the world of the artist, Provence and Côte d'Azur having an enviable reputation in nineteenth- and twentieth-century art: Van Gogh at Arles, Picasso at Antibes, Matisse at Nice, and many more of the greatest 'modern' artists were drawn here by the landscape and the light.

This guide not only recommends leisurely outings to the area's most interesting sites, but also a more in-depth exploration. Detailed information listing opening times, addresses and telephone numbers of places of interest is supplemented by listings of hotels and restaurants. A Facts for Visitors section lists practical information and useful tips to help you plan your visit both before you go and when you are there.

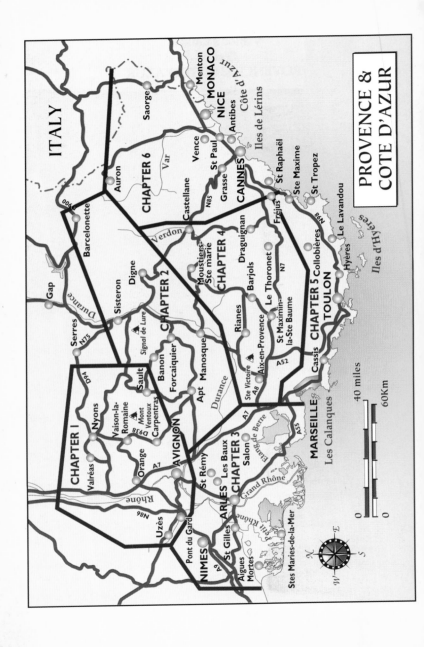

PROVENCE & COTE D'AZUR

ITALY

MONACO
NICE
Côte d'Azur

Menton
Saorge
Antibes
Iles de Lérins
Vence
St Paul

CHAPTER 6
Var
Grasse
Castellane
N85
CANNES
St Raphaël
Ste Maxime
St Tropez

Auron
Barcelonette
D900
Verdon
Moustiers-Ste marie
Draguignan
CHAPTER 4
Fréjus

Gap
Digne
Barjols
Le Thoronet
N7
Le Lavandou
N98
Hyères
Iles d'Hyères

Sisteron
Signal de Lure
Rianes
St Maximin-la-Ste Baume
CHAPTER 5
TOULON
Collobières

Serres
N75
Banon
Forcalquier
Apt
Manosque
Aix-en-Provence
Ste Victoire
A8
A52
Cassis
MARSEILLE
Les Calanques

CHAPTER 2
Signal de Lure
Durance

CHAPTER 1
Nyons
Vaison-la-Romaine
Mont Ventoux
Carpentras
Sault
D94
D938
A7
AVIGNON
A7
Salon
Etang de Berre
A55

Valréas
Orange
St Rémy
Les Baux
CHAPTER 3
Grand Rhône

Uzès
Rhône
N86
Pont du Gard
ARLES
St Gilles
Petit Rhône

NIMES
A9
Aigues Mortes
Stes Maries-de-la-Mer

40 miles
60Km
0
0

N
E
S
W

Visitor's Guide

FRANCE

PROVENCE

& Côte d'Azur

Richard Sale

Contents

Symbols Used In Margins And On Maps

𝗇 **Archaeological Site**

🏰 **Castle/Fortification**

🏛 **Museum/Art Gallery**

⛪ **Church**

🦇 **Caves**

🏛 **Building of Interest**

🌼 **Flora and Fauna**

✳ **Other Place of Interest**

🐃 **Zoo**

⛵ **Watersports/Boat Trips**

⚓ **Beach**

🏞 **Beautiful View/Natural Phenomenon**

Topography

☐ **Ground Level**

River/Lake

Town/Village

City

━━━ **Motorway**

━━━ **Main Road**

━━━ **Secondary Road**

━━━ **Minor Road**

How To Use Your Guide

Your Travel Guide has been designed in an easy to use format. Each chapter covers a region or itinerary in a natural progression which gives you all the background information to help you enjoy your visit. Distinctive margin symbols, the important places printed in bold type and a comprehensive index enables you to find the most interesting places to visit with ease.

At the end of each chapter, an **Additional Information** section gives you specific details such as addresses and opening times, making your guide a complete sightseeing companion.

The **Facts for Visitors** at the end of this guide lists practical information, including a comprehensive accommodation and eating out section, and useful tips to help you before you go and during your stay.

Introduction

For some people, the South of France is the whole French Mediterranean coast from the Italian to Spanish frontiers. For most, it is the southeast corner of France which encompasses Provence and the Côte d'Azur, two names with enticing associations. Provence suggests vines, olives and herbs, sun-filled open landscapes and a profusion of antique monuments. The Côte d'Azur is synonymous with luxury set in semi-tropical splendour. These stereotyped ideas are a little inaccurate but they are not entirely misleading since both areas share the Mediterranean's warmth and its brilliant light, so popular with artists.

The political map of France shows that Provence and the Côte d'Azur are made up of five *départements*. Each of these equates, very roughly, with a British county, although the head of a *département*, the *préfet*, is a powerful political figure, appointed by central government and responsible to the Minister of the Interior. The five *départements* are; in the north, Vaucluse (taking in the east bank of the Rhône), and, further east, the Alpes-de-Haute-Provence. South of these two are Bouches-du-Rhone, Var and Alpes-Maritimes, all of which border the sea.

To these is added here the southern strip of a sixth *département*, Drôme, that piece which totally surrounds a lopped-off bit of Vaucluse. Southern Drôme is part of the old

---

Previous page: Beaches, such as at Cassis, are very popular in summer

province of Dauphiné, but it is essentially Provençal. There are the same terracotta curled roof tiles — which are like skeins of unravelled orange and yellow wool; the same heavy-shadowed, arcaded streets in clustered villages. Grignan, St Paul-Trois-Châteaux, Buis-les-Baronnies and Montbrun-les-Bains think of themselves as *La Dauphiné Provençal*. The major town, conscious of its importance for tourists, proudly calls itself Nyons-la-Niçoise to emphasise — as do its olive groves — its climatic identity with the French Riviera.

Part of a seventh *département* must also be included. Just across the River Rhône is Gard whose Roman monuments link it to Provence. Finally, just to be sure that nothing the visitor is tempted by is excluded, there is an itinerary into the Ardèche Gorge, to good to be missed out just because a politically drawn line excludes it. It is, after all, normal for the French to include the Ardèche in Provence.

GEOGRAPHY

From the Rhône, which forms a natural frontier with neighbouring Languedoc, the distance to the Italian frontier is no more than 240km (150 miles) at the most. From Serre-Poncon in the north of Alpes-de-Haute-Provence to the islands south of Hyères, the southernmost islets off the Var mainland, is a distance of 160km (100 miles). It is not a vast territory, and is fully encompassed by Michelin 1:200,000 (1cm to 2km) No 245 which is more than adequate for most touring purposes, or by Michelins Nos 84 and 81, with just a small part of Nos 80 and 83, at the next larger scale.

Countless writers and artists have commented on how some part of Provence reminds them of one particular country or another. Katherine Mansfield was reminded of her native New Zealand by the mountains behind Menton. Vincent van Gogh saw in La Crau round Arles a replica of his Dutch home. The centenarian explorer, Alexandra David-Neel, living in the arid hills of Digne, felt she was almost in the Tibet she had got to know so well, Roy Campbell, the flamboyant rancher-poet, saw the Natal of his youth recreated in the Camargue.

The drawing of such comparisons is a form of flattery, but they also show how much Provence is a landscape of many distinct characters. They can safely be termed, in French, *pays*. The word is hard to translate; 'country' or 'district' cannot convey the intimacy and rooted possessiveness implicit in its French meaning. Stemming from the Latin *pagus*, it rightly carries a flavour of Provence's human antiquity. The diversity of these *pays* throw into relief innumerable contrasts within Provence, making it an endlessly rich region to explore.

As with all lands, the geography of Provence is dependent upon the underlying geology and, in geological terms, the region is as varied as any other of comparable size. There

are lush river valleys, though, as shall be seen, Provence is more usually associated with a less fertile vegetation. There are alluvial plains to the sides of the major rivers, especially the River Rhône, and there is that most dramatic of landscapes, the Camargue, a land where the normal boundary between land and sea has been blurred. In the Camargue, the visitor is never absolutely sure where the sea starts or stops, though gradual desalination of the salty lagoons is making the distinction a little easier with time. Hopefully though, the Camargue will be a curious in-between world for many years to come, a fascinating landscape made more so by the African nature of some of its wildlife.

Elsewhere in Provence, the meeting of water and land has allowed the limestone rock beneath the surface to be eaten away to form caves, the bigger and more accessible of these being among the best show caves in Europe. The rivers have also cut deeply into the limestone to form gorges, none more famous — and rightly so — than the Verdon Gorge which cuts its way through the limestone plateau of the Haute Provence.

It is interesting to note the contrast between the two great rivers of Provence. The broad Rhône is a fast-flowing frontier river, industrialised and impersonal, while its tributary, the Durance, once a seasonally destructive torrent but now tamed by dams, is still the true artery of Provence, as it coils snake-like and sluggishly past gravel islets along a broad valley.

West of the Verdon Gorge there are mountains, a complicated range where the Pyrennean and Alpine folds meet, and here is the 1,909m (6,260ft) Mont Ventoux, the highest peak in Provence, one that has featured prominently in the history of the annual Tour de France cycle race. How totally different are the green shadows and the cool, pyramidal hump of chalk-dusted Mont Ventoux, 'the giant of Provence', from the buckled, seemingly molten, ridges of Montagne Ste Victoire further south. To the east and north of the Verdon are other mountain ranges; the beautiful Provençal ranges of Maures and Esterel, together with the mountain wall of the pre-Alps that separates this area from real Alpine France.

In Vaucluse, the yellow soil suffuses the buildings of whole villages while around Aix the intense iron-oxide soil glows a vivid crimson-brown, especially after rain. Even the olive trees of one district hardly look to be the same species as those in another. In the Rhône Valley they are mostly pruned low and round, but behind Menton they are left to grow to a full and majestic height.

Those who think only of a monotonous coastline when they think of the South of France must also be prepared for surprises, for, in its coastal scenery, the area offers almost as many contrasts as it does inland. East from the Camargue there are the Calanques, stretching out eastwards from Marseille, tight, beautiful bays with sculpted limestone cliffs. East again there are well-sheltered harbours near Toulon and, by way of contrast, the extraordinary feature of the Presqu'ile de Giens (*Presqu'ile* means nearly island). Occasionally, flamingoes can be viewed here against a background of the French Navy.

Next comes the Maures Coast, where those mountains meet the sea, and the wide bays around Antibes before the Riviera coast begins. There, with roads running along platforms cut out of the rock of the Alps, the sea really does live up to its name, the turquoise sea of the Côte d'Azur. The name was coined in the late nineteenth century by Stephen Liégard in a poem that, like its author, has not stood the test of time. Only that most descriptive phrase for the coast is now remembered.

ANIMAL & PLANT LIFE

The rich variety of scenery produces a diversity of habitats which makes the whole country fascinating to naturalists. They now come to Provence in much the same way as medieval monks used to travel here to gather herbs and samples. Europe's richest concentration of avifauna is in the Camargue which has had enough exposure on television to be well-known by most visitors. Millions of birds migrate across Provence, though they rarely catch the casual eye. Dawn choruses are uncommon; it is a question of adjusting to different seasonal sound-cycles. Instead of waking to the songs of garden and woodland birds, sleep is

Top: wild flowers in the Mercantour National Park.
Butterflies of Provence: Amanda's Blue (centre left), Chequered Skipper (centre right), Provence Chalk-Hill Blue (lower left); Marbled White (lower right)

broken by choirs of nightingales. Early spring is tree-frog belching time, high summer is when the cicada's sizzling song splits the hot daylight hours, while in late spring and autumn, both days and nights are filled with the melodies of crickets.

Zoologists can study beavers, boars, tortoises, lizards, snakes — fortunately there are no adders below 1,000m (3,300ft) — and batracians. For botanists, hundreds of unfamiliar species and plant communities await identification. There is even an arctic flora clinging to the upper slopes of Mont Ventoux, despite the Mediterranean at its feet. The more serious horticulturist will want to make his own arrangements to visit some of the private and public gardens on the Côte d'Azur where exotic trees and plants from all the continents have been acclimatised.

As readers of J. H. Fabre will know, Provence is fascinating for entomolgists, but please refrain from collecting. Butterflies and moths appear in profusion but the survival of some species is precarious, and observation of habits must be considered pleasure enough. Large and showy insects attract the attention of every visitor; there are praying mantises, carpenter bees, locusts, scarab and capricorn beetles, as well as emperor moths, swallowtail and apollo butterflies, and the silent tracer-lights of fireflies.

ART & ARCHITECTURE

Nature is one magnet, the art and architecture of man through the different epochs of his time in Provence is another. The creative vision of the artist and the celebrated monuments to the stonemason's craft are achievements which draw admirers from great distances. There are prehistoric relics, a plethora of Roman monuments — which are among the finest the Roman world has to offer — medieval churches, Renaissance mansions, art museums which emphasise the long obsession of many artists with Provence, and the striking new coastal architecture. Off the beaten track, there are half-forgotten ruins, wayside shrines and Romanesque chapels. To stumble across them is the wanderer's delight, clearly remembered when better-known images have receded.

CLIMATE

It is tempting, with such a small area, to believe that it must be just a continuation of the France that you have crossed to reach it. Yet, however often it is repeated, an entry into Provence seems to be different. It is not because some administrative boundary has been crossed which identifies it, but because the physical features become different. A climatic frontier is crossed; the vegetation changes, and so does the quality of light. It is true that some man-made things change too, but Nature gives the chief clue as to why Provence, for all its undoubted Frenchness, is nonetheless a land apart. In place of soft, springy turf there is coarse hummocky grass, there are shrubs still, but now there are tall succulents and palms, and the deciduous trees give way to evergreen. At first sight, the conifers are a surprise, but here their needle leaves are a protection against the heat, not the cold.

Provence obeys the rhythms of the Mediterranean climate. Seasons follow in abrupt succession. Sudden autumn rains end the panting heat of summer and there are few autumn tints to please the eye, except among the vines and highland fruit trees and along river banks where poplars grow. Winters are mild, particularly along the sheltered parts of the coast.

Spring produces the year's most sustained rainfall. Dormant plant life explodes into growth, flowers and seeds before the rising heat of summer introduces a punishing drought which can last for three months. For the tourist these are the picture-postcard days when the scent of resin and herbs fills the air. Yet summer is when local life is threatened by dehydration.

The naturalist might say that Provence begins where anthills cease, but this is not to be taken too literally. It illustrates that in the north nature harvests warmth and drains off excess moisture — which is what anthills do — while in the south living things ward off the heat and aridity by searching for moisture in hidden crevices, on cooler, shaded north-facing slopes and underground where the little water that exists is stored.

Large areas of Provence lack water, though irrigation schemes have made much unproductive land fertile. Plants and animals which are not adapted to aridity do not survive. Even the non-naturalist can see how vegetation is dominated by dwarfed trees, as though to reach skyward would be injurious. There are conifers everywhere, their needles keeping summer respiration and subsequent water loss to a minimum. A gentle, sage-green colour paints the landscape all the year: there are holm and cork oaks; Aleppo, maritime and the aptly named umbrella pines; almonds and cypresses, and that quintessential symbol of the Mediterranean, the olive.

Where the forests have been thinned, a *maquis* — sandy scrub — undergrowth of tree-heather, strawberry tree, juniper, myrtle, broom, cistus, butcher's broom, mastic and turpentine trees, forms a nearly impenetrable mass of rough and prickly shrubs.

In wide clearings — and for thousands of years man has ruthlessly cut down forests for his many needs — rocks protrude, like ribs poking out of the carcass of the land. This is the *garrigue*, described by the writer Posidonius in the second century BC, who wrote, 'The country is wild and arid. The soil is so stony that you cannot plant anything without striking a rock.' In the thin soil of such clearings, grow the aromatic culinary herbs and low spiny shrubs such as kermes oak, gorse and ling. Here too, are the countless bulbs and tubers which flower so briefly yet profusely in the spring, then die back in the first parching weeks of sum-

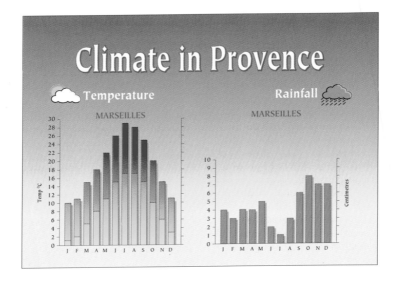

Climate in Provence

Temperature

MARSEILLES

Temp °C

Rainfall

MARSEILLES

Centimetres

mer to leave a tawny desert.

The feature that is common to these strange but attractive patterns of vegetation is that they have adapted so that they can retain moisture. The variety of ways which have been adopted to do this or, at least, to slow down the loss of moisture to the air is remarkable. Trees have thick and roughened bark. Leaves are usually small: sometimes they are reduced to mere thorns; sometimes they are curled inwards; they may be thick, leathery or shiny; or their undersides are covered with a down of pale hairs; and many exude protective oils. The long, scimitar-shaped leaves of the eucalyptus turn so as to keep only the narrow edges of their blades facing the sun. As with the eucalyptus, so with the grasshop-

pers. In cooler climates they tilt their flanks into the sun's rays like basking blackbirds. In Provence they face the sun head-on to ensure a minimum of exposure.

The climate is sometimes intemperate, and never more so than when the master-wind, the *mistral*, hurls itself down the funnel of the Rhône Valley and imposes its will on western Provence. It is most violent in late winter and early spring when low atmospheric pressures over the Mediterranean Sea suck down air currents from the snow-covered Massif Central. A chill, insistent wind blows for a few days, a non-stop wind that can drop temperatures by 10°C (18°F).

To gauge the effect of that wind on the inhabitants of Provence, look at how the old farmhouses (or *mas*) were constructed to withstand it. They are squat and massive, the north side often blank, with windows that are covered with hefty shutters — these also serving to keep out the summer's heat — and heavy roofs weighted with rocks. These defences are good, but do not entirely succeed in making the interior cosy; the *mistral* whistles through every cranny. Notice too, that farmers plant row upon row of stately cypresses or bamboo as windbreaks for the tender crops.

The winter *mistral* can be freezing and maddening — 'enough to pull the tail off a donkey' according to the people of Avignon and Marseille, who receive the fiercest lashings. However, the purity of light it brings draws distant hills, almost invisible at other times, into startling detail. From the Rhône delta, the wind fans east. The hills of Maures and Esterel break its power, and the Maritime Alps exhaust it to impotence. This fact, coupled with the heat-storing and radiating qualities of the rocks of the Côte d'Azur, explains why Cannes, Nice, Monaco and Menton became pre-eminent as winter resorts.

The *mistral* can blow in summer too; in 1989 it blew hard for several days, fanning fires that had started all too easily among the parched, tinder-dry forests of the coastal belt. When the smoke eventually cleared, there were still pockets of fire among the blackened stumps that had been forests, and the smell of wood smoke hung over the area for days. However, that is exceptional, and should not be allowed to deter the visitor.

This weather pattern occurs because Provence, to put it rather dramatically, is the most northerly perimeter of the Sahara Desert. Without the Mediterranean, that almost tideless and strongly salted inland sea, Provence would be literally Saharan. The summer that the visitor treasures is created by the hot air of tropical Sahara expanding northwards. As it does so, it reduces from its norm of six months without rain in Algeria to three months in Provence. This tropical air and the more polar air from the Alps have their 'dogfights' and that is what produces the occasional, but violent, downpours of summer. Sometimes, hot gusts from Africa, the *sirocco*, carry clouds of sand-particles, and the whole landscape is turned to an intense yellow or purple according to how the sun's rays are refracted. In winter, the Saharan air retreats and cold continental air presses into Provence, its effect being reduced by the warmth of the sea.

HISTORY

There are traces of men having lived in the area for millennia. This is no great surprise as the land bridge from Europe to Africa, over what is now the Straits of Gibraltar, survived until relatively recent times. However, the first impact that man had on the landscape was in Neolithic, New Stone Age, times, with the building of long barrow burial mounds. Skeletons have been unearthed which precede these mounds — some dated to 30,000BC, uncovered in the coastal Rochers Rouges outside Menton, were adorned with shell and fishbone necklaces and bracelets indicating a hunting, fishing, gathering culture. However, the burial mounds are the first tangible reminder to the layman.

In its original form, the barrow was a series of upright stones supporting a capstone and so forming a chamber. The dead would be laid within the chamber and then the whole structure would be earthed over to form a mound. Sometimes the mound still exists but usually it has eroded away to leave the stones of the chambers, gaunt and enigmatic. These curious objects attracted myth and legend: they have been considered the work of supermen or magicians. In Britain such chambers are normally called cromlechs, though the word dolmen is also used, and it is this latter word that is used in France. One such dolmen, and a superb one, is the Fairy's Stone, close to the town of Draguignan. It is not the only example, as sites exist all over Provence, though cave-paintings, which occur frequently in western France, are conspicuous by their absence. The terrain of southern Provence was too rough and the climate too warm to support the great mammals — bison, mammoth, woolly elephant, reindeer — which were hunted and immortalised in paint by the earlier (Upper Palaeolithic) cave-artists in Dordogne. Ibex, red deer and rabbits

were the staple meats of Provence, hardly heroic subjects to inspire masterpieces in cave-sanctuaries.

Quite suddenly, hunting gave way to a pastoral life, an event that coincides with the first domestication of wild animals in western Europe, which took place in south-west Provence. This precocious Neolithic revolution started a pastoral tradition which has been at the root of Provençal culture ever since, though industrialism has tried here, as elsewhere, to supplant it. Within the last twenty years, the tradition was still expressed by the *transhumance*, a slow, ritualised, month's trek on foot by thousands of sheep and their escorts. They left the lowland pastures as late spring began to shrivel the grass, wound their way to the lower Alps and returned as the first snows fell in October. Changes in the law then put an end to the tradition and the flocks were carried by train. Now the few animals that are still moved are moved by lorry.

On the stony plateaux around Bonnieux and Gordes there are beehive huts known as *bories* which, though mostly of relatively recent construction, are examples of how the earliest farmers built the first free-standing stone buildings. They were the work of the early semi-nomadic shepherds, perhaps driven to the plateau by other farmers who had settled on the richer, lower ground.

In the Vallée des Merveilles above Tende, there are tens of thousands of rock carvings, the earliest of which are thought to be evidence of Bronze

Age shepherds who came each summer to these inhospitable highland valleys. All these early semi-nomadic shepherds, along with traders in skins and salt, trod out the first recognisable tracks which became the waymarks for Roman engineers who arrived later to construct their stone-slabbed highways.

Until the coming of the Romans, Provence north of the Durance was occupied by Celtic tribes, while south of it were the Ligurians. The earlier quotation from Posidonius, giving the historian's views on the country of the Ligurians, continues with his observations of the Ligurians themselves. 'Work is an ungrateful toil, and daily hardships are such that life is truly difficult for these people whose bodies, as a result, are skinny and shrivelled. It sometimes happens that a woman gives birth in the fields, covers the young one with leaves, and then returns to her work so that a day will not be lost.' An unforgiving landscape indeed, and one in which the compensation of superb light might have been lost on the toilers.

The Ligurians built the first *oppida*, defensive positions of drystone walls at vantage points. Their residual heaps of stones can still be found on some hilltops, the one at Chastelard-de-Lardiers in the Lure Mountains was also a major religious sanctuary. Examples of the strange, yet strangely beautiful, Celto-Ligurian art can be found in many of the area's museums.

Traders from the Eastern Mediterranean had been sailing along the Provençal coast from at least 1,000BC, but it was not until 600BC that Phoenician navigators founded a Greek colony on the site of Marseille, which they called *Massalia*. They traded with the natives, introduced the vine and the olive, founded trading posts to both the east and the west along the coast, and peacefully penetrated the Rhône Valley. The Greek foundations of *Massalia* have now been laid bare and other Greek buildings can be seen at the open-air site of *Glanum* outside St Rémy-de-Provence. Most astonishingly, the Greek defensive wall at St Blaise is still in mint condition.

As Marseille expanded, its commercial power clashed with the interests of the Carthaginians and the Etruscans, so it was natural for the town to side with the Romans when the Punic Wars broke out. The Celts allied themselves with Carthage and, well-bribed by Hannibal, gave him and his elephants passage along the Rhône and into the Alps for his attack on Rome in 218BC. When Rome acquired provinces in Spain, Marseille assisted by keeping open the land route through Provence and subscribing a fleet which hastened the Carthaginian defeat at sea.

In 181BC, Antibes and Nice, both outposts of Marseille, came under threat from pirates but Rome came to the rescue. As time went by, Marseille found itself relying more and more on Rome's military might, so by 125BC, when Rome had largely subjugated the lands between the Alps and the Pyrenees, Marseille became Roman. Garrisons were installed and a huge *Provincia Romana* was created, of which today's Provence is only a fragment.

At about this time the strategic highways were built, traces of which can still be seen. *Via Aurelia* was the main artery between Rome and Spain, following the Italian coast to Nice and Fréjus, then going inland through Le Luc, Aix, Salon and Nîmes, essentially the same route that the RN7 takes now. The demi-god Hercules was supposed to have walked this way on his return from the Garden of the Hesperides, and Monaco was named after him, *Portus Herculis Monoeci. Via Domitia* descended the mountains by way of Embrun, Sisteron and Apt to join *Via Aurelia*, while *Via Agrippa* led north from Arles to Avignon, Orange and St Paul-Tros-Châteaux. Numerous branch roads were then constructed to give an effective network of communications.

As southern France became Romanised, there were tribal disputes, revolts against bureaucracy, taxation and commercial exploitation, but Julius Caesar was to govern the region for seven years with skill and authority. With the decline in the power of Marseille — hastened by its mistaken support of Pompey in his struggle with Caesar — Arles gained supremacy.

Provence can be said to have prospered under Roman rule, particularly during the reign of Augustus when agriculture, stock-breeding and trade expanded. At this time, Arles became the granary of Rome. Goods were transported across the sea by the powerful guilds of boatmen (called *utriculariae* because they kept their cargoes afloat with inflated animal bladders) based in the Rhône Delta.

Natives could become Roman citizens, and Roman law was tolerant of alien religions as long as Rome's absolute authority was not questioned. Christians, who first appeared in Marseille in AD95, did not acknowledge this authority and suffered persecution until Christianity was made the official religion by Constantine the Great, early in the fourth century. He settled in Arles, which was by then the second city of the empire and known as 'the little Rome of the Gauls'. The Romans gave the whole of France south of the River Loire the Low Latin *Occitan* tongue of which Provençal is a derivative, a language used by all classes, and the medium in which the troubadours of the Middle Ages expressed their formalised lovesongs.

Attracted by the wealth of Arles, the Visigoths began the first of many sieges of the city and Marseille in AD413. They were unsuccessful, but they heralded the disintegration of the Western Roman Empire, a disintegration which lead to Provence coming under the rule of the Franks in AD536, though they left it as a semi-autonomous state.

When the Arabs crossed the Pyrenees they were not halted until Charles Martel defeated them at Poitiers in AD732. To stop them crossing the Rhône, he invaded Provence and the region called on the

Walking in the Maritime Alps

Arabs for help. After seven long and bloody years, Martel was victorious, returning a sacked and massacred Provence to the firm administration of the Frankish Empire. The eighth century was one of the most tragic in Provençal history. Saracen raids were continuous, not only from the sea but from their settlements near Hyères and St Tropez, until their final defeat in AD972.

Long periods of anarchical feuding, depopulation and pestilence ensured the economic and moral decline of Provence. However, early in the thirteenth century, the wise rule of Raymond Berenger V unified and modernised the country and gave it a sense of identity.

In 1246, a combination of intrigue and marriage gave Provence to Charles of Anjou who became Charles I of Provence and King of Sicily, an act of inheritance which the port of Marseille turned to great profit. This was the period of the great religious pilgrimages. St Louis set off on the Seventh Crusade from Aigues-Mortes in 1248, which saw the building of splendid Romanesque churches such as St Trophime at Arles and that at St Gilles, as well as many rural churches and chapels. The art of the troubadours flourished at the Courts of Love, of which Les Baux was one of the most famous.

In 1229, the territory of Comtat Venaissin — which approximated to present-day Vaucluse, though it excluded Avignon, Orange and some other bits of land — was bought for

80,000 florins by the Pope and so became detached from the rest of Provence. In the following century, the Popes acquired more territories, including Valreas, now a little enclave of Vaucluse surrounded by Drôme. These enclaves remained the possession of the Holy See until 1791. As a result of these purchases, this corner of Provence, hitherto unimportant in the wider affairs of Europe, held centre stage. In 1309, a French Pope, Clement V, fled Rome, settled at Avignon, and installed the Holy See in what was to become the massive fortified Palace of the Popes. Five Popes ruled from there until 1377 when the Papal Court returned to Rome. The Comtat Venaissin was then administered by papal legates for more than 400 years.

In this phase of pomp and power, Avignon attracted the political, financial, intellectual and artistic elite of Europe. While the rest of Provence suffered incursions from Gascons, Spaniards, English, and the freebooters of Du Guesclin — all part of the devastating effects of The Hundred Years' War — the presence of the Popes ensured a measure of protection to the papal territories.

In the fifteenth century, an economic and artistic upsurge came under the impetus of René d'Anjou, a poet and artist with neither political nor military gifts who is remembered as Good King René. After his death in 1480, Provence (excluding the Comtat Venaissin and Monaco) entered into formal union with the crown of France, royal power being exercised through the Parliament of Aix. Official transactions now had to be conducted in French, not Latin, to the resentment of many Provençaux who felt they were being deprived of their cultural heritage and identity by this centralisation. Resentment simmered until it found creative expression in the Provençal Renaissance of the nineteenth century under the leadership of the poet, Frédéric Mistral.

In the mid-sixteenth century, the Luberon Hills saw massacres and the total destruction of villages. The victims were the Vaudois, a fundamentalist heretical sect akin to the Albigensians in Languedoc who had been dealt with most cruelly early in the thirteeenth century. All Protestant settlements in Provence provoked equal hosility with the Catholics, the two sides becoming embroiled in the Wars of Religion between 1560 and 1598, even though the Edict of Nantes (revoked in 1685) was supposed to give freedom of worship and conscience. In fact, not until the Edict of Toleration in 1787 were Protestant minorities freed from the fear of persecution.

With the opening of the eighteenth century, it looked as though stability and prosperity would return. Instead of this, Provence found itself devastated by the worst of many visitations of the plague. In 1720, a ship from the Levant brought it to Marseille. The main towns were decimated; 90,000 people died in two years. The authorities of the papal estates put up a wall, 100km (62 miles) long, with frequent sentry boxes, in the hope of confining the plague to the Provençal side, and traces of the wall can still be found near Pouraque, south of Venasque. St Sebastian transfixed by arrows, a common pictorial theme in churches and chapels, symbolically represented the dreaded plague.

Yet prosperity came in the wake of distress. Merchants from Marseille and Aix built their handsome *hôtels* or town mansions, country seats, new churches and public buildings, and Aix became a centre of elegance and learning. Even the Seven Years' War (1756-63) had an unforeseen benevolent consequence. Nice and its *Comté* belonged to the Dukes of Savoy and the King of Sardinia, allies with Britain in maritime rivalry with France. British families lived in Nice and Tobias Smollett, learning of the delights of its climate, visited Nice for his health in 1763-5 and wrote his influential (and still very readable) *Travels*. Publication marked the beginning of the British association with the Côte d'Azur. A century later, Lord Brougham 'discovered' Cannes, while Dr Henry Bennet did the same for Menton.

A gradual convergence of social and economic unrest throughout the country precipitated the French Revolution in 1789. Factors included flagrant inequalities; selfish and absentee landlords; despotism; corruption; mal-administration and unfair taxation; high grain prices, particularly in Marseille and Toulon, as well as a grain failure after a cold winter. In 1788, the Parliament of Aix had protested against the privileges and perquisites enjoyed by the nobility and clergy. Passions were inflamed in Provence by Count Mirabeau, a powerful orator, through his *Address to the Provençal Nation*. Violence was widespread, the Parliament of Aix held its last meeting and with that ended the constitution of Provence.

In 1789, the National Assembly in Paris abolished the Aix Parliament by decree, the administration of the province being effected from then onwards by three newly created *départements* — Bouches-du-Rhône, Var and Basses-Alpes. Two years later, during which time there was virtual civil war in the region, the Comtat Venaissin was given up by the Popes and became the fourth *département*, Vaucluse. Nice and Monaco temporarily joined the new *département* of Alpes-Maritimes.

In 1792, a contingent of volunteers marched from Marseille to Paris in support of the revolutionary cause. At a farewell banquet in their honour, someone sang a revolutionary song, the battle song of the Army of the Rhine and actually composed by Rouget de Lisle, a young sapper officer, in Strasbourg. It was a hit with the 500 volunteers and they sang it frequently during their long march to Paris. By the time they had reached the capital, the song, a rousing one, had become a nationwide symbol of the new era. Today it is known as the *Marseillaise*.

Broadly speaking, the revolution was espoused by the urban working classes in Provence, who were known as 'The Reds'. Conservative rural communities tended to have monarchical sympathies and were called 'The Whites'. When the king was executed in 1793 there was widespread revulsion against the Revolution, and Toulon even opened its port to the young Republic's enemies, the Anglo-Spanish fleet. The Convention in Paris sent an army to recapture Avignon and Marseille where 'The Whites' briefly dominated. After weeks of siege, Toulon was also recaptured, with a young officer, one Captain Napoleon Bonaparte, distinguishing himself.

For all the great social and legal reforms introduced by Napoleon, his relations with Provence were not happy. Royalists felt affronted when he proclaimed himself Emperor and commercial interests suffered as a result of the Allied blockade his campaigns brought about. On the way to his Elban exile, the Provençaux threatened his life. When he landed at Golfe-Juan in 1815, at the start of the 'Hundred Days', the first part of his journey towards Paris along stony tracks — which approximate to the proudly named Route Napoleon (RN85) — was that of a fugitive, abused and cheated. It was not until he reached Gap that he heard his first cheers.

With the collapse of Napoleon's empire, royalists in Provence started a brief reign of 'White Terror' by assassinating Bonapartists in Marseille and Avignon. From these events, and for fifty years afterwards, Parisians convinced themselves that the Provençaux were brutal, reactionary fanatics. The restoration of the Bourbon monarchy in 1814 led to the July Revolution of 1830, and the next king from the House of Orleans gave birth to the greater upheaval of 1848. Neither regime sensed the mood of the people and the growing ideas of socialism. The next king, Napoleon III, nephew of Bonaparte, was popular for a while in most of France, but not in Provence.

Only after the ill-judged Franco-Prussian war of 1870-1, when a new republic was established, did the government reflect the long-held egalitarian and democratic traditions, and the new-found patriotism of Provence.

New industrial technologies — metallurgical and chemical among others — came to Provence. Bridges were thrown across the Rhône and the Durance; bauxite was first mined at Les Baux; railways, canal systems and marshland drainage were extended; and steam navigation favoured the growth of Marseilles. Agriculture, still the mainstay of Provençal life, suffered mixed fortunes. Wheat, sheep and olives remained static staples but the silkworm cottage industry was destroyed by disease. Vineyards were ruined by phylloxera and their slow recovery was largely due to Pasteur's discoveries; the madder dye industry was quickly supplanted by German chemicals. Rural depopulation gathered pace as youth was drawn to the coast and to industry, and the Basses-Alpes became one of the poorest *départements* of France.

World War I left the territory of Provence untouched but bled its

Walking in the Mercantour National Park

manhood and bequeathed stagna-
tion. World War II saw the Italians
occupy the Côte d'Azur and the
French fleet scuttling itself in Toulon.
After 1942, the Germans occupied
the whole of the Midi which was to
know deprivations, deportation, the
Maquis (resistance movement), Allied air attacks, destruction by the
retreating German divisions, airborne and seaborne landings, libera-
tion and recriminatory vendettas.

The Algerian War brought large
numbers of French refugees to Provence who have been absorbed into
the social, commercial and political
life of the province. A whole town,
Carnoux, was built for them. At different periods, influxes of Italians,
Spaniards and Algerians have supplied the unskilled and semi-skilled
labour on roads, building sites and
in vineyards.

Provence, whose existence as a
political reality was erased by the
Revolution, has been reborn officially, though its geography and political intentions are different. In
1956, the central government created a series of economic regions in
France. Provence was resurrected as
Provence-Côte d'Azur-Corse: the
five *départements* that this book covers, plus Corsica and Hautes-Alpes;
the latter thought to be an error of
judgement for traditionalists.

Great changes have been wrought
in thirty years. Now only a small

percentage of the population works on the land, but agricultural productivity has been vastly increased. Industry has tended to concentrate along the Rhône Valley. It includes petro-chemicals, electronics, hydro-electrics, iron, steel, aluminium, cement, nuclear fission for civil and military purposes, food production and tourism.

The tourist may not be interested in this face of Provence but it is a face of prosperity which has put the region in the forefront, and no longer the backwater, of European affairs.

ACCOMMODATION

Tourist hotels are classified officially by the government in star categories which range from four-star 'L' — the fabled 'palace' hotels of the Côte d'Azur, and the elegant and often beautiful 'Relais et Châteaux' — through three intermediate grades, to one-star, which is of moderate, but quite adequate, comfort. These are objective ratings based on facilities in relation to the number of bedrooms; they are not in themselves recommendations of quality.

The one- and two-star hotels are reasonable as to both price and comfort. They may not offer the chintzy, armchair comfort frequently expected of hotels in Britain, but traditionally the French have been less interested in comfort than the British, though things are changing. These one- and two-star hotels make up most of the largest hotel-chain, the *Federation Nationale des Logis et*

Auberges de France or *Logis de France* for short. This is a loose and fundamentally independent association of nearly 5,000 hotels. All of them undertake to provide a good standard of welcome, comfort, cleanliness and food at reasonable, inclusive prices. They are small and medium-sized (many have less than twelve bedrooms) family hotels in rural areas and small towns. *Auberges* are small and simpler than *logis* and so tend to be cheaper. It is worth remembering that in France there is no sacrifice of individuality as a result of belonging to a chain.

To give an impression of what an authentic Provençal hotel is like means piecing together a composite picture because they are all so very different. Perhaps the shell of the hotel is an eighteenth-century town house; grave and restrained to look at from the outside. The interior retains the old, high-ceilinged beams. The bedroom furniture is polished walnut with ornately moulded baroque panels. On the bed is a cover of strong yellow, green or red, dotted with contrasting motifs of such charm as to make you want to go out and buy one at once. With luck, the bed-linen will be rough, white and lavender-sweetened. Copper pots hang on the restaurant walls and each table has a blaze of welcoming colour from the tablecloth and is finished off with polished glasses. The floor is surfaced with hexagonal terracotta tiles, smelling of beeswax.

The annual handbook of these useful hotels is free to callers at the French Government Tourist Offices (see Useful Addresses in the Further Information of this book).

Many other more modest, non-tourist hotels exist in most towns and villages, as do furnished rooms and flats to let. Properly equipped country houses, villas, cottages and farms (or self-contained parts of them) can be rented as holiday homes (*gîtes rurales*). Well-equipped camp and caravan sites, sometimes in very lovely settings, can be found everywhere.

The months of July and August are the hot, high season when it is unwise not to have booked holiday accommodation in advance. Both earlier and later in the season, the hotels in popular centres, whether inland or by the sea, tend to be fully booked. This is particularly so in September when the stored warmth of late summer attracts many visitors.

FOOD & DRINK

Traditional Provençal food is distinctive, being based on olive oil, herbs and garlic. Garlic is milder in the south of France than it is to the north and, when properly cooked in Provençal dishes, tends to enhance the flavour of the dish rather than leaving an unpleasant smell or taste. Those who do not like garlic may have a little difficulty with the local fare in which 'the truffle of Provence', otherwise known as the 'Friend of Man' or the 'Divine Condiment', features prominently.

Restaurants, like hotels, run the whole gamut from the magnificent to the simple. Some of the most prestigious restaurants in the world can be found in this area. Gastronomes come from far and wide to l'Oustaù de Baumanière at Les Baux; to La Bonne Auberge at Antibes and Le Moulin de Mougins at Notre Dame-de-Vie, outside Mougins to name only those to whom experts have given the highest accolades. A meal at any of them is an experience, but it is best to go prepared neither to quibble nor blanch at the cost.

Most visitors, looking for a more modest yet still memorable experience, turn to the annual *Michelin Red Guide*'s recommendations of restaurants which provide 'good food at moderate prices'. Over the years many have found these reliable, though an even better source of information can be the place where one is staying. Fall into conversation with a French family familiar with the local area, and good advice as to where the food is choice and the price is right will usually be forthcoming.

Substantial and inexpensive meals are provided by *Les Relais Routiers*, which are mostly on main roads. Orginally, these catered for lorry-drivers, now passing motorists patronise them as well. However, do not expect opulence as well as nourishment; at some of these roadside cafés the surroundings are stark.

The menu which is displayed outside the door of your chosen restaurant will include a fixed-price tourist menu, usually a basic, inexpensive three-course meal. A second *table* d'hôte will have more choice. A third, a *menu gastronomique*, including regional specialities, will also be shown. All the dishes appear on an *à la carte* list. It is almost invariably cheaper to choose the *table d'hôte*.

Before leaving for France, it might be best to consult one of the excellent books that are now available in English on regional French cooking so as to be alert to local Provençal specialities, of which only some can be mentioned here.

Near the coast, fish and seafood dishes naturally take pride of place. It is a well-known saying of the region that while fish live in the sea they die in olive oil. The classic fish dish is *bouillabaisse*. Experts disagree as to its vital ingredients, but basically it is a stew of a variety of Mediterranean fish, garlic and saffron. It must be ordered the day before and should be consumed with gusto and ritual by a party of four or more. Like some other great Provençal dishes, it is not for the budget-or calorie-conscious traveller.

The second great dish is *bourride*. Again, it is a stew, made with grey mullet, sea-bass, whiting and other white fish, topped with *aïoli*, an unctuous mayonnaise of garlic and olive oil known as 'the butter of Provence' — though the great Mistral himself referred to the mix as 'insipid jam' ! *Aïoli* transorms plates of plain vegetables or hard-boiled eggs into a feast.

Every restaurant serves *soupe de poisson*. It can be something mediocre out of a tin or packet, but at its best it is a stock of various fish, pun-

gent and peppery, served with toasted cubes of bread, cheese and a rust-coloured sauce of garlic, hot peppers and saffron called *rouille*, which also means rust in French.

Brandade de morue is pounded, dried salt cod, made creamy with olive oil and milk; if it is on the menu at all it is likely to be on a Friday. Other sea fish which are seen on the slabs at market or in restaurants are John Dory (*daurade*), sea-bass (*loup de mer*) and red mullet (*rouget*).

Nice, on account of its long political association with Italy — which lasted until 1860 — has a distinctive, Italianate cuisine. Look out for *soupe au pistou*, a vegetable soup thickened with a *pommade* of pounded basil, garlic and olive oil. For a substantial picnic, buy a *pan bagnat*, French bread with olive oil, spread with chopped anchovies, tomatoes, onions and peppers. An alternative is *tourte aux blettes*, an open-crust pastry covered with leaves of *chard* (rather like spinach). Another alternative is the local vegetable flan called *tian*. It is also worth trying *anchoïade*, an open sandwich, eaten hot or cold, with anchovy paste and oil, garlic and vinegar. Two dishes with Niçois names are known everywhere: *pissaladière* (akin to the Italian pizza), and *salade niçoise*.

The Camargue supplies the cattle for *boeuf en daube*, stew in red wine with aromatic herbs, as well as for *boeuf gardianne*. Rice-growing (the area now produces most French rice) gives a local risotto dish, *riz de Carmargue*, made with mussels and other sea-foods. Eels are bred in vast

Produce from Provence: lavender (top left), olives (top right), sunflowers (lower left), garlic (lower right)

numbers in the Carmargue, a local dish has them stewed in wine and served with tomatoes and potatoes.

From the herb-covered hills comes succulent lamb, the small grey snails called *cantareu* in Provençal, rabbit, thrush and blackbird pâtés and, but no longer frequently, wild boar.

A splendid variety of early vegetables makes salads and *crudités* — raw vegetables which when attractively dressed and presented are a much-appreciated first course since the quantity of cooked vegetables with the main course is sometimes small. Tomatoes, cabbages, marrows, lettuce, dandelions, aubergines, pumpkin, artichokes, asparagus and pimentoes stuffed or combined in a variety of ways ought to avoid any complaints about repetitious meals.

The fresh fruits of Provence are famous. There are olives, figs, cherries, peaches, apricots, grapes and melons, as well as the ubiquitous golden and red delicious apples. Try the thirst-quenching *pastèque à la provençale* — chilled water-melon filled with either a fine red or *rosé* Provençal wine. Fritters made with flowers such as mimosa or marrow make agreeable sweet courses.

Cheese boards may be loaded with a variety of French cheeses, but those from Provence will be few, though the disc-shaped *Banon* goat cheese should be among them. Its flavour is delicate yet distinct, and no wonder, for it is first wrapped in the leaves of the herb savory, then dipped in *eau-de-vie* before receiving its final wrapping of vine or chestnut leaves and being tied with straw.

Allied to *Banon* is *poivre d'âne* or ass's pepper (*pebré d'assé* in Provençal), its peppery flavour is imparted by finely ground savory leaves on the outside. Look out too for the particularly strong ewe's milk cheese, *cachat*, usually only found in season, between May and November.

For the sweet tooth, the delicately almond-flavoured *calisson d'Aix* biscuits are a temptation, as are the crystallised fruits of Apt, Spanish chestnut purée and *marron glacé* from Collobrières. There are also candied flowers and figs from Grasse and Nice; caramel sweets called *berlingots* from Carpentras, with a more fragile flavour than our boiled sweets; and the famous nougat of Montélimar, whose ingredients are the high quality regional honey and almonds. Nougat is also made in smaller quantities at Draguignan, Sault and Sisteron.

Finally, there are the wines. For the most part, wines produced in the broad coastal belt of southern Provence have no great merit beyond, perhaps, their high alcohol content. These are the Côtes de Provence, Coteaux d'Aix and Coteaux du Var. Quantity rather than quality is the rule, but the reds go well enough with the robust meat dishes of Provence, and the whites and *rosés* adequately accompany fish.

Exceptions are the strong red and white wines of Bandol; the very dry Cassis white; Palette from near Aix produces red, white and *rosé*, of which the red from Château Simone is most highly regarded. Château Vignelaure, its neat vineyards curving up at a bend in the D561 between Rians and Jouques, produces a respectable red; Bellet, behind Nice, also makes red, white and *rosé* wines in small quantities — it is a chic drink.

More interesting wines are found further afield. Stray into Gard to taste Tavel, the best dry *rosé* of all, at Tavel itself. Its near neighbour, Lirac, also produces a distinguished rosé. Near Aigues-Mortes is the 'wine of the sands', Listel *gris-de-gris rosé*. Also in Gard — if one dare mention it in the same breath — some 16km (10 miles) southwest of Nîmes, is the Perrier factory. The famous mineral water rises as a spring from a subterranean lake and is bottled under pressure. The plant can be visited most weekdays of the year.

Cross to the north bank of the Durance and you are in Vaucluse, the southern part of Côtes du Rhône country. Châteauneuf-du-Pape is the only classic wine of Provence, of which a little white is also produced. Gigondas is a good red from the slopes a few kilometres north-west of Châteauneuf. When Côtes du Rhône labels are hyphenated with one of a dozen communes in Vaucluse, a bold, smooth wine is promised. Visan is a faintly sparkling *rosé* which gives a brief, champagne-like lift. Coteaux du Tricastin, Côtes du Luberon and Côtes du Ventoux have been exported for a number of years now, during which time their quality has improved.

A sparkling wine is made in Drôme by the *méthode champenoise*. This is Clairette de Die, which comes both *brut* and *demi-sec*. One of the lightest fortified sweet wines is Beaumes-de-Venise, drunk either as an aperitif or as a dessert, as is its close neighbour, Rasteau.

The most popular aperitif — the 'national drink' of Provence — is the aniseed-flavoured *pastis*, clear until water is added and tasting innocuous to begin with. Beware, the kick comes a little later. The shelf of most bars will display a bewildering variety of *pastis* bottles, and it takes constant practice for the taste-buds to distinguish them all. The indigenous variety is Ricard, a name associated all over Provence, not only with this drink but with Paul Ricard's leisure and sports centres as well. Recently, a non-alcoholic Ricard *pastis*, thick and sweet, has come on to the market. The other locally made aperitif is the quinine-based St Raphaël; the red is full and sweet, the white is drier and less fruity. Something of a rarity is a yellow, punget, herb-flavoured liqueur called Sénancole, originally developed to a secret formula — as these liqueurs always are — by the monks of the abbey of Sénanque, not far from the village of Gordes in Vaucluse.

Wine-tasting and the comparing of notes can be one of the delights of a Provençal holiday, but the truth has to be told — wine prices in restaurants are sometimes as high as they are back home. A local wine is not necessarily cheap for being local. Some restauranteurs still include a carafe of wine in the price of the meal. In the *Michelin Guide* this is indicated by the letters 'bc' (*boisson compris*) following the price of the meal. Others provide an acceptably priced carafe or jug (*pichet*) of *vin de table* or *vin du patron*.

Wine in groceries or supermarkets is still cheap, as it is at wine co-operatives, the *caves co-operatives* or *vinicoles*, which are dotted about the wine-growing districts. A small *bonbonne*, a glass demi-john encased in whicker, holds 10 litres, the more pratical *cubitaine*, the now familiar wine-box, is sold in various capacities from 10 litres to 33 litres. Wines which have been enjoyed on holiday can be bought in this way and stowed in the boot of the car. Even if customs duty has to be paid, the purchase is worthwhile, all the more so if the quality of the wine is good because the tax is always the same.

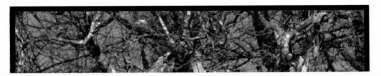

The Rhône Valley

The traditional highway from the north into Provence is the valley of the River Rhône. Until the railways came, the produce of the region was loaded on to great barges at Avignon and hauled by teams of horses to Lyon and beyond. Visitors came south by boats which had to shoot the twenty-five arches of the still-standing medieval bridge at Pont St Esprit. A swift current demanded considerable skill and sobriety of the pilot, as well as steady nerves of his passengers. Most people now travel in rather more haste, taking the Autoroute du Soleil (A7), a journey that calls for equally steady nerves. Those with rather more time to spare can follow either of the Rhône's banks, the west bank's N86 getting the motorist as rapidly into Provence as does the N7 on the east bank.

A more rural route climbs out of Vienne and follows the edge of the Dauphiné foothills through Romans-sur-Isère, Crest, Nyons, Carpentras and so to Cavaillon. As far as Nyons this is the D538.

Nyons is in Drôme, yet is good preparation for Provence proper. French families stay there in both summer and winter, as the rounded, shrub-dotted hills shelter the resort from the *mistral*. In summer, the cooling *pontias* breeze blows down the Aygues Valley, a river whose name is sometimes written as Eygues or Aigues — all of these variants mean water.

Arcaded streets on the northern side of the town lead to the Quartier des Forts, built in the Middle Ages. The beautiful, covered Rue de Grands Forts leads to an old gateway, once ❊ part of the town's protective castle, but it is best just to wander at will through the narrow streets. South-west of the church the River Eygues is crossed by Pont Roman, thirteenth ❊ century despite its name, with a single 40m (131ft) arch that many believe to the finest in Provence. When you leave, take the narrow road known as the Promenade des Anglais north-west out of Nyons to complete a circular trip that offers the best view of both the town and the valley. Those interested in the olive oil industry and the local cuisine, can pursue that interest in the town. Nyons is a local centre for oil-making and several of the oil mills in the town offer tours to visitors. One of the best of these is Moulin Autrand which ❊ stands on the northern bank of the Eygues close to Pont Roman. Here traditional methods of making oil are still employed, using eighteenth-century mills. To the west of the town there is also an excellent museum to the olive oil industry. 🎦

The richly fertile Plateau de Vaucluse, lying north of the valley of the River Coulon (taken by the N100 as it passes through Apt) was acquired by the Papacy during the Middle Ages, and as the Comtat Venaissin it was held by the Popes when they transferred the Papacy to Avignon. Later, the Avignon Popes bought land around Valréas and, intent on linking it with the Comtat, tried to buy the strip of land that separated the two. Alarmed by this erosion of his kingdom by a potentially hostile state the French king vetoed further sales, leaving Valréas and the land surrounding it as an 'island' of Papal land. This oddity still exists, the island now being an enclave of the *département* of Vaucluse entirely surrounded by the *département* of Drôme.

Valréas, the chief town of the Vauclusian enclave, stands on a hill, its circular boulevards overhung by plane trees. At the heart of the town is a sixteenth-century clock tower topping an eleventh century *donjon*, all that remains of Château Rupert. Nearby are the town church, Notre-Dame-de-Nazereth in eleventh century Provençal Romanesque style and the White Penitents' Chapel, five centuries older and beautifully decorated. To the south, the town hall occupies Château de Simione, an eighthenth-century mansion with painted ceilings and superb woodwork. The *château*, which is open to visitors, also houses a collection of the work of the Austrian artist Schorf who died in the town.

In the nineteenth century Ferdinand Revoul, a local businessman, began making cardboard boxes for a silkworm breeding friend. Recognising the potential of the new packaging, Revoul began to sell to jewellers and pharmacist. A small factory was set up and soon Valréas became a centre for cardboard box making and packaging. The town is still a centre for the industry, and its development is illustrated in a most unusual museum to the west of the town hall.

Grignan, 9km (5½ miles) to the north-west, is a place of literary pilgrimage for admirers of the Marquise de Sévigné, whose letters about seventeenth-century court life in Paris and the Provençal countryside are still read. The letters were written to her daughter who was married to the Count of Grignan, a man the Marquise described as being 'very ugly, but one of the most honest men in the kingdom'. It is debatable whether the Count viewed this as a compliment. The Marquise wrote her letters at the castle, which can be visited. It is an elegant, and beautifully decorated, Renaissance mansion that offers a superb view over Mont Ventoux. The Marquise loved it: it was, she wrote, 'fine and magnificent' and offered shelter from the mistral 'that bitter, freezing and cutting wind'.

The D538 south of Nyons enters Vaucluse at **Vaison-la-Romaine**. A hundred years ago, Baedeker did not mention the place, its fame arising only with the excavation of Roman Vasio in 1907. A patrician city, it was founded as a Roman town (there had been a Ligurian settlement) in the fifth century and retained its position until the Franks destroyed it 400 years later. The Roman town, excavated as the Quartier du Puymin, includes a fine villa, the House of Messii, which shows how well the senior officers of the Empire lived. Pompey's Portico is an elegant public promenade, while the Nyphaeum, the town's water-source fountain

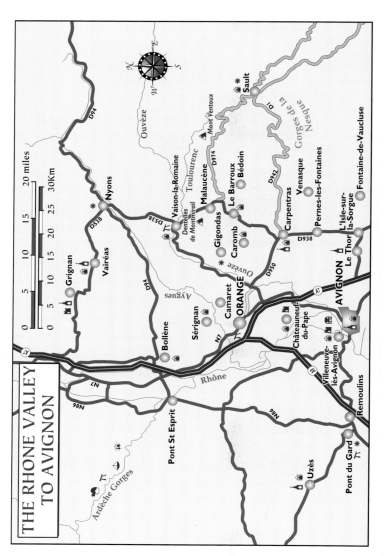

THE RHONE VALLEY TO AVIGNON

Sault

Fontaine-de-Vaucluse

Mont Ventoux

Gorges de la Nesque

Vaison-la-Romaine

Toulourenc

Le Barroux

Bédoin

Venasque

Pernes-les-Fontaines

Nyons

Dentelles de Montmirail

Malaucène

Carpentras

L'Isle-sur-la-Sorgue

Gigondas

Caromb

Le Thor

Grignan

Vairéas

Ouvèze

AVIGNON

Camaret

ORANGE

Châteauneuf-du-Pape

Sérignan

Villeneuve-lès-Avignon

Bollène

Remoulins

Rhône

Pont St Esprit

Uzès

Ardèche Gorges

Pont du Gard

Ouvèze

Aygues

20 miles

30Km

and the elegant theatre give a good impression of why the Romans are considered a civilised race. The site museum houses the best of the excavated finds. Sadly, in September 1992 the River Ouvèze, swollen by

The mountains of North Vaucluse

Mont Ventoux from Chalet-Reynard

high rainfall, burst its banks and flooded Vaison. Over thirty people were killed and the Roman remains were damaged, though restoration has limited the permanent damage.

Medieval and Roman Vaison are surrounded by the modern town on the right bank of the River Ouvèze. The one-time cathedral of Notre Dame de Nazareth, which was also damaged in the 1992 flood, dates from the twelfth and thirteenth centuries, and gives a good idea of the simple strength of Provençal Romanesque architecture. It stands on the site of a sixth-century church, parts of which are preserved in the structure of the later building. To reach the Upper Town, which has a maze of old streets and houses, occasional fountains and a seventeenth-century chapel, cross the single-span Roman bridge, miraculously undamaged by the flood, over the Ouvèze. At the heart of the old town is Place du Vieux-Marché with its delightful fountain. Here, on Sunday mornings in summer, a typical Provençal market is held. From the square, the tight, steep Rue des Fours leads up to the ruins of a twelfth-century castle of the Counts of Toulouse, the feudal owners of the town. Sadly, it is ruinous, and is not open to the public.

The prime excursion from Vaison is to the top of 'The Giant of Provence' — Mont Ventoux 1,909m (6,260ft). Be sure to choose a clear day because the summit of the mountain — rounded, smoothed and blasted white by the weather — often wears a thick halo of cloud. The direct route is by **Malaucène**, its main streets massively guarded by plane trees. Clement V, the first of the Avignon popes, had the church built early in the fourteenth century, and Malaucène (the name means 'bad sands', on which it had been built) was his summer residence. The church is on the site of one founded by Charlemagne and has an iron-plated door, a memory of the time it served as a stronghold during the Wars of Religion. The clock tower that reaches above the old town, topped by a delicate wrought iron bell-cage, served as a look-out during the same period. The D974 passes a delightful twelfth-century chapel — one of hundreds all over Provence — and then the source of the Grozeau Stream, harnessed by the Romans through a now vanished aqueduct.

It is 21km (13 miles) to the top of Ventoux, first through forest, then pasture and finally over bare, stony slopes. The descent passes Chalet-Reynard: beyond, go right, through St Estève to **Bédoin**, a large village of ochre-coloured houses and little squares. It is from here that time trials were started which aimed at discovering the abilities of the newly introduced motor cars by driving them up the hill. Just before World War I, the record stood at just under 18 minutes. Today it is closer to 9 minutes, an average speed of nearly 90mph. From Bédoin, a narrow, interesting, road leads to **Caromb**, with an equally interesting museum of old tools. The museum is one of the few in the area which is free.

A little to the west of Caromb, take the D13, is **Barroux**, a village dominated by a restored *château* in fine Renaissance style. From it there is an excellent view of both Mont Ventoux and the Dentelles de Mont-mirail, further to the west.

While the views from the top of Mont Ventoux are spectacular, there are even more satisfactory ways of savouring its majesty. From Vaison make for Entrechaux and turn right just before Mollans-sur-Ouvèze. An east-west road above the poplar-lined Toulourenc Valley now runs for about 20km (12½ miles) along the northern flank, allowing the travel-ler to keep Mont Ventoux in sight all the way. Steep slopes rise sheer to the top, buttressed by huge pyra-mids of grey limestone and yellow sandstone which seem to cement the whole mountain into place.

Turn up the hill to see the precari-ously balanced village of **Brantes** which commands an extended view of the bare, flat ridge of Ventoux. A very fine walk from the village crosses the Toulourenc Stream and climbs Ventoux, following the marked GR9 track all the way, but it is only for the fit and well-prepared. In June, the locals around Brantes gather lime blossoms which are dried and made into *tisane* herbal drinks.

Continue eastwards to reach Reilhanette. Beyond here a right turn reaches **Sault** whose belvedere looks on to the sunbaked, southern face of Ventoux. In July, great acres of lav-ender perfume the town. The town museum houses a small collection of prehistoric, Gallo-Roman and medi-eval finds.

From Sault it is 45km (28 miles) by the D942 to Carpentras. A consider-able length of the route is taken up by the gorges of the Nesque. From the first signposted belvedere, the trav-eller can see the Rocher du Cire (Rock of Wax) where generations of wild bees have nested, coating the rock with wax. Frédéric Mistral, in his epic poem *Calendau* wrote of the Rocher du Cire, and the lines are quoted on the stele at the viewpoint.

At the end of the deeply incised gorge, the landscape opens out on to the Plain of Comtat Venaissin. At Villes-sur-Auzon another excursion can be made up the Combe de l'Hermitage which rejoins the D942 near Sault, a narrow, winding but attractive route.

On the eastern outskirts of **Mazan**, there is a cemetery along whose re-taining walls are ranged sixty-two Gallo-Roman sarcophagi, taken from the Carpentras to Sault road-side. The sacophagi at Arles are more famous, but Mazan's can be inspected in tranquillity. Also in the Mazan cemetery is the half-buried chapel of Notre Dame de Pareloup (Our Lady Protectress against Wolves), first built in the twelfth century to exorcise demons in the guise of wolves which devoured buried corpses. At the time when the chapel was built, real wolves did prowl freely in these parts during cold win-ters. The history of the chapel, and other aspects of local history and folklore, are explored in a small mu-seum in the town.

Mont Ventoux

Travellers heading south have always looked for Ventoux, the peak traditionally marking the gateway to Provence. Geologically, the Ventoux ridge is the western extremity of the Alps and, at 1,909m (6,260ft), is the highest peak between the Alps and the Pyrenees. On clear days — ther best chance is at dawn or dusk — both Mont Blanc and the Pic du Canigou in the Roussillon Pyrenees are visible. But be sure to take a jacket, the peak usually living up to its name: in Provençal this is *Ventour*, the Windy One: a little below the summit on the road to Chalet Reynard, is the aptly named Col des Tempêtes. The wind has scoured the summit area of the peak, blasting the stones clean and white, but in protected hollows a few hardy plants take root, alpine poppy, trumpet bellflower and a form of saxifrage that also grows on Spitsbergen, an island only 1,000km (625 miles) from the North Pole.

At the summit are an observatory, radar station and TV mast, the little chapel of Ste Croix, often snow-filled in summer, a café and a souvenir shop. Occasionally stalls selling sweets, including nougat from Sault line the summit road. At such times the top would be unrecognisable to the poet Petrarch who, with his brother, and two servants made the first known ascent of the peak on 9 May 1336. Petrarch climbed from Malaucène and came to enjoy the view — the first Provençal tourist. He must have had a clear day as the panorama took his breath away.

A little below the summit, on the road to Chalet Reynard is a memorial to a much sadder event. The simple, dignified relief carving commemorates the death, in 1967, of Tom Simpson during a stage of the Tour de France. The official verdict on Simpson's death, one of very few in the world's greatest cycle race, blamed heat exhaustion and drugs: on the day the thermometer at Chalet Reynard, at the foot of the climb, is said to have reached 54°C (129˚F). The cyclists who today use Ventoux as a test-piece, frequently stop and, in a moving tribute, add a cap, a stone or other memento to the collection below the memorial.

Nearer to Carpentras, on the right, the traveller passes a handsome aqueduct with forty-eight arches. It is 729m (2,400ft) long and was built between 1720 and 1729 to supply the town's water. **Carpentras** is a lively town, ringed by boulevards, and lying in a fertile market-

Château le Barroux

Sault nougat for sale on the summit of Mont Vantoux

BONBONS ASSORTIS PATES de FRUITS
NOUGAT de SAULT

gardening plain. The town has always been important, having been the capital of the Memini, a local tribe of Gauls who traded with Greeks and Phoenicians travelling up river from Marseilles. Later, under the Popes of Avignon, it was the capital of Comtat Venaissin. Today, the town, sometimes called 'The Crucible of Mont Ventoux' for the way the mountain watches over it, is the local market centre.

Most of the interesting sights are in the narrow streets of the Old Town, close to the cathedral. Friday mornings are market days and there is a both a general market and a flea market. Between November and late March there is also a truffle market, for truffles are something of which Vaucluse is justly proud.

The only vestige of the ramparts put up by the Popes in Avignon in the fourteenth century is the Port d'Orange, a 27m (90ft) high fortified and restored tower near where Boulevard Leclerc and Boulevard du Nord meet. Outside the circling boulevard, an eye-catching building in Place Aristide Briand is the elegant eighteenth-century hospital, the Hôtel-Dieu, whose upper balustrades are surmounted by carved oriflammes. Inside is a graceful monumental stairway and a pharmacy, little changed since the eighteenth century, can be visited. Within it, local and Italian faïence-ware stands in cabinets decorated with paintings of monkey apothecaries.

The Gothic cathedral of St Siffrein is entered by the south door. The dedication is to the patron saint of Carpentras who appears in no orthodox hagiography but may have been a sixth-century monk, Siffred or Siegfried, who came to evangelise the area. The south door is the Jews' Door by which Jews, recently converted to Christianity, went to worship. Above the door is the *boule aux rats*, a globe carved with rats that has, to date, defied explanation. Is it a play on the town's name (*carpere ras* means nibbling rat) or a comment on a world over-run by sin?

Inside the cathedral are figures by the sculptor Jacques Bernus (1650-1728) from Mazan, the greatest Provençal sculptor after Pierre Puget. There are also paintings by two artists whose works hang in innumerable churches and museums in Provence; Nicolas Mignard (1606-68), Provençal by adoption, and Pierre Parrocel (1664-1739), one of a large family of Parrocel painters. The treasury has several superb medieval wooden statues and some excellent gold and silver plate from the eighteenth century.

Next to St Siffrein is the seventeenth-century Palais de Justice whose court rooms — which can be visited — are decorated with striking friezes. Tucked behind, is the Roman Municipal Arch, erected in the first century AD during the reign of the Emperor Nero. It marked the entrance to the Gallo-Roman town, originally called *Carpentoracte* and changed to *Forum Neronis*. Although not well preserved, its bas-reliefs of two prisoners are distinct; they commemorate the victories of Augustus in Germany and the east.

A little to the north-east and reached by Rue d'Inguimbert, is the oldest synagogue in France, although it has been much reconstructed. The first building was erected in 1367 when the Popes at Avignon were heavily dependent on Jewish financiers and gave Jews sanctuary in Comtat Venaissin after they had been expelled from France and the rest of Provence. Consequently, the town, like Cavaillon, had a flourishing Jewish ghetto. Baths for ritual purification, called in Provençal the *cabussadou* ('head first'), are in the basement. Ovens for baking unleavened bread can be seen. Carved woodwork, panelling, wrought ironwork, candlesticks and other liturgical objects impart an air of delicate elegance.

For the non-specialist, the Comtadin Museum in Boulevard Albin-Durand is enjoyable. Objects that were in daily use many years ago make it an agreeable bygones collection. Of particular interest are the bells used for the age-old sheep-drives, the *transhumance*, because Carpentras was the centre where generations of bell-makers from the Simon family worked. Bells of different shapes and tones for sheep, rams, goats, donkeys and horses were made to harmonise musically as in a carillon, for the sheep-drive was conducted in a recognised order of procedure, almost as a religious ritual. So great was the Simons' reputation, that no other bells but theirs were sold in the market stalls throughout Provence. Above the Comtadin Museum is the Duplessis

Museum of paintings by local artists. Within the same building is the Inguimbertine Library, named after the founder of the Hôtel-Dieu hospital, with about 250,000 volumes and 5,000 manuscripts, some very rare.

Nearby, to the west, is the Sobirats Museum, a delightful reconstruction of an eighteenth century town mansion, while to the north, housed in a building that was once a convent and then a chapel of the Grey Penitents, is the Musée Lapidaire with a collection of local archaeological finds.

The return to Vaison from Carpentras gives intriguing glimpses of the Dentelles de Montmirail which calls for a separate excursion. This is a small range of dramatic, naked rock towers, elegantly eroded into a lacework (hence the name) that is ideal for rock-climbing. They rise to a little over 730m (2,400ft) but look much higher, and are virtually encircled by the roads between Vaison, Malaucène, Beaumes-de-Venise, and Sablet.

Leave Vaison by the D938 and, just before Malaucène, turn right and follow a scenic road upwards past the Cirque de St Amand. There is a backward look along this view to Mont Ventoux's western end which, while not having the dramatic appeal of the view from the north, is a fine sight. The road now continues through Suzette, Lafare and the wine-village of Beaumes-de-Venise. A beautiful run at any time, this journey is particularly so in early summer when the evening sun slants behind the sharp, white Dentelles and sets the scented yellow masses of Spanish broom ablaze.

Beaumes-de-Venise, named after the local caves (*baume* in Provençal) has been producing Muscat wine since at least the fourteenth century when the Avignon Popes had a vineyard here. The addition of 'de-Venise' to the village's name recognises this early ownership. In July and August the village hosts a wine festival. The local vineyards all set up stalls, so that the visitor needs only a glass and a strong constituion to try all the Muscat vintages. Stalls selling local goats' cheese, foie gras and the famed Beaume melon and Muscat sorbets add variety.

From Beaumes the D81, and then the D7, turn into the road which runs on the west side of the Dentelles. On the right, a grass track leads to the rural chapel of Notre Dame d'Aubune whose tall, square belfry is ornamented with three fluted pilasters and carved decorations on each face, an unusual, much admired design. Some believe that the chapel dates from the twelfth century, but others believe that it is much older, perhaps dating from the ninth century. Either way, it is one of the most attractive buildings in this area of Provence.

Folk-legend has it that Charles Martel, having defeated the Saracens outside Poitiers in AD732, fought them again during their retreat in the vicinity of the Dentelles. The Tour Sarrazine (Saracens' Tower) is said to be a ruined, eighth-century signal tower. It lies up the valley from the hamlet of Montmirail, above the spring which once provided cura-tive waters for a long-forgotten spa. The Saracens' Cemetery stands on a little plateau just above Notre Dame d'Aubune, marked by the ruins of the chapel of St Hilaire that most agree dates from the seventh century. There may be no historical evidence for these names. It is just as likely that 'Saracen' refers to gypsies for, since the fifteenth century, the Provençaux, seeing a physical resemblance, have called gypsies *sarrasins*.

On the D23 is **Gigondas**, whose Grenache is second only to Châteauneuf-du-Pape as a red wine of quality. The road continues past another delightful rural chapel of St Come and St Damien whose external apse-roofs are covered with fish-tail tiles while the main roof is weighted with massive blocks to hold off the *mistral*. Higher still is Hôtel Les Florets, an Alpine Club centre for horse-riding, walking and rock-climbing.

After Sablet on its hillock, it is worth making a small detour uphill to **Séguret**, snuggling under a sheer wall of rock, for a stroll about its alleys, washhouse, old gateways and views over orchards and vines to the plain. To the west of Séguret, beyond the D977 and the Ouvèze river is **Rasteau**, one of the main villages of the *Côtes du Rhone* appellation. Here, at the Domaine de Beaurenard, the visitor can explore the tools and processes of viniculture and wine production.

To the south, the next town is Orange with its Roman monuments. But before we reach that town, we cross the A7, straying from our area

Farm carts near Rasteau

The Roman Theatre, Orange

for just a while, in order to visit the Ardèche Gorge. Though hardly Provençal, every visitor who comes as far as Orange should see it.

Though the whole of the Ardèche Valley is worth exploring, it is the lower section, between Pont St Esprit and Vallon-Pont-d'Arc, that holds the main interest. There the river has carved a narrow way through a limestone plateau, producing spectacular scenery and gouging out a number of excellent caves that have been opened up for the visitor. The best of these is the Orgnac Aven which lies out of the gorge on the limestone Plateau d'Orgnac. The cave is huge — the Upper Chamber itself is over 250m (820ft) long, 125m (410ft) wide and nearly 40m (130ft) high in places — and has a number of fascinating features. Both the Chaos Chamber and the Red Chamber certainly live up to their names. The site's prehistory museum displays the finds from excavations of the caves. Man lived here from Paleolithic (Old Stone Age) times until the early Iron Age, a period of some 300,000 years.

In the gorge itself, the best cave is that of St Madeleine. However, Marzal Aven, a little to the north of the main gorge, is better and includes a museum of underground exploration and a prehistoric zoo with all sorts of life-size (but plastic) dinosaurs.

Throughout the gorge there are fine viewpoints. Visitors will find their own, but everyone should follow the High Corniche in the central region of the gorge where there is a succession of excellent viewpoints. The alternative is to take a boat down the gorge, which gives the low level view. It is possible to borrow boats and canoes for the journey, but it is a long one, and not for the inexperienced. It is better to join an organised trip which will not only guarantee a dry journey, but will also return you to the start. Boat trips are available from Vallon-Pont-d'Arc and all along the riverside from the village to the famous Pont-d'Arc itself, an exquisite arch of white limstone framing the river.

Orange, from where Provence was left for a quick trip up the Ardèche, was the Celtic capital, *Arausio*. It was later colonised by veterans of the Roman Second Legion who built the theatre, the triumphal arch, temples, baths and other public buildings the Romans regarded as essential in their major cities. The present name dates from a much later period when the town was the property of the House of Orange. The Princes of Orange held it for 400 years until the French attacked and took it in 1689. Today it is more peaceful, even more so since the A7 *autoroute* has removed the bulk of the traffic that used to use the N7.

Before exploring, there is a good general view of the town, the Rhône and the nearby mountains, from the top of Colline St Eutrope by the Montée des Princes d'Orange-Nassau. At its foot is the Roman theatre whose circular tiers of seats., which could hold up to 10,000 people, were set into the hillside. The huge façade of red sandstone, 36m (120ft) high and 103m (340ft) long, was said by Louis XIV to be 'the finest wall in my kingdom'. In its heyday, this magnificent stage backdrop in three tiers was decorated with seventy-six columns, friezes, niches and statues. A great awning was held aloft by poles whose supports are still visible. The statues have all vanished except the one of Augustus, 3.5m (11½ft) tall, discovered in fragments and lovingly pieced together. Today the Emperor even has his baton. The statue was placed high in the central niche, a Gaul grovelling for mercy at the Emperor's feet; the Romans were always a little tactless in their reminders to the local populace as to who their overlords were.

Vandals, time and wind may have eroded the wall but the acoustics are still excellent. In Roman times the acoustics were aided by the use of hollow doors which acted as soundboxes for the actors' voices, by placing sounding boards beneath seats to act as loudspeakers, and by the careful design and construction of the amphitheatre and awning. These intricate details, the equally intricate ornamentation of the original wall and the sophisticated scene-shifting machinery are carefully explained if you take a guided tour. An international music festival is held in the theatre during the last two weeks of July.

In the municipal museum opposite the theatre are items which have been removed during excavations. Perhaps the most interesting one is a cadastral plan engraved in AD77. On a huge marble slab are recorded the configuration of the region, the boundaries of the properties of the Roman veterans and the Gaulish inhabitants (who had the poorest land). Names of owners, bondsmen, tax rates (6 per cent surcharge on arrears), show how efficient Roman bureaucracy was.

From the museum head north along the N7 to reach the triumphal arch. It stands now in the middle of a roundabout at the centre of the busy road, at the north-east end of Orange. It is a rather inconvenient site for today's visitor but it has to be remembered that the route now taken by the N7 was once followed by the Via Agrippa to Lyon. Military and naval (the latter is unusual for the Romans) motifs are carved in rich profusion over the whole edifice to make it one of the masterpieces of the Roman Empire. Carvings of naked and hairy Gauls are again in evidence, further powerful advertisements of Roman mastery.

As an antidote to all that Roman architecture, the visitor should see the ex-cathedral of Notre-Dame and the streets of old Orange. This large Romanesque church was built in the twelfth century, but needed considerable rebuilding after it was damaged in the Wars of Religion. Old Orange — take Rue Caristié northwards from the Roman Theatre — is a delight, little streets linking typically Provençal squares, each with a fountain and plane trees shading the pavement cafés.

From Orange, an essential excursion for naturalists is to the village of **Sérignan-du-Comtat**. Go 3km (1¾ miles) along the N7 past the Roman arch, turn right on to the D976 and cross the vine-filled plain. On the outskirts of Sérignan, on the right, is a high wall behind which the entomolgist Jean-Henri Fabre (1823-1915) lived and worked between 1879 and his death. The 'Homer of the Insects' is universally remembered by the translation of his important observations in the *Souvenirs Entomolgiques* which give a lucid insight into the complex lives of the insects of Vaucluse, in a style both intimate and elegant. Fellow-scientists tended to dismiss him because of his refusal to accept Darwin's theory of evolution by natural selection. However, the most recent views about the theory may yet go some way to rehabilitating Fabre, showing him to be not quite the arch-reactionary he was held to be in his lifetime.

Fabre's house and garden are now a museum run by the Natural History Museum in Paris. His laboratory, collections, primitive research equipment, and child's writing desk are all on view. Fabre is buried in the cemetery outside Sérignan, and his statue stands in the village square.

Going south-west, rather than north-east, from Orange, the visitor can see another of the area's splendid Roman remains, the **Pont du Gard**, claimed to be France's third most visited site after the Eiffel Tower and Versailles. The D976 leaves Orange and almost immediately goes above the A7 (Autoroute du Soleil) and runs more or less parallel to the other autoroute, La Languedocienne, which branches off at Orange. Keep right at Roquemaure and on through Remoulins, set among orchards, to the aqueduct, 38km (24 miles) from Orange.

Although the rule imposed by the Romans was imperious, stern and sometimes brutal, the sight of this great work goes some way towards accepting Rome as a civilising influence. Six lower arches span the wooded banks of the River Gardon. Above them are eleven wider, lighter arches by the side of which runs the roadway. Uppermost are thirty-five small arches, 275m (900ft) long, which 2,000 years ago carried the water-duct. The watercourse, which used both aquaducts and tunnels bored through hills, ran from the source of the Eure near Uzès to the Roman town of *Nemausus* (Nîmes) 50km (31 miles) away. It was so accurately engineered that a drop of 1mm per metre was maintained thoughout its length. Four hundred litres of water a day were channelled over the Pont du Gard for every inhabitant of *Nemausus*, more than is considered necessary today. For 400 years, the conduit was regularly maintained before it fell into neglect and lime deposits choked the water channel. In the nineteenth century, Napoleon III had the aqueduct restored.

Near the aqueduct there is a large car park from which marked paths wind their way upstream for the best views. The aqueduct can also be crossed on foot, but it needs a head for heights as there is no safety rail.

Vineyards & Wines

It is believed that the Phoenecians brought the first vines to Provence and the Greeks brought the Persian Shiraz (Syrah) grape to grow on the banks of the Rhône. Certainly wine production in the area has a long history and it was here that the naming and control system for French wines began. In 1923 the growers of the Châteauneuf-du-Pape area sought exclusive use of the village name. The legal case took years, but the result, in 1935, was the creation of the AOC (*Appellation d'Origine Contrôlée*) system, with only strictly defined areas being allowed to use a given name. Strangely, despite Provence being one of the major production areas it was granted an AOC only in 1977. The other major AOC is Côtes du Rhône (with Châteauneuf-du-Pape its heart and Côtes du Rhône Villages, as a small sub-district of the large appellation).

In the label says *cru* it is wine from a vintage year, if *grand cru* then it is a magnificent wine and the price will reflect it. Below AOC are other names to grade the quality of the wine: VDQS (*Vin de Qualité Supérieure*) is good, but not as good; Vin de Pays, will come from a guaranteed region and will be better than Vin Ordinare, the table wines.

Today's growers at Châteauneuf use up to thirteen species of grape and are unique in planting their vines well apart and filling the spaces between them with white Provençal limestone pebbles. These refect the sun, producing a micro-climate around the vine which gives the wines their high alcoholic content and unique flavour. Today Châteauneuf produces around 13 million bottles annually, about 650,000 of them white, the rest the famous reds.

Provence produces red, rosés and whites, and other wines that have a little extra: Muscat from Beaumes-de-Venise is a sweet apéritif wine while Rasteau also produces a sweet fortified wine based on the Grenache grape.

Recommending wines is a disaster-prone area and best left to 'experts'. To obtain something *you* like, visit the local *caves*, looking out for *dégustation* and *vente*, tasting and selling. Offering to pay for your trial glasses usually results in your being taken seriously and being offered better vintages to try. Your money will not, in any case, be accepted. But rememeber that after several glasses of good quality local wine it is best to have someone else drive you and your new purchases back to your accomodation.

The Pont du Gard is a feast for the eyes; with its setting, its bold dimensions, and the warm colour of the rough, dressed drystone blocks. Its vitality and beauty derives from the fact that the arches are deliberately, though only slightly, irregular in span. Thankfully the site has been spared the souvenir kiosks and cafés that often seem inevitable, so the visitor can really appreciate the aqueduct. The protruding stones held the scaffolding required for its construction, but imagine the effort of lifting 6-ton blocks of stone into position.

Uzès, where the water for Nîmes started its journey, is a fine town, virtually a living museum of seventeenth- and eighteenth-century architecture. The town became rich through its interests in the silk trade and there is a superb street of fine houses around every corner. The Ducal Palace overshadows everything, an excellent castle with sections dating from between the eleventh and the seventeenth centuries. From the top of the palace's Bermonde Tower — reached by a spiral staircase of almost 150 steps — the view of the town and the garrigue landscape that surrounds it is excellent. To the south of the palace is the old clocktower, dating from the twelfth century and topped by a delightfully wrought-iron bell cage, and, on again, the picturesque, arcaded Place aux Herbes.

Opposite the palace's north-east corner is the crypt, an early Christian cell hacked out of the rock and with a carved relief of John the Baptist.

From the crypt, continue along Rue Boucaire and Rue Rafin to reach the fine eighteenth-century mansion of the Baron de Castille, to the left. Ahead, across the main road, is the ex-cathedral of St Théodorit, built in the seventeenth century but remodelled 200 years later. To the right of the cathedral is the Tour Fenestrelle, dating from the twelfth century and unique in France as a round bell-tower. The tower, named for its numerous windows, is all that remains of an earlier cathedral destroyed during the Wars of Religion.

Beside the tower the Promenade Jean-Racine offers a shady walk and fine views of the country to the south. The name commemorates the seventeenth-century writer who spent a formative year in Uzès.

Another write associated with the town is André Gide, the Nobel laureate, whose family is commemorated in a collection in the town musuem housed in the old Bishop's Palace beside the cathedral. Gide's father and uncle were from Uzès and André spent many holidays here with his grandmother, visits that form the basis of *If I die ...* , one of his most popular works. The museum also has collections of local flora, fossils and on the history of the town.

Finally, those visitors with an interest in horses can visit the French National Stud which lies about 2 miles (3½ km) outside the town beside the D981 to Alès.

The distance from Roman Orange to medieval Avignon is less than 30km (18 miles). Take the D68 which reaches a village in 10km (6miles) whose name is familiar to every wine-lover — **Châteauneuf-du-Pape**. Rows of green vines rise out of a sea of large pebbles once rolled by the Rhône. They act as a furnace which reflects the sun's heat onto the ripening grapes that produce the well-known red wine. Up to thirteen varieties of grape may be used in making the wine. As might be expected, there is a museum to the wine trade in the town.

Above the village are the imposing ruins of a fourteenth-century castle built by Pope John XXII as his summer residence. It has been plundered down the years, the last assault was by German troops who blew up most of the huge keep in 1944.

Avignon has a long and enviable history. It was inhabited, though obviously not as a city, in the Bronze and Iron Ages, and has a Celtic history too. It grew prosperous due to its position at the confluence of the Rhône and Durance Rivers, but made the mistake of choosing the wrong side in the Albigensian Wars. The wrathful French king, who was victorious, dismantled its defensive walls. At a later stage of the wars the city was taken by the Holy Roman Empire and in the early fourteenth century the Papacy was transferred to here from Rome. During this period the city's greatest architectural treasures were built. Despite the return of the Papacy to Rome, the city's future was assured, and it thrived, even after 1791 when it finally passed back to France.

Today Avignon is a large town of 90,000 inhabitants, the great majority of them living outside the intact medieval ramparts — the medieval town wall is complete, all 5km (3 miles) of it, together with its thirty-nine defensive towers. If outer Avignon is bustling and banal, the Old Town's narrow streets enclose the sense of history. The chief place of interest is the Palace of the Popes.

Built mainly by Benedict XII and Clement VI during the years from 1334 to 1352, the palace is actually more fortress-like, a design that mirrored the Pope's insecurities. The palace is huge, extending over about 2½ acres, and externally it is a marvel of grey stone, all high, filled arches and soaring walls. Internally it is equally grand; the Grand Courtyard is spacious, and leading from it is a myriad of interesting rooms. The Robe Room is hung with fine tapestries, while the Papal Bedroom is painted with birds and vines. More impressive murals are found in the Stag Room, which also has a superb wooden ceiling. The Great Hall on the lower floor is breathtaking for its sheer size alone. It is unfurnished, but that seems merely to add to the beauty.

The Grand Courtyard is also the venue of an international drama festival during the last three weeks of July. Its great prestige draws enthusiasts from all over the world to see productions which some consider too avant-garde and elitist.

Within the Palace Square is the Petit Palais, originally a cardinal's palace, then a bishop's palace and now a fine museum. Here there is a

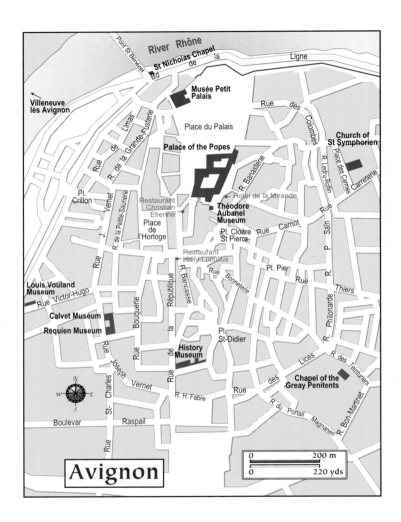

River Rhône

St Nicholas Chapel

Ligne

Port St Bénézet

Bd de la

Villeneuve
lès Avignon

**Musée Petit
Palais**

Rue des

Colombes

Place du Palais

R. de la Grande-Fusterie

Limas

Rue

de

Vernet

**Church of
St Symphorien**

R. Ledru-Rollin

Place des Carmes

Carreterie

Palace of the Popes

R. Banasterie

Pl.
Crillon

R. de la Petite-Saunerie

Restaurant
Christian
Etienne

Place
de
l'Horloge

Hotel de la Mirande

**Théodore
Aubanel
Museum**

Pl. Cloître
St Pierre

Rue

Carnot

R. Salin

P.

Restaurant
Hiély-Lucullus

Rue

R. Bancasse

Rue

Bonneterie

Pl. Pie

Rue

Thiers

R. Philonarde

**Louis Vouland
Museum**

Rue Victor-Hugo

Calvet Museum

Requien Museum

Rue

Bouquerie

République

la

de

Rue

Pl.
St-Didier

Rue

Joseph

St- Charles

Vernet

**History
Museum**

Rue

de

R. H. Fabre

Rue

des

Lices

R. des Teinturiers

**Chapel of the
Greay Penitents**

R. du Portail

Magnanen

R. Bonnmarmet

Boulevar

Rue

Raspail

0   200 m

0   220 yds

Avignon

---

good collection of Romanesque and Gothic sculpture, and some fine early paintings, chiefly by Tuscan artists. Elsewhere in the town there are other excellent museums: the Muséum Requien is of natural his-tory, named after the naturalist Es-prit Requien who lived in the town. The herbarium has almost 250,000

Opposite: Bastille Day celebrations in Avignon

species of plant, while the library is one of the most important in the world. Next door the Musée Calvet, currently being restored, has a fine collection of paintings, including works by Utrillo, Dufy and Modigliani, and Greek sculptures. Musée Vouland concentrates on the decorative arts, particularly eighteenth-century French furnishings, while Musée Aubanel — named after Théodore Aubanel, a friend of Frédéric Mistral — is devoted to Aubanel's printing business, with some interesting old printing machinery. There is also a small collection of paintings. Finally, the Musée Lapidaire has a collection of sculptures and carvings dating from the area's Greek and Roman periods.

From the huge square in front of the Places of the Popes — the centre for excellent outdoor theatre and street-theatre productions around Bastille Day — old Avignon is easily reached. A stroll through almost any part of the old town is worthwile, revealing the architectural styles of 200 and 300 years ago in the façades of mansions (hôtels) of wealthy merchants and the nobility and some newer touches, with artists at work in the squares, especially in Place de l'Horloge. The square is usually alive with folk, chatting in the plane tree-shaded cafes or admiring the trompe-l'oeil paintings on the surrounding walls which illustrate scenes from Avignon's history.

Two of the most picturesque streets are Rue Banasterie (Weavers' Row), and Rue des Teinturiers (Dyers' Row) where the River Sorgue flows gently past inert, ancient mill wheels. The latter street, in the south-east corner of the Old Town, is widely believed to be the finest that Avignon has to offer, and should not be missed. Numerous churches and chapels of different periods are scattered about the Old Town. So many churches are there that the skyline is dominated by bell towers, which lead Rabelais to describe Avignon as la ville sonnante, the ringing city. One of the best of the old chapels is that of the Grey Penitents, now restored to its sixteenth-century glory.

For many though, the chief place of interest is the bridge, immortalised in song. It, or rather what is left of it, stands beyond the town wall to the north-west. The dancing in the song actually took place on an island under the bridge, not on it (sous le pont not sur le pont), but that makes little difference to the visitor who comes to relive a childhood memory. Today's visitor will readily see that the bridge was too narrow for dancing. It was built in the late twelfth century for carriages. The legend is that a local shepherd boy claimed to have been told to build it in a vision and proved the story to a sceptical townsfolk by miraculously picking up a huge stone to start the work. The church promptly gave money for the bridge's completion. Over the years, floods have reduced the bridge to half its length. The chapel of St Nicholas on one pier is all that remains of medieval fortifications.

If there is a temptation to sentimentalise Avignon's past while admiring its ancient remains, the fulminations of one who served at the papal court — Petrarch — will restore the balance. He left to posterity his view that Avignon was a living hell, a sink of vice with neither faith, nor charity, nor religion; the city was odious, pestilential when there was no *mistral*, insufferable when it blew.

Across the Rhône from Avignon is **Villeneuve-lès-Avignon** (*lès* here meaning 'near'), once connected to Avignon by the shepherd boy's bridge. Belonging to the Kingdom of France, it was built (as a *ville nueve*, a new city) and fortified by the French kings to keep frontier watch on Avignon which was then part of the Holy Roman Empire. Interestingly, the French king owned the river, endearing himself to the Avignon folk by charging them rent every time it flooded their houses!

When the Popes came from Rome to Avignon, the cardinals chose the rising ground of Villeneuve to build their summer palaces, but most of these were destroyed at the time of the Revolution. One that remains is the fourteenth century palace of Cardinal Pierre du Luxembourg, now a museum, in Rue de la République. The collections include a magnificent fourteenth-century ivory Vir-gin and some excellent medieval paintings.

Villeneuve is a quieter place to stay than Avignon. Be sure to stand at the top of the Tour de Philippe le Bel as the sun begins to set: it throws Avignon and the palaces into a warm relief and illuminates the distant hump of Mont Ventoux. Fort St André can also be visited. It is reached through a fortified gate that experts claim to be the finest example of its type in France. Inside is the Abbaye St André, standing in fine Italianate gardens.

Be sure, also, to visit the nearby Chartreuse (charterhouse) of Val-de-Bénédiction. The charterhouse was one of the richest in France, but the last monks were evicted during the Revolution. Today it is a cultural centre hosting many events.

Finally, go east from Avignon to the village of **Le Thor** which has a fine thirteenth-century church and, nearby, the Thouzon Cave, a fine show cave. East again is L'Isle-sur-la-Sorgue, where the River Sorgue divides into five branches, each of which once drove a mill wheel. Today the mills are gone, but one waterwheel still turns in the village's public gardens, a moss-covered reminder of the past.

Palais des Papes (Palace of the Popes), Avignon

The famous Pont St-Bénézet, Avignon

ADDITIONAL INFORMATION

PLACES TO VISIT

Ardèche Gorge

Grotte de la Madeleine
Open: July and August daily 9am-
6pm; September to June daily
9.30am-12noon, 2-6pm
☎ 75 04 22 20

Aven du Marzal, Musée du Monde Souterrain & Zoo Prehistorique
Open: April to October daily 9am-
12noon, 2-6pm; March and November Saturday 10am-12noon, 2-5.30pm
☎ 75 04 12 45

Aven d'Orgnac
25km (16 miles) north-west of
Bagnols-sur-Cèze
Open: April to September daily 9am-
12noon, 2-6pm; March, October to
mid-November 9am-12noon, 2-5pm
☎ 75 38 62 51

Musée Prehistorique
Aven d'Orgnac
Open: July and August daily 10am-
7pm; April to June, September daily
10am-12noon, 2-6pm; March,
October to mid-November daily
10am-12noon, 2-5pm
☎ 75 38 65 10

Avignon

Le Palais des Papes
Place du Palais
Open: June to September daily 9am-
7pm; October to May daily 9am-
12.15pm, 2-6.15pm; closed on official
holidays. Guided tours available (in
French) approximately every hour
☎ 90 86 03 32

Chapelle St Nicolas
Pont St Bénézet
Open: May to September daily except
Tuesday 9am-6.30pm; October to
April daily 9am-5.30pm. Closed on

official holidays
☎ 90 82 65 11 or 90 85 60 16

Musée du Petit Palais
Place du Palais
Open: All year, daily except Tuesday
9.30-11.50am, 2-6.15pm. Closed on
official holidays.
☎ 90 86 44 58

Musée Lapidaire
27 Rue de la République
Open: All year, daily except Tuesday
10am-12noon, 2-6pm. Closed on
official holidays.
☎ 90 85 75 38

Musée Requien
67 Rue Joseph-Vernet
Open: All year, Tuesday to Saturday
9am-12noon, 2-6pm
Library open: Monday to Friday 9am-
12noon, 2-6.30pm
☎ 90 82 43 51

Musée Calvet
Rue Joseph-Vernet
Currently closed for restoration
☎ 90 82 65 11 for information

Chapelle des Pénitents-Gris
Rue des Teinturiers
Open: All year, Monday, Wednesday
to Saturday 8am-12noon, 2.30-7pm;
Tuesday 8.30-9.30am, 3.30-7pm

Musée Louis Vouland
17 Rue Victor Hugo
Open: July to September Tuesday to
Thursday 10am-1pm, 3-6pm, Friday
10am-1pm, 3-8pm; October to June
Tuesday to Friday 2-5pm. Closed on
official holidays.
☎ 90 86 03 79

Musée Théodore Aubanel
Near Eglise St Pierre
Open: All year except August
Monday to Friday 9am-12noon
☎ 84 84 46 26

Musée Pierre du Luxembourg
Rue de la République
Villeneuve-lès-Avignon
Open: June to September daily 10am-12.30pm, 3-7.30pm; March to May and October to January daily except Thursday 10am-12noon, 2-5pm
☎ 90 27 49 66

Philip the Fair's Tower
Villeneuve-lès-Avignon
Open: April to September daily 10am-12noon, 3-7.30pm; March and October to January daily except Monday 10am-12noon, 2-5pm
☎ 90 27 49 68

Fort St André
Villeneuve-lès-Avignon
Open: July and August daily 9.30am-7.30pm; April to June and September daily 10am-12.30pm, 2-6.30pm; October to March daily 10am-12noon, 2-5pm
☎ 90 25 45 35

Abbaye St André
Villeneuve-lès-Avignon
Open: July and August daily 9.30am-7.30pm; April to June and September daily 10am-12.30pm, 2-6.30pm; October to March daily 10am-12noon, 2-5pm
☎ 90 25 55 95

La Chartreuse du Val-de-Bénédiction
Villeneuve-lès-Avignon
Open: April to September daily 9am-6.30pm; October to March daily 9am-5.30pm
☎ 90 25 05 46

Carpentras

Hôtel-Dieu
Place Aristide Briand
Open: All year Monday, Wednesday and Thursday 9-11.30am
☎ 90 63 00 78

Treasury
St Siffrein Cathedral
Open: Easter to September daily

except Tuesday 10am-12noon, 2-6pm; October to Easter daily except Tuesday 10am-12noon, 2-4pm;
☎ 90 63 04 92

Palais de Justice (Law Courts)
Place du Général de Gaulle
Open: All year Monday to Friday 9am-12noon, 2-4pm
☎ 90 63 00 78

Musée Lapidaire
Rue Stes Maries
Open: Easter to September daily except Tuesday 10am-12noon, 2-6pm; October to Easter daily except Tuesday 10am-12noon, 2-4pm;
☎ 90 63 04 92

Musée Comtadin/Musée Duplessis/ Inguimbertine Library
234 Boulevard Albin-Durand
(Adjacent to the Musée Lapidaire)
Open: Easter to September daily except Tuesday 10am-12noon, 2-6pm; October to Easter daily except Tuesday 10am-12noon, 2-4pm;
☎ 90 63 04 92

Musée Sobirats
Rue du Collège
Open: Easter to September daily except Tuesday 10am-12noon, 2-6pm; October to Easter daily except Tuesday 10am-12noon, 2-4pm;
☎ 90 63 0492

La Synagogue
Place de l'Hôtel de Ville
Open: All year Monday to Friday 10am-12noon, 3-5pm (4pm Friday)
☎ 90 63 39 97

Town Museum
Mazan
(4 km east of Carpentras on the D942)
Open: June to September daily except Tuesday and Sunday 3.30-6.30pm; October to May By appointment only.
☎ 90 69 74 27

Châteauneuf-du-Pape

Musée du Père Anselme
Open: March to December daily 9am-12noon, 2-6pm
☎ 90 83 70 07

Comtat Plain (near Avignon)

Grotte de Thouzon
3km north of Le Thor on the D16
Open: July and August daily 9.30am-7pm; April to June, September and October daily 10am-12noon, 2-6pm March and November Sundays and public holidays 2-6pm
☎ 90 33 93 65

Musée National d'Histoire
L'Harmas Village, near Serignan-du-Comtat on the N976
Open: May to September daily except Tuesday 9am-11.30pm, 2-6.30pm; October to April daily except Tuesday 9am-11.30pm, 2-4.30pm
☎ 90 70 00 44

Grignan

Le Château
Open: July and August daily 9.30-11.30am, 2-6pm; September, October and April to June daily 9.30-11.30am, 2-5.30pm; November to March daily except Tuesdays and Wednesday mornings 9.30-11.30am, 2-5.30pm
☎ 75 46 51 56

Mont Ventoux

Le Château
Barroux
Open: July and August daily except Wednesday 11am-12noon, 3-6.30pm
☎ 90 63 00 78 for information

Town Museum
Sault
Open: Mid-June to July Monday, Wednesday and Saturday 4-6pm; August to mid-June by appointment only
☎ 90 64 02 30

Musée des Vieux Outils (Museum of Old Tools)
St Marc Cellar
Caromb
Open: All year except during the grape harvest daily 8am-12noon, 2-6pm
☎ 90 62 40 24

Nyons

Moulin Autrand (Olive Oil Mill)
Avenue de la Digue
Open: All year, Tuesday to Saturday 9.30am-12noon, 3-7pm; Monday 3-7pm; Sunday 9.30am-12noon
☎ 75 26 11 00

Moulin Ramade (Olive Oil Mill)
Open: All year Monday to Saturday 9am-12noon, 2-7pm
☎ 75 26 08 18

Oil & Wine Cooperative
Place Olivier-de-Serres
Open: All year Monday to Saturday 9am-12noon, 2-7.30pm; Sunday 9.30am-12noon, 3-6pm
☎ 75 26 03 44

Olive Museum
Avenue des Tilleuls
Open: April-December Tuesday to Sunday 10am-12noon, 3-6pm
☎ 75 26 12 12

Orange

Théâtre Antique
Open: April to September daily 9am-6pm; October to March daily 9am-12.30pm, 1.30-5.30pm. Closed on official holidays.
☎ 90 34 70 88

Musée Municipal
Place des Frères Mounet
Open: April to September daily 9am-17pm; October to March daily 9am-12noon, 1.30-5.30pm. Closed on official holidays.
☎ 90 51 80 06

Uzès

Town Museum
Bishop's Palace
Open: February to December daily
except Monday 3-6pm
☎ 66 22 68 99

Le Duché (Ducal Palace)
Open: Easter to October daily
9.30am-12noon, 2.30-6.30pm
☎ 66 22 18 96

La Crypt
Open: July and August daily 9.30am-
12noon, 2-6pm
☎ 66 22 68 88 for information

French National Stud
Route d'Alès
Open: All year daily except Sunday 2-
5pm
☎ 66 22 33 11

Vaison-la-Romaine
Quartier du Puymin
Open: All year daily 9am-1pm, 2-6.45pm
☎ 90 36 02 11

Musée du Vigneron
(Wine Growing Museum)
Domaine de Beaurenard
Rasteau (6km south-west of Vaison
along the D975)
Open: April to September daily 10.30am-
6pm
☎ 90 46 11 75

Valréas

Château de Simione (Town Hall)
Place Aristide Briand
Open: Mid-July to August Monday to
Saturday 3-7pm; September to mid-
July Monday to Saturday 2-5pm
☎ 90 33 00 45

Musée du Cartonnage et de l'Im-
primerie (Packaging Museum)
Mairie de Valréas
Open: April to September Wednesday
to Saturday 10am-12noon, 3-6pm,
Sunday 10am-12noon; October to
March Wednesday to Saturday 10am-
12noon, 2-5pm, Sunday 10am-12noon
☎ 90 35 58 75

Upper Provence & Durance Valley

2

From the direction of Grenoble, two routes make for the heart of Provence. One is the N75 which goes over the Col de la Croix Haute 1,176m (3,860ft) in the Devoluy Range to Serres. The other, more easterly, road is the N85 which traverses the Col Bayard 1,246m (4,090ft) in the Campsaur Range, and leads to Gap. They converge just north of Sisteron.

Sisteron is a theatrical gateway into Provence. The harsh Dauphiné Mountains are to the north, while to the south the valley opens on to richer, warmer land. At the town, the Durance river has barged its narrow way through buckled and striated mountains. This weathering process was aided by the last Ice Age because the glaciers of the Alps never reached further than Sisteron, though their melting debris, tons of sharp angular rocks, helped carve the gorge. The town is cleverly set where the Durance joins a lesser stream, the Buech, and is built into the rocks on the west side of the gorge facing the towering Rocher de la Baum. This is a vast natural defence to approaches from the east, its town-side face composed, it seems, of candles of rock, so intense has been the geological folding in the area. Today the town is bypassed by the road, the main route on into Provence being taken under the Rocher by tunnel. This has left the town more peaceful than it used to be, giving the visitor time and space to breathe.

Previous page: Sisteron

The strategic importance of the site was not lost on the Romans who fortified it, called it *Segustero* and ran the *Via Domitia* past it. Such was the site's importance, however, that very little remains of that 'first' town, later settlers having laid waste the early work while building their own defences. In the thirteenth century, it was still considered 'a grandiose portal dividing Provence and Dauphiné', though at that time it was also the place that sealed the fate of Provence forever. Here, in a Franciscan monastery that had been built near the town, the Count of Provence, Berengar V, signed his will. He left Provence to one of his daughters who later married Charles of Anjou, taking her proud possession with her and so making the region a part of France.

As late as 1944, the strategic importance of the town was re-emphasised when it suffered from Allied air attacks which destroyed some of the medieval quarters. Thankfully, they have been reconstructed.

Near the Place de la République are the town hall, church, and the four remaining fifteenth-century towers whose ramparts have all but disappeared. The Museum of Old Sisteron is also close by, its archaeological items were discovered during reconstruction work after the bombing raids.

The full name of the one-time cathedral is Notre Dame-des-Pommiers, a strange looking name, and one that has nothing to do with apples, but is a corruption of *pomerium*, an area which must be left free. Its architecture reflects Sisteron's geographical position; the octagonal tower and its external gallery have both Lombard and Alpine influences. The perfect alignment of the masonry is characteristically Provençal.

A warren of narrow streets, stepped and vaulted (*andrônes*), and linking tiny squares, make up the old quarters. Where the main street enters a tunnel there is a bust of Paul Arène (1843-96), a Sisteron writer of lightness and charm who, under a pseudonym, wrote the famous *Lettres de Mon Moulin* with Alphonse Daudet in 1866. In Rue Saunerie, at No 20, Napoleon took lunch on 5 March 1815 on the route — now known as Route Napoleon — that led from Elba to Waterloo.

The citadel of massive ancient fortifications, started in the eleventh century and added to later, stands supreme above the town. The initial climb to the site can be avoided by taking a little electric tourist train, which also runs around the best of the old town. A curtain wall on a narrow ridge and supported by high arches leads to the citadel which is reached by a steep climb (for which no help is available), with a panorama at the top identified by a viewing table. The final climb, up a steep staircase, reaches the Devil's Tower, the descent from which includes an underground staircase. Both the citadel and the rock are floodlit on summer evenings, when broadcasts in French explain Sisteron's history. In the guardroom at the entrance, there is a museum of local wartime resistance.

Sisteron is a good starting place for excursions into the scenically interesting local countryside. Pride of place must go to a visit to the Vançon Valley, to the north-east of the town. This is a drive that some might call interesting, others choosing a more colourful adjective. It all depends on how you find the hairpins of the D3 that soon leaves the D951 and heads east and sharply upwards. Soon you reach the Pierre Ecrite Gorge, steep sided, narrow and with a strange Roman inscription carved in one of its rocky walls that implies, most improbably, that there was once a city in the valley. Beyond the gorge, the valley continues in fine style, the road being easier, but never easy. Look out for the eleventh-century pilgrimage chapel standing beneath the Rocher du Dromon.

There are other fine excursions to both the east and west of the River Durance. As a rule, the eastern ones are more Alpine in character because they penetrate valleys whose peaks are over 2,000m (6,560ft), while the valleys to the west run into lower peaks and are more open and Mediterranean in aspect.

If, instead of entering Provence on the route to Sisteron, the traveller has left the side of Lac de Serre-Poncon and taken the D900, then a pleasant drive leads to **Digne**, a popular stopping place, well-supplied with hotels and a spa for the treatment of rheumatism. Digne does not quite have the feel of a Provençal town, its mountainous setting of steep and sombre crags making it seem more Alpine. Yet, for

The church of Notre-Dame and the ancient fortifications at Sisteron

all that, it is a centre for the growing of fruit and flowers, and especially of lavender. Each year, in September, there is a lavender fair.

Digne is, in fact, the capital of a vast area where lavender is grown. Several types grow in Provence. True (or common) lavender is the plant from which the finest essence is distilled. Aspic, which flowers in late August, is not cultivated but hybridises with true lavender to give *lavandin* which yields great quantities of inferior essence. Lastly, French lavender, found mainly on silica soils like those of the Maures Mountains, has deep purple flowers but is of no commercial value.

Boulevard Gassendi, in Digne's Ville-Haute, is the main artery of activity and interest. On each side of it are car parks. At one end is the Grande Fontaine, its Doric structure buried under tufa and moss. At the ✳ centre of the Boulevard is the Place Charles de Gaulle and a statue of ✳ Pierre Gassendi (1592-1655), philosopher and polymath, born at nearby Champtercier. Gassendi is little known to the layman, though one of his debating partners, René Descartes, has become famous, if only for his proclamation 'I think, therefore I am'.

The old part of the town lies to one side of Boulevard Gasssendi. The municipal museum, housed in a former hospice, provides a visual survey of Digne's prehistory and the Gallo-Roman period. Paintings by

Route Napoleon

Following the disastrous invasion of Russia and the consequent retreat from Moscow, during which half a million men of the Grande Armée were lost, Napoleon Bonaporte abdicated as Emperor of France. Louis XVIII was restored to the throne and Napoleon accepted a pension and retirement to the island of Elba off Italy's Tuscan shore. But a life of idleness and reflection did not suit him and with a small band of followers he returned to France. On 1 March 1815 he landed at Golfe Juan. It was not the tumultuous homecoming he had wanted and, probably, expected. The French were worn out by years of war and privation. They had cheered their new king, but without much enthusiasm, and felt no more enthusiasm for a vanquished emperor.

Napoleon rested the night in Cannes. Advised that local commanders were hostile, he did not take the obvious route up the Rhône Valley, but sent an advance guard northwards to gauge his likely reception. He moved cautiously, reaching Grasse on 2 March, Catellane on 3 March and Digne the next day. His advance guard discovered that Sisteron was unguarded, a crucial discovery as it opened the route through the Durance Gorge: Napoleon lunched at the town on 5 March and moved on. On 7 March he was stopped by a hostile commander at Grenoble. For a moment the situation looked bleak for the old emperor, but the men hailed him despite their commander, and he entered Grenoble. The long road to Paris was now open. Louis fled, but Napoleon's triumph was short-lived: the road beyond Paris led to Waterloo.

In 1932 a road following Napoleon's route was opened. This is the Route Napoleon, identified by frequent symbols of an eagle above an 'N', and with frequent information boards giving details of Bonaparte's progress. The eagle symbol derives from Napoleon's off-quoted remark on his return from Elba that 'the eagle will fly from steeple to steeple until he reaches Notre-Dame'.

local artists are augmented by better-known painters such as Natoire and Ziem. A natural history collection includes specimens of unusual local moths.

Notre-Dame-du-Bourg, once a cathedral, stands at the northern outskirts, and the Lombard and Alpine influences that were apparent at Sisteron are seen again. This majestic building has a particularly fine rose window, but now the church is only used for funerals, and the caretaker has to be found at the cemetery if you want to get in. This is not the grandest way to spend a holiday, so you should settle for a look at the outside and a walk around the old town. Close to Digne, the Haute Provence Geological Reserve has been set up, covering almost 400,000 acres (more than 150,000 hectares) of one of the most interesting areas of Europe for geology and fossil remains. The geology is explored at the Geology Centre at St Benoît, which houses the largest collection of specimens in Europe. An alternative is the Museum of World War II somewhat inappropriately positioned in Place Paradis — Paradise Square.

Also in the town, and a must for all readers of the works of early explorers, is the collection of the work of Alexandra David-Néel, the famous explorer. Alexandra studied oriental languages at the Sorbonne, then travelled to Lhasa, the first European woman to do so. On her return she became one of the West's foremost Tibetan scholars. She moved to Digne at the age of 59 but 10 years later left to spend a further 9 years in the Himalayas. She returned to Digne but in 1968, just after her 100th birthday, she renewed her passport for a long trip to China. Sadly it was not to be, and she died in the town in 1969. The collection of the Fondation Alexandra David-Néel includes many important pieces from the Himalayan kingdoms and Tibet.

From Digne the N85 heads south,

then turns eastwards to **Barrême** where there is another geology museum. From Barrême the N85 (and Route Napoleon) heads south-east to Castellane. Turn left in Barrême to follow the N202 is **St André-les-Alpes** at the head of the man-made Lac de Castillon. The lake is popular with watersports enthusiasts. This, and the nearby alps of Haute Provence make St André a popular centre for outdoor enthusiasts. The area is so good for hang gliding, and the village so well-sited for flyers at the end of a successful day, that one local wine producer advertises his vintage as the 'Wine for Eagles'.

From St André the D955 carves a beautiful route northwards, following the Verdon river through Haute Provence to **Colmars**. Here the Romans built a temple on a hill and dedicated it their god Mars. *Collis Martis* gave its name to the town, though it was Vauban, Louis XIV's military architect, who gave Colmars its present day appearance. Set where the kingdom of France met that of Savoy, Colmars was strategically vital, defending what was called the Barcelonnette Gap. Vauban's Fort de Savoie is massive and, with the town's ramparts, presented a formidable barrier to any invading army. From Porte de France, a path reaches an earlier defensive work, the Fort de France.

North again, the road continues beside the Verdon river, edging the Mercantour National Park — explored later when it is reached again behind the Riviera. To the right is Mont Pelat, the highest peak in the

Provençal Alps at 3,051m (10,007ft). The Col d'Allos, beyond the village of Allos, is a difficult climb and can be blocked by snow until late June, but the descent is easier. Just before Barcelonnette is reached, the D902 heads off southward, going through the National Park and rounding Mont Pelat to cross the Col de la Cayolle, continuing to reach Guillaumes at the head of the Gorges de Daluis.

Barcelonnette is named after Barcelona, its founder — Count Raymond Berenger V — having been Count of Barcelona and wanting to create a smaller version of the Catalan city. Little Barcelona is a pleasant airy town, very alpine in character, yet having several elegant mansions with distinct Mexican features. These reflect the fortunes of the three Arnaud brothers who emigrated to Mexico and made considerable fortunes. Their travelling companions returned, spreading the tale of New World prosperity. As many as 5,000 locals are believed to have followed the Arnauds — who have a street named for them — a population of some 40,000 Mexican now claiming Provençal descent. Some of those who emigrated returned with their fortunes, these being responsible for the Mexican flavour of the town. One of these fine mansions houses the Musée de la Vallée which explores the history of the Ubage Valley, in which Barcelonnette stands, and the town's Mexican connections.

The N202 from St André-les-Alpes soon crosses Lac de Castillon,

continuing over the Col de Toutes-Aures and then through the Gorges de Golange to reach **Annot**. This beautiful village seems to grow from the surrounding rocks — huge sandstone boulders, the *grès d'Annot*, littering the streets have been incorporated into some of the houses. On Sundays in July and August a steam engine pulls the Belle Epoque train along the line from Puget-Théniers to here. The line, part of that travelled by the *Train des Pignes* linking Digne to Nice, travels through marvellous scenery — though the section between St André-les-Alpes and Annot, where the train is pulled by conventional engines, is equally splendid — and offers a view of Entrevaux, the most easterly town in this tour of Haute Provence.

Entrevaux also sits where France once met Savoy and, as the river gorge narrows to just a few hundred metres, was ideal as a defensive position. The defences are one of Vauban's masterpieces and have created the almost perfect medieval fortified village, a Hollywood producer's dream. An arched bridge leads to a twin-towered bridge beyond which there are old barracks and powderhouses, and a defended, zig-zag path rising to the fort. These features have aided Entrevaux's recent prosperity, the village now being firmly, and rightly, established on the tourist trail. To add to its appeal there is a regular summer programme of events in the town.

From Sisteron an attractive secondary road, D951, passing the villages of Mallefougasse and Cruis,

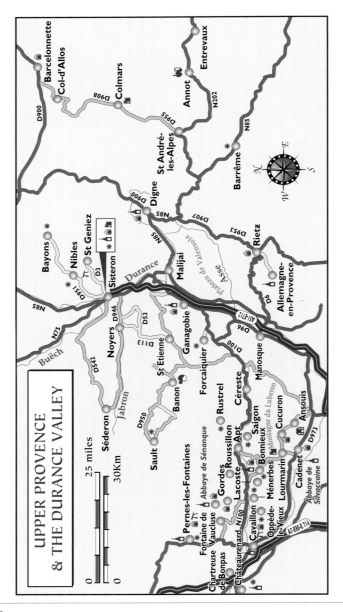

UPPER PROVENCE
& THE DURANCE VALLEY

Montagne de Lure

reaches St Etienne (St Etienne-les-Orgues on some maps) at the foot of the southern slope of the Montagne de Lure. In medieval times, the village was famous for country remedies made from herbs that grew — and still do — on the flanks of the Lure. These remedies were sold far and wide.

The Lure Range, crossed by a road rising through oak and conifers, that links St Etienne and Sisteron, is the natural extension of Mont Ventoux, separated from it by the depression at Sault. It, too, is a limestone mass riddled with underground caves (*dolines*) into which streams vanish abruptly. Walkers will love the Lure — although it is only slightly lower than Mont Ven-

toux, it is a friendlier range with its easier slopes. The summit of the range, Signal de Lure, 1,826m (5,990ft) high, is reached by the GR6 which goes from Sisteron to Tarascon. This is a magnificent walk, but there is no need to complete it to reach the top nor, in fact, to do too much walking at all, as the D113 allows less intrepid walkers to drive to within about 20 minutes of the summit. To the right as you follow the road upwards from St Etienne, a stony, but drivable, track leads to Notre-Dame de Lure. St Donat had a hermitage here about 500AD and a monastery was founded in the twelfth century. Today a small Romanesque chapel surrounded by old lime trees occupies this peaceful spot.

The road goes no higher than 1,700m (5,580ft) and from its high point a steep climb reaches the Signal de Lure. Some dwarf juniper, beech and gorse are scattered near the barren summit. Saxifrages, fritillaries and Mont Cenis violets appear as soon as the snows melt and later orchids appear. Butterflies are quite plentiful with about 70 per cent of them being either Alpine or central European and Asiatic species. The really lucky visitor might also spot a short-toed eagle. After climbing the last few metres, visitors are treated to the best panorama in this area of Provence. The view is dominated by Mont Ventoux, but also includes Mont Viso and Mont Pelvoux as well as a good section of the coast.

Those who have visited the summit and feel invigorated, can try the brusque, zig-zag descent into the Jabron Valley. However, this section of road is closed between mid-November and the end of May.

From St Etienne, two attractive roads go to Forcalquier, while a longer westward journey of 2km (1¼ miles) aims for **Banon**, near which is one of the deepest caves in France. The Gouffre du Caladaire, 480m (1,575ft) deep, is reached on foot. Close to it is the romantically abandoned village of Montsalier-le-Vieux.

By turning right 9km (5½ miles) out of St Etienne, in the direction of Banon, the traveller can take the D12 which leads to tiny **Lardiers**. On a nearby hilltop are the remains of an important Gallo-Roman shrine, the *oppidum* of Chastelard-de-Lardiers.

A double wall enclosed some 20 acres which surrounded a sanctuary. Vast deposits of gold, silver and bronze rings and 50,000 tiny clay lamps — all votive offerings to Mercury, the patron of travellers — have been excavated.

The road from Lardiers continues northward to Saumane and then swings back to Banon. **Simiane-la-Rotonde**, about 10km (6 miles) to the south-west, is a real fairytale village when viewed from a distance, but one that has been the centre of some historical controversy. The problem is the rotunda that tops off this superbly concentric, rising village. It could be a mausoleum, a defensive structure or even a chapel. Some say the lords of Simiane built the rotunda in imitation of the castles erected by Crusaders in the Holy Land; others think it is a likeness to the circular kitchens of medieval abbeys. To see for yourself, enquire for the key in the village. There is a curious, lantern-like hexagonal tower that certainly dates from the twelfth century, built into the remains of a castle, and furnished with a cone-like roof. Inside, the rotunda is irregularly twelve-sided, formed by twelve blind arcades. Below is a crypt, while above is an ornamented chamber. Stairs built in the thick walls give access to upper terraces of this strange building. One thing is certain; aesthetically, the rotunda is in just the right place, whatever its original purpose.

A stay at **Forcalquier** (*Furnus calcarius* in Latin or *Fourcalquier* in Provençal, each name deriving from the Middle Ages when local lime-kilns provided employment) usually begins with a visit to the impressive but darkly brooding church of Notre-Dame, begun in 1196. In front is a fifteenth-century fountain surmounted by an octagonal pinnacle with a plaque commemorating the marriage in 1235 of Provence's Eleanore and England's Henry III. By then, the town was the capital of the local area of Haute-Provence, and a very powerful town it was, a seat of counts and famous for its court where Provençal troubadours kept the revellers happy. The court of Count Raymond Berengar was especially famous for its revelry. Each of his four daughters married a king. It was said that, on one occasion, all four kings were in the town together. This, and other aspects of Forcalquier's history are explored in the museum in the town hall, Place du Bourget.

On markets days, the square in front of Notre-Dame is thronged with stalls. Nearby is an excellent restored Franciscan monastery, the Couvent des Cordeliers, founded in 1236. The community was one of the earliest Franciscan houses in France, though the building is older, having been built as a mansion. A visit to the monastery is well-worthwhile, especially for a walk in a restored section of the cloisters. A stroll, through the town's old quarters, where there was once a Jewish community and a synagogue, leads to the citadel and on to the church of Terrasse Notre-Dame-de-Provence with fine views of the town and surrounding hills.

Forcalquier's cemetery, about 1km (½ mile) north of the town, is sufficiently unusual for a French cemetery for it to have become a tourist attraction in its own right. The terraces are lined by tall and ancient yews, neatly clipped and shaped into arched niches and topiaries. It also contains small, cylindrical, drystone buildings with pointed roofs called *cabanons*.

In all directions from Forcalquier there are charming villages: St Maime, Dauphin (a good example of a perched village), Limans and Sigonces. To the south, near the village of Mane, is the beautiful sixteenth-century Benedictine Priory of Salagon with a museum that explores the old way of life in Haute Provence. The priory garden has many of the local herbs that were, and are, important in herbal medicine, while the buildings include an old blacksmith forge from Lourmarin, collections of old tools and other reminders of the old ways.

To the south of Mane, the N100 passes close to Château de Sauvan, widely regarded as the most beautiful classical *château* in Provence. Further south again, but still on the N100, a right turn leads to the Haute Provence Observatory, built here in the 1930s after a survey had shown the site to have the lowest incidence of fog and the clearest air in France. The observatory, which includes the National Astrophysics Conservatory, can be visited.

From Sisteron, the main road to Forcalquier, the N96, follows the Durance river and offers an excellent view of the Penitents des Mées, to the left, across the river. These spectacular towers of pebbles and cement-like earth, looking like giant termite nests, stand up to 100m (330ft) high and are the product of glacial and weather erosion. They are named after Mées, the village that stands beneath them, (the village itself being named after the towers, from the Latin *metae*, a milestone). An old legend recounts that some of St Donat's monks (*penitents*) from the Lure fell in love with the Saracen women who had been captured and brought back to Forcalquier. Outraged by this, St Donat turned his love-sick flock to stone.

Further south along the N96 a turn right winds uphill to the Priory of Ganagobie, one of the most peaceful sites in Provence. The priory stands on the tree-filled plateau, where there are holm oaks and pine, together with broom and lavender (alive with butterflies in summer), as well as a balcony view of the valley. Originally this plateau was the site of a Ligurian settlement on top of which a town was built in the early Middle Ages. The Benedictine Monastery was founded in AD980, rebuilt in the twelfth century but partially destroyed in 1792. Today it is an interesting site with a unique triple-arched doorway decorated with oriental-looking carvings. A Christ in Majesty decorates the lintel of this striking doorway.

Inside, visitors can see the marvellous twelfth-century mosaics and a Virgin in the nave painted by Adolphe Monticelli (1824-86) who spent his orphaned childhood at Ganagobie. Although this is not one of his better paintings, it is a reminder that this highly original artist, whose jewel-like brushwork fired Van Gogh with admiration, was partly responsible for the Dutchman coming to Provence for two momentous years.

Manosque, 23km(14 miles) south of Forcalquier, and set above the sluggish coils of the Durance, has grown rapidly and prosperously as the marketing centre for early vegetables, fruit and truffles, and as the home for workers at the Cadarache nuclear power research centre — now branching out into the field of robotics — downstream where the Verdon joins the Durance.

Two fourteenth-century fortified gateways, Porte Saunerie and Porte Soubeyran, mark the bounds of the old town. The curious names for the gates derive from the Provençal words for 'salt' and 'superior', Saunerie being near the town's medieval salt store and Soubeyran at its highest point. Porte Saunerie is the gate by which the French king François I entered the town on a day when it earned the title 'Modest Manosque', a title that it still bears, though more now in disparagement than in respect. The king was presented with the keys to the city by a local girl renowned for her beauty. At the time this seemed a good idea, but the king was more than a little taken with the girl and became adamant that *droite de seigneur* should be added to his gifts. The city's mayor, the girl's father, was appalled by the

Above: Ochre cliffs near Roussillon

Above: Roussillon

Below: Roussillon

Below: Gordes

idea. Not even for a king would his daughter suffer such a fate as to lose her virtue outside of marriage. He promptly threw acid into her face to cruelly mutilate it. The king was horrified when he saw her and lost all interest. The mayor was presumably satisfied, but history does not record how the girl felt about it.

Elsewhere in the town, be sure to see the handsome wrought-iron belfry which surmounts the square tower of St Sauveur church. Such eighteenth-century campaniles are common in Provence and are poetically spoken of as 'God's sheep bells'.

North-eastwards, Manosque rises to the Mont d'Or, the place where the poet and novelist Jean Giono (1895-1970) lived for most of his life. Incidentally, he claimed that François I never visited the town and that the story of the mayor's daughter was an evil gibe. Many of his novels used his native landscape as being representative of elemental forces. Readers of these books will conjure vivid images from the names that recur in them: Vachères, Banon, Le Revest-du-Bion, Ste Tulle and Manosque itself. Giono is buried in Manosque's cemetery. The Jean Giono Centre has material — written and on film — on the writer's life.

From the town, cross the Durance Canal and River and take the D6 which rises through wooded country to the open plateau of undulating hills covered by bristling rows of lavender and almond trees around **Valensole**. Distant peaks jut coyly beyond the rim of the plateau, and the Luberon Range, across the Durance, is a luminous blue in this limpid light. Valensole is one of the main centres for lavender production, the town and local farms offering numerous chances to buy locally made honey, its distinctive flavour arising from the bees' work in pollinating the precious crop. At the Musée Vivant l'Abeille, the working life of the honey bee is explored, with visitors being allowed to accompany the beekeepers as they work among the hives.

Leave Valensole — where Admiral Villeneuve, Nelson's opponent at the Battle of Trafalgar was born — by continuing along the D6 to Riez.

When the Burgundians invaded this part of Provence, **Riez** was *Reia Apollinaris* — an important administrative centre in the Roman Empire. It was *Julia Augusta Reia Apollinaris* in full, but that was too long even for the Romans. Arriving from Valensole, on the right are four columns of grey granite with Corinthian capitals and an architrave of white marble, the remains of a first-century Roman temple, presumably dedicated to Apollo. The nearest quarry of grey granite was at Pennafort near Callas in Var, 117km (73 miles) away.

Another uncommon relic is the baptistry at the edge of Riez on the road to Allemagne-en-Provence (named after *Alemona*, a fertility goddess). Experts disagree about when it was erected, though most favour the fourth century. Outside it is square with a later dome; it is octagonal inside with four apsidal chapels let into the thickness of the walls. A ruined baptismal font is surrounded by eight Corinthian columns of grey granite (as at the temple), again surmounted by marble capitals. A collection of sarcophagi, a taurobolic altar, slabs with inscriptions, carved masks and fragments of pillar can be seen through the iron grille.

There are some charming places in Riez and a sundial of 1806 in Place St Antione bears a reflective message, 'The most serene moment is marked by a shadow'. The town's Musée Nature en Provence explores the geological history of Provence with over 3,000 samples of rocks, minerals and fossils. The best of the fossils is an almost perfectly preserved wading bird found in marl deposits in the Luberon hills and dates back 35 million years.

After visiting the baptistry, continue along the same road, the D952, to reach **Allemagne-en-Provence**, worth visiting to see its Renaissance *château*, looking like a refugee from another part of France. Further along the D952 is **Gréoux-les-Bains**, where the thermal waters have been used since the Romans were here in the first century AD. The town, dominated by the ruins of a twelfth-century castle of the Knights Templar, was most prosperous during the early nineteenth century when the visiting of spas was the high point of the social calendar. Today the warm, sulphurous waters are used in the modern spa buildings for the treatment of arthritis, rheumatism and respiratory problems.

North of Riez lies an empty corner of Provence where the Asse Valley cuts the Plateau de Valensole in two. One or two farm roads meander across this more severe part of the plateau. To savour this isolation, take the D953 past Puimoisson, then the D8 northwards from Bras d'Asse through the Ravin des Cardaires to reach the River Bléone opposite Malijai on the Route Napoleon (the N85).

To the west of Manosque lies the Montagne du Luberon, the N100 defining its northern edge. Visitors following the N100 southwards from Forcalquier pass Mane and the turning to the Haute Provence Observatory, and then the turn to the fine perched village of **Reillanne**. To the west is Céreste, enclosed in its walls, while a valley road leads to Carluc priory, an early Christian necropolis cut from rock.

Apt is next, a village that demands more time. The name was Celto-Ligurian, *Hath*, before the Romans changed it to *Apta Julia.* Today, the town is known for its crystalised fruits and for its lively Saturday morning market.

Two archaic crypts, one above the other, are the curiosity in the ex-cathedral of St Anne. The upper was hollowed out in the eleventh century but an even earlier altar rests on a Gallo-Roman monumental pillar or cippus. Six small, thirteenth-century ossuarial sarcophagi fit neatly into niches.

In the lower crypt, the relics of St Anne, mother of the Virgin Mary, were supposed to have been found in AD776 after having been brought from Palestine. This was the year that Charlemagne came to consecrate, so it is said, the earlier church on the site. The original church was erected in the fifth century using the foundations of a Roman temple. Archaeologists have unearthed fourth-century Christian sarcophagi in the vicinity, so where St Anne's stands was one of the earliest organised Christian communities in the whole of Gaul. This may also have been the first church in the Occident to venerate the Virgin's mother: it was certainly the first in France dedicated to the saint.

Not surprisingly, Apt became a place of pilgrimage. Anne of Austria came here in 1623, prayed to be made fertile — though it took 15 years for her prayer to be realised — and bequeathed valuable reliquaries which are in the treasury and St Anne's Chapel. There is still an annual pilgrimage, on the last Sunday in July.

Close to the church, in Rue de l'Amphitheatre, is the Archaeological Museum with local Roman items that include a fragment of the arena and some pottery. The town now also houses the Luberon Regional Park Centre with an information centre on the park. Here, too, is the Musée de Paléontologie.

The best preserved Roman bridge in France, Pont Julien, is reached by going west from Apt along the N100. After 8km (5 miles), turn left on to the Bonnieux road which almost immediately crosses the humpback bridge over the River Coulon. It was built in the first century AD to carry the *Via Domitia* across what must

then have been a turbulent stream, for the pillars of the three powerful arches have openings which allowed floodwater to flow more freely and so relieve stress on the structure.

Turning right, rather than left over Pont Julien, follows the D108 north to **Roussillon**, surrounded by now-abandoned quarry pits of various ochre colours, the most startling one being an intense red-brown. All these shades also appear on the façades of the houses. On entering the village there is a car park up the steep, narrow and people-filled road to the right. From it, cross to the superb modern sundial/sculpture for your first view of the beautiful ochre rocks. The best views are from viewpoints to the south of Rue des Bourgades from where the Aiguilles du Val des Fées (the Needles of the Fairies' Valley) can be seen. Climb through the town, with its numerous art galleries, and past the church to reach the castrum and another fine view of steep, banded ochre cliffs. The quarries close to Roussillon are no longer worked, but there are still working quarries to the east, producing ochre, a mixture of sand and iron oxide, as a pigment for paints. The ochre is of such high quality that the area is one of the most important production sites in the world.

Also to the east, there are even more spectacular quarries near **Rustrel**, about 19km (12 miles) away — reached via St Saturnin-d'Apt — on the edge of the Plateau de Vaucluse. Rustrel Colorado, as the quarries are known, can be visited on foot

Bories

Scattered over the Luberon Hills and the Vaucluse Plateau are about 3,000 *bories*, the traditional hut of this area of Provence. The *borie* is beehive-shaped and constructed of the flat slabs of limestone, called *lauzes*, that litter the fields. The construction was drystone, with walls up to 1.5m (4.5ft) at the base to support the height. The shape allowed a roof to be constructed by a technique known as false corbel vaulting, with each *lauze* overhanging the one below slightly as the construction rose. The final hole was closed by a single large slab. To prevent rain water entering the hut the *lauzes* were tilted at a slight angle.

Bories were used from the Iron Age through to the eighteenth century, both as dwellings and as tool sheds or animal pens. At their most sophisticated they were two storey, and grouped together to form small villages centred on a communal bread oven. The advantages of the *borie* are clear: they could be made from stones acquired simply by clearing fields for cultivation, and the temperature inside them remains remarkably constant, evening out the changes from summer's heat to winter's cold that occur outside. However, some experts still argue that the true purpose of all *bories* is not understood, maintaining that some could have been burial mounds and some places of worship.

after leaving the car near the Dôa Stream. Columns of red ochre, capped with clay like giant mushrooms, are bizarre features in the landscape.

Back on the N100 a right turn, the D103, leads towards Gordes. This road soon reaches the Musée du Vitrail/Moulin des Bouillons. The stained glass museum was set up to honour the work of Frédérique Duran, but also illustrates the history of stained-glass window production. The museum is in a modern building next to a pond that is home

to black swans. Close by is the Moulin des Bouillons, a sixteenth-century olive mill that now houses a museum to the olive oil industry. The finest exhibit is a huge olive press, weighing over 7 tons, made from a single oak tree. The history of lighting, with oil lamps playing a prominent role, is also explored.

Just to the west of the museums' site is the tiny village of **St Pantaléon**. The church here is hewn from the rock. Beside it is a rock necropollis with tombs mainly of children. Legend has it that if new-born children who died before baptism were brought here they came back to life during a baptismal mass. They died again when the mass ended, but could then be laid to rest in a baptised state.

North of the museums — take the road for Gordes — is a village of *bories* (traditional Provençal peasant hovels), which can be reached by parking and walking up a marked path. At the site the restored huts are grouped around an old bread oven.

Beyond is **Gordes**, a medieval village of some importance, which seems to clamber up the hillside. Gordes was overtaken by events and declined in the 1920s, only to make a recovery under the impulsion of the artist, André Lhote. It was severely damaged in the war in 1944, but its fortunes were revived, again because of artists, when peace came. Today Gordes flourishes and attracts many visitors.

Its *château* enjoys a lofty perch and is, like many others in Provence, a mixture of medieval and Renaissance, with finely proportioned rooms, decorations and stairway as well as an exuberant chimney-piece. It contains the striking Vasarely Museum. Here, the versatile, Hungarian-born artist Vasarely, who restored the *château*, and did much to restore the town's fortunes, is remembered by some 1,000 of his own works. Geometric, undulating designs of pure colour express his notion of continuous movement. Also on show are some of his earlier figurative works.

North of Gordes, along the D177,

is Sénanque Abbey, the first of the 'Three Sisters of Provence', a trio of fine abbeys, the second of which, Silvacaine, is to the south of the Luberon. Sénanque was founded in 1148, legend having it that the church was built by just twelve monks. In keeping with the rules of the Cistercian Order to which they belonged, the monks built a church with almost no ornamentation, though the lines and the setting more than compensate. The roofs of *lauzes* (stone slabs) are original and very beautiful, as is the tiny bell tower. Inside the barrel-vaulted ceiling is a real delight, as are the cloisters with their arcaded walkways. The abbey's greatest period was during the thirteenth century, but in 1544, during the war against the Vaudois heretics many of the monks were hanged by the Vaudoes. The abbey's fortunes never revived: by the end of the seventeenth century there were just two monks. The abbey was sold in 1791, but thoughtfully restored. After several attempts to re-establish the monastic order, the present community took up residence in 1989. On the first floor of monks' dormitory there is a permanent exhibition on the Tuareg people of the Sahara.

West of Gordes is **Fontaine-de-Vaucluse**, which is reached by taking the D15, the Cavaillon road, turning right after 6km (4 miles) to Cabrières-d'Avignon, then taking the D100 and D100A to the village.

The 'fountain' of the name is the resurgent River Sorgue which appears as a lake at the cavernous foot of a huge semi-circular crag. *Son et lumière* shows are given here on summer evenings, looked over by the ruined castle of the bishops of Cavaillon. What looks like a placid lake and stream turns into a foaming torrent when the heavy rains of winter and spring have seeped into the fissured limestone rocks of Mont Ventoux, Lure and Luberon. The underground streams come to the surface through this powerful siphon. The remains of the Roman aqueduct which carried the waters of the Sorgue to Arles are visible by the roadside of the D24 near the village of Galas.

In Fontaine-de-Vaucluse itself, is the Norbert Casteret Speleological Museum, named after the great French cave explorer. The museum houses Casteret's own collection of stalagmites and stalactites, together with reconstructions of typical sections of cave systems and a history of the explorations of the Fontaine resurgence. Close to the museum is the Vallis Clausa paper mill. Paper has been handmade in the village since the fourteenth century, today's process being essentially the same as that used for the last 400 years, a process that includes the use of flowers.

The column in the square honours the Italian poet Petrarch who retired to this spot from Avignon between 1327 and 1353. Here he wrote many of the poems which speak of his unrequited love for Laura of Avignon, and his attachment to the solitude (as it then was) of Fontaine-de-Vaucluse — his *Vallis Clausa*, the Closed Valley. Of the Sorgue he wrote that it 'must be numbered among the fairest and coolest, remarkable for its crystal waters and its emerald channels … none other is so noted for its varying moods, now raging like a torrent, now quiet as a pool'. A small Petrarch Museum stands on what is thought to be the site of his house.

Over the centuries, men of letters have come here in pilgrimage out of respect for a major innovative poet and his romantic attachment to Laura. He has been called the first modern man, the one who took the step away from medievalism's fearful submission to divine authority and towards the individualistic Renaissance assertion of man as the measurer of values.

Also in the village is a museum that explores aspects of World War II: the Resistance movement in Vauchese, life in occupied France, *La Liberte de l'Esprit* (the Freedom of the Spirit), and a collection of writings and paintings illustrating the French striving for freedom.

To the west of Fontaine is **L'Isle-sur-la-Sorgue**, a mecca for antique hunters. The Hôtel Donadeï de Campredon, a beautiful eighteenth-century mansion, is worth visiting for its decoration, in French classical style, and the occasional exhibitions held there. The mansion lies to the north of the town church: to the west, the old hospital has delightful eighteenth-century wood and wrought ironwork with Moustiers pottery jars in the old pharmacy. Finally, almost any walk along the River Sorgue is worthwhile as at several

Olives & Olive Oil

The olive tree was brought to Provence by the Greeks, a necessary introduction as they believed that the last row of olive trees formed the border between the civilised world (their world) and the lands of the barbarian. Today olive groves are a very common sight and are easily picked out, the leaf, one side silver, the other a delicate dark green, being one of the most distinctive and the most beautiful of Provençal trees. There are several types of tree, some producing olives for oil, others for the table. Harvesting of olives for eating is still laborious, involving hand-picking, for green olives, or tree-shaking (again by hand) so that riper, black, olives fall on to carefully arranged mats. For oil production mechanical harvesters are used as damage to the olive is less of a problem. The machine grips the tree and shakes the olives loose, collecting them in a hopper.

After collection the olives are washed and then pressed. Originally this was carried out by mechanical presses, the olives collected on to *scourtins*, rush mats, but hydraulic presses are now used. The first pressing produces Extra Virgin oil, with an acidity below 1 per cent, water is then added and the olives are pressed again, producing Fine Oil (acidity about 2 per cent). More water and a final press produces Semi-Fine or Pure Oil (acidity 3 per cent or higher).

For the table the olives must be cured in a mixture of water and wood ash for a week or so before being pickled in brine. By common consent the black olives of Nyons are the best in Provence, though this, of course, is a matter of taste.

points around the town there are old waterwheels, now moss-grown, but a reminder of the town's history as a centre for olive oil and silk making.

North-west of Fontaine is **Pernes-les-Fontaines**, a village grouped around an ancient clock tower, but with another tower — Tour Ferrande in Rue Gambetta — that is thirteenth-century and contains some quite beautiful frescoes dating from the last quarter of that century.

Back on the main road, the next town is **Cavaillon**, set on the right bank of the Durance in the flatlands at the foot of the Petit Luberon. It is a thriving commercial centre for the early season fruit and vegetable market, and its name is associated

Opposite: Pernes-les-Fontaines

with fragrant, pink melons. The thirteenth-century former cathedral of St Veran is a good example of the Provençal style. A pentagonal external apse is dominated by an octagonal tower. All the side chapels contain paintings and carvings in wood and stone. Walk along the Grand Rue from the church to reach the Archaeological Museum, housed in the chapel of an old hospital, which has a display of prehistoric finds, a reconstruction of Cavaillon's Roman arch, and a room showing 500 Greek, Gaulish and Roman coins found on Colline St Jacques above the town.

To the south of the museum is a beautifully preserved eighteenth-century synagogue. What were known as the four Holy Communities of Avignon, Carpentras, l'Isle-sur-la-Sorgue and Cavaillon, ensured the protection of Jews from early in the fourteenth century until the French Revolution. Consequential, the Comtat Venaissin came to be known as 'the Jewish paradise', under the direct authority of the Popes and administered by elected chiefs called *baylons*. Below the synagogue, in the part reserved for making unleaven bread, is a small Judeo-Comtadin museum.

South of the old cathedral the first-century Roman arch in Place du Clos was moved stone by stone in 1880 from the wall of the church in which it had been embedded. Unlike arches commemorating victories, this one, though richly decorated, is conspicuously lacking in military motifs.

From Place du Clos, a 15-minute walk up a stepped path takes the visitor to the top of the abrupt rock of Colline St Jacques. Neolithic and Ligurian tribes inhabited the site on which the seventeenth-century chapel of St Jacques now stands. Then it became a powerful Celtic op*pidum*. Later, the Greeks of *Massalia* (Marseille) set up a trading post for their goods, which were carried up the Durance river by boatmen who were the forerunners of the powerful guilds formed under Roman rule. In about 42BC, the Romans founded *Cabellio* in the plain below.

Finally, in the Durance valley, we go west from Cavaillon to the Chartreuse of **Bonpas**. A beautiful little chapel is almost all that remains of a thirteenth-century monastery. The village name is interesting. Originally it was *malus passus* as it represented a possible, but difficult, crossing of the Durance. When the first monks arrived, they built a bridge and the name was changed to Bonpas.

At nearby **Châteaurenard**, the remains of the hilltop castle are still impressive, and a climb to the top of the remaining tower offers a fine view of the Durance Valley.

Like other Provençal ranges the Montagne du Luberon, to the north of the Durance valley, is east-west and is gently concave in the middle. The area is a regional park, created to preserve the area's natural assets. The limestone of the hills and the wild untouched landscapes are rich in both flora and fauna. Many species of orchid, some quite rare, grow here as well as other rareties such as black-berried honeysuckle. Bird life includes several rare raptors including Bonelli's eagle and the eagle owl.

A much more intimate mountain than either Ventoux or Lure, Luberon is 65km (40 miles) long, divided into Grand Luberon east of the Combe de Lourmarin with Bonnieux at the col, and Petit Luberon to the west. Once a walker's preserve, a road along the crest of Grand Luberon has more recently opened out its expansive vistas to the motorist.

There is an almost secret atmosphere here. Dozens of varied villages repay a visit; no two are alike in character and architecture, though many have shared the suffering of sixteenth-century massacres. Members of the Vaudois sect, who were followers of the twelfth-century fundamentalist Petrus Valdo, seeking to escape persecution in Piedmont, settled in the Luberon in the fourteenth century. The Popes at Avignon declared the Vaudois to be heretics and the repression of their 10,000 homes took place in 1545 with fanatical inhumanity. Some of the villages were never allowed to be rebuilt, their names extirpated from maps and records. Old Mérindol, the religious centre of the Vaudois, is still just a heap of stones.

The chief village of the Luberon is **Bonnieux**, set close to the top of the road that separates Grand and Petit Luberon, and reached from Apt, Pont Julien or a turning further west along the N100. Positioned on terraces linked by tightly turning streets, and between the old and new churches, the village is extremely attractive, especially when view from the west. The new church has some good paintings, and nearby there is a Bakery Museum. For many visitors the smell and taste of fresh-baked bread is the essence of France. Although Bonnieux's museum does not offer either, it does offer a fascinating look at the history of the baking trade.

From Bonnieux there is a fine view of **Lacoste** to the west, nestling below its partially ruined castle. In the eighteenth century the castle passed to the Sade family. The Marquis de Sade (1740-1814), Lord of Lacoste for 30 years and infamous for his erotic writings, escaped here to avoid prison, but ultimately spent more time in prison than in the castle.

To the west of Lacoste is **Ménerbes**, a sprawling, somewhat elusive village. The castle and church are ruinous and cannot be visited, but the old, upper village with its tight alleys has changed little since the sixteenth century when Catholics besieged the Protestant villagers for over five years. The villagers used a secret passage to replenish their food, a passage never discovered by their besiegers who were constantly amazed by the village's powers of survivals.

West again is **Oppède-le-Vieux**, perhaps the most extraordinary of all the Luberon villages. During the Wars of Religion the Lord of Oppède was Catholic, while his village tenants were Protestant. He sent 800 villagers to slavery in the galleys of Marseille, the almost totally de-

Bonnieux

Lourmarin

Cadenet

Silvicane Abbey

populated village falling into disrepair. About 100 years ago Oppide was rediscovered and has since become popular with artists and holidaymakers. The restoration work has been carefully conceived so that today Oppède is an almost intact medieval village, its houses seemingly growing from the rocky spur on which they sit.

To the south of Bonnieux the D943 that traverses the Luberon passes through glorious scenery, a lush green coombe — sometimes quite narrow — studded with rocky outcrops. The next village is **Lourmarin**. The *château* here is part medieval, part Renaissance: its hexagonal tower can be climbed for a panoramic view of the Luberon, the Durance Valley and Montagne Ste-Victoire beyond. The *château* was once owned by the Agoult family, one of whom — the Countess of Agoult — married the Hungarian composer Franz Liszt. One of their three children married Richard Wagner.

Within the village, one road is named after the writer Albert Camus. The house where the writer lived will be pointed out to you by locals. Camus won the Nobel Prize for Literature in 1957, three years before he died in a car accident. He is buried in Lourmarin cemetery, a little way out of the town, in a simple grave. The cemetery is also the resting place of Henri Bosco, a less well-known Provençal poet.

Moving eastwards from Lourmarin, the traveller passes through a series of delightful villages. There is **Cucuron**, with an interesting museum devoted to the history and culture of the Luberon, and **Ansouis**, with a fine fortified *château* and a museum that claims to be 'extraordinary' but is hardly earth-shattering. The museum is largely to underwater life, with a recreated underwater cave. There is also Provençal furniture and a collection of paintings by the museum's creator, Georges Mazoyer. The village itself is rather more interesting: a pretty place, well-situated on the Luberon.

Go east again, rounding an edge of the Grand Luberon to reach the twelfth-century priory of Carluc at the end of a short, peaceful valley. Next comes Castellet, a hillside hamlet, and Auribeau where a road leads off up towards the high Luberon. From the road's end, the motorist can turn walker and follow GR92 to the summit of Mourre Nègre, at 1,126m (3,400ft) the highest point of the Luberon. The walk will take about 1 hour, but the view makes the effort worthwhile, with the Durance Valley, the Lure and Mont Ventoux, as well as part of the coast, being visible.

To the south of Lourmarin is **Cadenet**, its square dominated by a wonderfully vibrant statue of André Estienne, born here in 1777, and famous as the drummer boy at the Arcole Bridge battle in 1796. The battle was part of Napoleon's Italian campaign, fought to expel the Austrians from northern Italy. The French army had stormed the bridge several times, but each time had been driven back by stout defence.

With defeat looming, André swam the river, placed himself behind the Austrian defenders and beat a rapid tattoo on his drum. Believing themselves attacked from behind, the Austrians fell back, allowing the French to pour across the bridge. During World War II the Germans began to confiscate similar statues for melting down, but a group of Partisans hid the drummer bay until peace came. Their exploit is recorded on the statue's plinth.

While in the village, be sure to visit the Musée de la Vannerie, an interesting museum of basket making set up in an old basket workshop. Cadenet was a centre for basketwork in the nineteenth and early twentieth centuries.

From Cadenet the D543 crosses the Durance en route to Aix-en-provence, but we make one more visit, turning right along the D561, following the river for a short while, then going left to reach **Silvicane**
Abbey. This is the second of the 'Three Sisters of Provence': Thoronet, the third 'Sister' is visited later. The abbey's name is from the Latin *Silva Cannorum* (forest of reeds) because the area was a swamp when the Cistercian monks arrived in the eleventh century. In 1289 during a violent ownership dispute with the Benedictine monks of Montmajour Abbey, there were fights and several monks were held as hostages. An ecclesiastical inquiry was needed to decide that the Cistercians rightfully held Silvacane. They held it for a further two centuries, but the abbey was then abandoned and became a parish church. Later it became a farm, but is now state-owned and has been restored. Externally, the abbey is plain Romanesque, but inside the roof is a wonder of the stonemason's art, with high-soaring ribs supporting stone vaulting, the ribs themselves supported on elegantly twisted columns.

PLACES TO VISIT

Apt

Musée Archéologique
Rue de l'Amphithéâtre
Open: June to September Monday,
Wednesday to Saturday 10am-
12noon, 2-5.30pm; October to May
Monday 2-5pm, Saturday 10am-
12noon, 2-5pm
☎ 90 74 00 34

Musée de Paléontologie
1 Place Jean-Jaurès
Open: All year Monday-Saturday
10am-12noon, 2-5pm
☎ 90 74 08 55

Cavaillon

Musée Archéologique
Grand Rue
Open: All year daily except Tuesday
10am-12noon, 2-6pm (5pm from
October to March)
☎ 90 76 00 34

Synagogue/Jewish-Comtadin Museum
Rue Hèbraïque
Open: All year daily except Tuesday
10am-12noon, 2-6pm (5pm from
October to March)
☎ 90 76 00 34
A joint ticket is available for the two
museums.

Cucuron

Musée Marc Deydier
Open: All year daily except Tuesday
mornings 10am-12noon, 3-7pm
☎ 90 77 25 02

Digne

Musée Municipal
64 Boulevard Gassendi
Open: July and August daily 10.30am-
12noon, 2-6pm (5pm on Sundays);
September to June Monday to
Saturday 2-6pm, Sunday 10am-
12noon, 2-5pm
☎ 92 31 45 29

Museum of World War II
Place Paradis
Open: April to October Tuesday,
Wednesday and Thursday 2-6pm
☎ 92 31 45 29/92 31 54 80

Fondation Alexandra David-Néel
27 Avenue du Maréchal Juin
Open: July to September, tours at
10.30am 2, 3.30 and 5pm; October to
June, tours at 10.30am, 2 and 4pm
☎ 90 31 32 38

Geology Centre
St Benoît
Open: April to November Monday to
Friday 9am-12noon, 2-5.30pm
(4.30pm on Friday)
☎ 90 31 42 73 for information

Fontaine-de-Vaucluse

Le Monde Souterrain de Norbert Casteret
(The Underground World of Norbert
Casteret)
Open: February to mid-November
May to August daily 10am-8pm;
February to April and September to
mid-November Wednesday to
Sunday 11am-6pm
☎ 90 20 34 13

Petrarch Museum
Open: June to September daily
except Tuesday 9.30am-12noon, 2-
6.30pm; mid-April to May and first 2
weeks of October daily except
Tuesday 10am-12noon, 2-6pm;
mid-October to December and March
to mid-April Saturday and Sunday
10am-12noon, 2-6pm
☎ 90 20 37 20

1939-45 Museum
Open: July and August daily except
Tuesday 10am-8pm; mid-April to
June and September to mid-October
daily except Tuesday 10am-12noon,
2-6pm; March to mid-April Saturday
and Sunday 10am-12noon, 2-6pm;
mid-October to December Saturday
and Sunday 10am-12noon, 2-5pm
☎ 90 20 24 00

Vallis Clausa Paper Mill
Open: June to September daily 9am-
5pm; October-May Monday to Friday
9am-5pm
☎ 90 20 31 72

Hotel Donadeï de Compredon
2 Rue Dr Tallet
L'Isle-sur-Sorgue
6km west of Fontaine on the D938
Open: June to September daily except
Tuesday 10am-1pm, 2.30-6.30pm;
October to May daily except Tuesday
9.30am-12.30pm, 2.30-5.30pm
☎ 90 38 17 41

L'Hôpital
Rue Jean-Théophile
L'Isle-sur-Sorgue
6km west of Fontaine on the D938
Open: All year Monday-Friday, guided
tours only, between 2pm and 6pm
☎ 90 38 01 31 ext 137

Tour Ferrande
Pernes-les-Fontaines
10km north of Fontaine on the D938
Open: by request only — inquire at
the Tourist Office (☎ 90 61 31 04)

Forcalquier

Le Couvent des Cordeliers
Boulevard des Martyres
Open: July to mid-September Wednesday to Sunday 10.30am-12noon,
2.30-6pm; May, June, mid-September
to October Sunday and Public Holidays
2.30-6pm
☎ 92 75 02 38

Town Museum
Town Hall
Place du Bourget
Open: July to September daily 10am-
12noon, 3-7pm
☎ 92 75 10 02

Observatoire de Haute Provence
St Michel l'Observatoire
10km to the south-west off the N100
Open: April to September Wednesday and first Sunday of the month
10am-5pm
☎ 92 70 64 00

Conservatory of Ethnic Heritage of Haute Provence
Salagon Priory
Mane
3km to the south on the N100
Open: July to September daily 10am-
12noon, 2-7pm; April to June daily 2-
6pm; October to mid-November
Saturday and Sunday 2-6pm
☎ 92 75 19 93

Château de Sauvan
5km south of Forcalquier on the N100
Open: all year Saturday and Sunday
3-6pm
☎ 92 75 05 64

The Rotunda
Simiane-la-Rotonde
20km west of Forcalquier on the D51
Open: all year at any reasonable time
☎ 92 7590 60

Gordes

Musée Vasarely
Le Château
Open: All year daily except Tuesday
10am-12noon, 2-6pm. Also open on
Tuesdays in July and August
☎ 90 72 02 89

Village de Bories
2km south of Gordes on the D15
Open: June to September daily 9am-
8pm; October to May daily 9am-5.30pm
☎ 90 72 03 48

Musée du Vitrail Frédérique Duran
(Duran Stained-Glass Window Museum)

Moulines des Bouillons
(Olive Oil Museum)
4km south of Gordes on the D103 off the D2/D15
Open: May to mid-December daily except Tuesday 10am-12noon, 2-6pm; February to April daily except Tuesday 10am-12noon, 2-5pm.
Joint ticket available for the two museums
☎ 90 72 22 11

L'Abbaye de Sénanque
8km from Gordes on the D177, off the D15
Open: All year daily except Sunday mornings and religous holidays 10am-12noon, 2-6pm (5pm from December to February)
☎ 90 72 02 72

Haute Provence

Musee Louis Maurel
(Geology Museum)
Barrême
Open: All year daily 10am-12noon, 2-6pm
Telephone before visiting as the museum is not continuously manned.
☎ 92 34 21 10

Fort de Savoie
Colmars
Open: July and August daily 10am-12noon, 2-5pm; June and September by appointment only
☎ 92 83 41 72

Musée de la Vallée
Villa Sapinière
Avenue de la Libération
Barcelonnette
Open: All year Wednesday, Thursday and Saturday 3-6pm (7pm in July and August)
☎ 92 81 27 15

Belle Epoque Stream Train
Puget-Théniers to Annot
Trains run on Sundays in July and August
☎ 92 83 23 03 for details

Train des Pignes
Dignes to Nice
There are four trains daily
☎ 92 31 42 73 for details

Lower Durance Valley

L'Abbaye de Silvacaine
Off the D561 north-west of Aix
Open: April to September daily 9am-7pm; October to March daily except Tuesday 9am-12noon, 2-5pm
☎ 42 50 41 69

Chartreuse de Bonpas
10km north-west of Cavaillon on the D973
Open: gardens only — all year daily 9am-12noon, 2-6.30pm (5.30 from October to April)

Tour du Griffon
Châteaurenard
Open: May to September Monday to Thursday, Sunday 10am-12noon, 3-6.30pm, Saturday 10am-12noon; March, April and October Monday to Thursday, Sunday 10am-12noon, 3-5pm, Saturday 10am-12noon
☎ 90 94 23 27

Luberon

Château Sabran
Ansouis
Open: All year daily 2.30-6pm.
Closed on Tuesday October to March
☎ 90 09 82 70

Musée Extraordinaire de Georges Mazoyer
Rue de Vieux Moulin
Ansouis
Open: June to September daily except Tuesday 2-7pm; October to May daily except Tuesday 2-6pm
☎ 90 09 82 64

Musée de la Boulangerie
Rue de la République
Bonnieux
Open: June to September daily except
Tuesday 10am-12noon, 3-6.30pm;
March, April, October to December
Saturdays, Sundays and holidays
10am-12noon, 3-6.30pm
☎ 90 75 88 34

Musée de la Vannerie
(Basket Making Museum)
La Gioneuse
Avenue Philippe-de-Girard
Cadenet
Open: All year daily except Tuesday
and Sunday morning 10am-12noon,
2.30-6.30pm (5.30pm from November
to March)
☎ 90 68 2444

Le Château
Lourmarin
Open: June to September daily
10.30am-12noon, 2.30-6.30pm;
October to May daily 10.30am-
12noon, 2.30-5.30pm (but closed
Tuesdays November to March)
☎ 90 68 15 23

Manosque

Centre Jean Giono
1 Boulevard Elémir Bourges
Open: All year Tuesday to Saturday
9am-5pm
☎ 92 72 76 10

Prieuré de Ganagobie
25km north of Manosque on the D30,
off the N96
Open: All year daily 9.30am-12noon,
2.30-5pm
☎ 92 68 00 04

Musée Vivant l'Abeille
(Bee Museum)
Route de Manosque
Valensole
Open: All year except February
Tuesday-Saturday 10am-12noon,
1.30-5.30pm (4pm on Saturday)
☎ 92 74 85 28

Riez

Musée Nature de Provence
4 Allée Louis Gardiol
Open: All year Tuesday to Saturday
12noon-6.30pm
☎ 92 77 82 80

Sisteron

La Citadelle
Open: April to October 9am-6pm
☎ 92 61 12 03

Musée de Sisteron
Off the Place de la République
No official opening hours. Ask at the
Tourist Office (Hôtel de Ville, Avenue
de la Libération, ☎ 92 61 12 03) for
permission to visit.

Arles & The Camargue

3

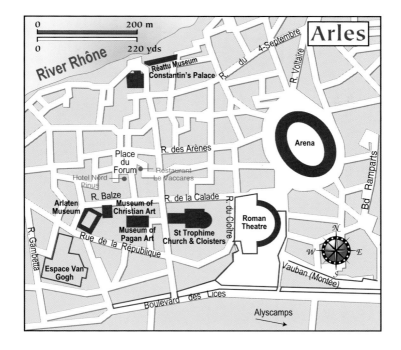

Arles, 38km (24 miles) south of Avignon, is a popular centre, perhaps the most Provençal of all the region's towns. It is full of reminders of its illustrious past, reminders that cover the centuries, from the Arena of the early Roman Empire to the blazing yellow cornfields of Vincent van Gogh's paintings.

The town has a Celtic-Ligurian past, though it is with the Greeks that the first positive records arrive. Then it had two names, *Theline* (the Provider), which was replaced by

Opposite: Daudet's windmill, between Arles and Les Baux-de-Provence

Arelate (the town in the marsh). Both are apt, as the land around the town is remarkably fertile, while to the south there are the swamps of the Camargue, swamps that seeped closer to the town 2,000 years ago. Its position on the Roman roads to Gaul meant that it was important when the Romans finally subdued the area, and it soon rivalled the nearby Phoenician port of *Massalia* (Marseille). The rivalry grew when Arles took the side of Julius Caesar in his feud with Pompey, and when Caesar emerged victorious it is possible to imagine that the noise of the cheering in his town was rivalled only by that of falling masonry as the defences of Pompey's town were dismantled.

Thereafter, Arles became increasingly important. Originally, when the town was the first Roman foundation in Gaul, it was known as 'the granary of Rome', a somewhat disparaging title which implies that it existed only to fill its master's bread basket, though an interesting flashback to the Greek name. Later, Arles gained a better title, 'the little Rome of the Gauls'.

By the fifth century, Arles had become so prosperous that 'all that the Orient, or unguent Arabia, luxuriant Assyria, fertile Africa and fecund Gaul produce is to be found there'. As soon as the Romans had retreated from this area of Gaul, pulling in their horns as the barbarian hordes poured in on Rome, this wealth brought others keen to replace the town's Roman masters. First came the Goths, then the Franks. Finally, in the early eighth century, the Saracens arrived. They did not stay long, freedom for the townsfolk of Arles being apparently heralded by the arrival of Charles Martel's army. Martel attacked the town, routing the Saracens at first but facing stiffer opposition when they barricaded themselves in the Arena. Martel lost many men in taking that last defence and, when the dust had settled, he took out his anger and frustration by slaughtering the townsfolk. The poor people must have wondered if they should have been so enthusiastic when Martel arrived.

Today Arles is a museum city, proud of its Roman and medieval heritage. Savour its atmosphere on foot; a car is of no help in the narrow streets. Start in the tree-lined Boulevard des Lices, which is thoroughly modern, with thronged cafés and restaurants, and make for the Place de la République where there is a Roman obelisk of Egyptian stone. This was moved here from the chariot racecourse in a suburb of Trinquetaille.

On one side of the square is the seventeenth-century *hôtel de ville*, on another is the west façade of St Trophime church. The west porch is a delight of Romanesque art. There are elaborate carvings in great rhythmical patterns and borrowed motifs from Syrian, Persian, Nordic and antique Roman sources. Illiterate pilgrims, on their way to St James of Compostela in Spain, received the carved messages of election and damnation as effectively as a television advertisement today. Those pilgrims retraced a route followed by St Trophime himself who, it is said, reached the city in the first century, arriving just as the townsfolk were preparing to sacrifice three youths to their pagan gods. The saint hurled himself at the crowd and pagan priests, shouting that the true ethic was to love, not slaughter, your fellow man. The priests fled and the city was converted to Christianity. In the first church that stood on the site, St Augustine was consecrated as the first Bishop of England.

The interior of the church of St Trophime is equally as fine and strong as the exterior. An unusually narrow nave lends exaggerated height to the vaults. Paintings, carvings in wood and ivory, Aubusson tapestries and sarcophagi adorn the church, giving it a rich, but not overly ornate feel. It is also possible to visit the cloisters of the one-time town cathedral. They are superb: two of the four sides are twelfth-century and are pure Romanesque, while the other two sides were added two centuries later and are Gothic, not quite as pure in their form as there was some attempt to match the earlier work. The carvings, in particular, are exquisite.

Just north of Place de la République is the small and shady Place du Forum with a statue of the poet Frédéric Mistral; the wrought ironwork surrounding it is in the form of a *ficheiroun*, or trident, traditionally used by the cowboys or *gardians* of the Camargue. Embedded in the angle of the wall of the venerable Hôtel Nord-Pinus are two Corinthian columns which once formed part of a temple adjoining the Roman forum.

The Place du Forum is a reminder of Vincent van Gogh's brief stay in Arles, between February 1888 and May 1889, when his painting reached full maturity. Unfortunately, there is no museum to Vincent van Gogh in Arles. The problem now is that the town, which is very conscious of the tourist value of the artist, could not afford to cover even one wall with paintings. The town does, however, have two buildings named after him: the Espace van Gogh has an extensive library of books on the most

famous inhabitant and holds occasional exhibitions. The Foundation Vincent van Gogh-Arles, close to the Espace, was opened as a tribute to Vincent's dream of an artists' community in Arles. It houses a collection of contemporary art — paintings, sculpture, designs, photography, music and writings — inspired by van Gogh — donated by the artists concerned. The works include pieces by Frances Bacon, Christian Lacroix and Kerel Appel. When the permanent collection is on tour, there are exhibitions of contemporary art.

After van Gogh, the next biggest attractions are the Roman remains. The Arena, or Amphitheatre, is the chief place of interest. It is truly impressive, a statement in stone of the Roman Empire's feelings about its own permanence. In size, the Arena is about twentieth of those that survive, being 137m (450ft) along the long side of its oval, 107m (350ft) across the short side. When completed, it could have seated over 25,000 spectators to watch the events and contests. Below the walls of the Arena, the visitor can still see the caged areas where animals would have been kept before they went to the arena to kill or be killed.

Today it is bulls that are led to the Arena. Usually, the events here and at nearby Nîmes are Provençal, the nimble bulls of the Camargue being used. In this event, the bull has a rosette attached to its forehead and is put in the ring with several *rasetteurs*, each dressed in his uniform of white shirt and trousers, who try to remove the rosette while preserving life and

The Roman Arena, Arles

Pont 'Van Gogh', Arles

Van Gogh at Arles

Vincent Van Gogh, born in Groot-Zundert, Holland on 30 March 1853, arrived in Arles from Paris in February 1888. His room, in a small hotel above a café with a central billiards table, had two straw-covered chairs and a narrow bed, as all who love his paintings will know. He painted continuously — the Alyscamps, the drawbridge on the canal, the Arles cafés — and wrote almost as often to ask his Parisian friends to join him. Only Paul Gauguin came, but their friendship soon turned sour, van Gogh's increasingly irrational behaviour creating an insurmountable hurdle. He hurled a glass at Gauguin, threatened him with a razor and, finally and famously, cut off part of one of his ears and gave it to Gauguin wrapped in paper. Not surprisingly Gauguin left Arles hurriedly.

Left alone, van Gogh suffered from hallucinations and increasing bouts of insanity. He was hopitalised (in what is now the Espace van Gogh) producing some of his best work there. Although released for a short period, his health deteriorated and he was transferred to an asylum in St-Rémy-de-Provence in May 1889. Here he found peace and seemed well when, after his release in May 1890 he arrived in Paris. He move to Auvers-sur-Oise and there, on 27 July 1890, he shot himself with a revolver borrowed on the pretext of shooting crows.

During his 15-month stay at Arles van Gogh painted some 200 pictures, but did not sell one. Legends have it that for years after his death his paintings would turn up — as a board across a broken window, as part of a chicken coop and so on. It is ironical that paintings the citizens of Arles thought so little of are now so expensive that neither the Espace van Gogh nor the Foundation Vincent van Gogh-Arles can afford one, with the result that there are now none of his paintings in the town.

The setting for van Gogh's *Café Terrace at Night* is now a furniture shop and that for *The Yellow House* in Place Lamartine, which he shared with Paul Gauguin, was destroyed by bombs in 1944. However, the cemetery of the Alyscamps remains much as it was when he painted it. The famous drawbridge (the Pont de Langlois, erected by an earlier Dutchman) over the Marseille and Rhône Canal just south of Arles was sketched and painted into immortality by Vincent. It was pulled down in 1926, only to be reconstructed later. It no longer moves, as the original did, but is no less appealing for that. The Arlesian costumes he painted are no longer seen today, except on rather self-conscious folkloric days.

limb. The bull is never harmed, though the same cannot be said of the *rasetteurs*, many of whom have been severely gored. The event raises ethical questions for animal lovers, but at least in Provençal bullfighting there is no final killing. However, bullfights of the Spanish variety are also held both at Arles and Nîmes. These involve a larger, more dangerous bull that is killed at the end of the contest, either by the matador or by ring men.

The Arena was erected in the first century AD, though there was probably an earlier wooden one on the same site. That would have dated from around the first century BC, the same time that the Theatre was built. The Theatre, built when Augustus was emperor, was sumptuously decorated with statues and marble facings, and was designed to hold about 7,000 people. Sadly, it was badly damaged in medieval times and only some columns and seating now remain. Constantine's Palace, which is actually the public baths and occasionally known as the Trouille Baths, is much later, dating from the fourth century, the time of Constantine the Great. The water to supply the baths was brought by aqueduct from Eygalières, 25km (15½ miles) away.

The last significant Roman site is the Alyscamps, the remains of a necropolis that survived its original users. The name derives from the Latin *Alysii Campi*, Elysian fields, the abode of the dead. At the end of the site is a large ruin that was once the church of St Honorat. Over a period of about 900 years — though chiefly in three periods, in the fourth, eighth and twelfth centuries — this was one of the most famous necropolises in the world and thousands of burials took place here. In Roman times the Aurelian Way led past the tombstones to reach the gates of the town. The area's greatest period was post-Roman, however, when miracles were said to have occured around the tomb of St Genesius, beheaded by the Romans. As the fame of Genesius spread, more and more Christians demanded to be buried here. The site was later used as a convenient quarry, but the best of the stonetombs can now be seen in the Museum of Christian Art. The Museum of Pagan Art holds the better objects from Arles' pre-Christian period.

Other museums include the Réattu which has a large collection of tapestries, furniture, ceramics and paintings, including works by Gauguin, Léger and Vasarely. There are also a large number of drawings by Picasso. Behind the museum, a really good walk along a bank of the Rhône is possible. The Arlaten Museum was created in 1896 by the traditionalist poet Mistral as 'the true museum of the living life and people of Arles', and enlarged with the money he won as Nobel Prize Laureate for Literature in 1904. He packed the thirty rooms with anything which recorded the culture of his beloved *pays d'Arles*, all the items being labelled in Provençal in his own hand. From herbs to costumes, poems to furniture, theatre programmes to life-size tableaux; here is yester-year's Provence.

Finally, the visitor should take the D35 southwards, turning left from it to see van Gogh's drawbridge over the canal, and should then take the N570 northwards, turning off right along the D17 to visit the abbey of Montmajour. The abbey was built on rising ground above what had been marshland drained by the monks. Founded in the tenth century, it fell into a long decline and is now being restored. The keep is a powerful and commanding presence, in sharp contrast with the demure twelfth-century cloister and the church, whose crypt is partly hewn out of the rock.

While at the site, do not miss the tiny burial chapel of Ste Croix in the form of a Greek cross in a field just below the abbey. It is a gem of Provençal Romanesque art and is surrounded by tombs cut out of the rock.

The Roman and medieval impressions gained in Arles can be extended by visiting St Gilles and Nîmes in Gard. **St Gilles**, 16km (10 miles) west of Arles on the N572, was also a stopping-place for pilgrims on their way to St James of Compostela in northern Spain. Three rounded doors fill the entire width of the west front of the abbey-church, and the effect is even more impressive than at St Trophime. Indeed, the west front is thought by many to be the finest example of Romanesque sculpture in southern France. The carvings surrounding them were completed in the late twelfth and early thirteenth centuries and depict scenes from the life of Christ, together with some scenes from the Old Testament. St Gilles' tomb is in the crypt which is an early example (eleventh-century) of ogival vaulting.

A belfry contains a spiral staircase — Le Vis de St Gilles — whose fifty steps are roofed with stone like a curving tunnel, an early example of the stonemason's craft. It is said that stonemasons come from far afield in order to view the staircase, so perfect is its execution, some of them leaving graffiti on the stonework. Close to the abbey, the Maison Romane, is worth visiting. The house, birth-place of Guy Foulque, elected Pope Clement IV in 1265, has an interesting collection of excavated stonework from St Gilles Abbey and a collection of old tools from local crafts.

North-west from St Gilles, the D42 passes the Garons airfield and enters Nîmes, but first go west once more to visit **Aigues-Mortes** (the town of the dead waters). From a distance, the town appears to rise out of the surrounding marshland — which originally gave it its name — as though it were the painted backdrop for a Disney cartoon. It was built almost from nothing as there was only a very tiny fishing village here when Louis IX came in the mid-thirteenth century. The king needed a Mediterranean port so that he could take his army on a crusade but, as France was fragmented, he did not have one until he found a fishing village nestling among the dead waters of the Western Camargue. The

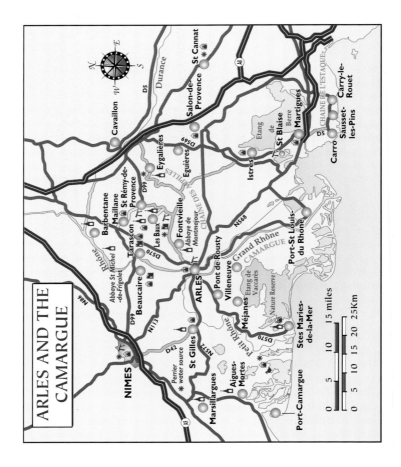

ARLES AND THE CAMARGUE

king built his port, and that is what we see today; it is virtually untouched, its ramparts are still complete and, since the population is less now than it was then, the village is still confined within them.

To walk the ramparts — especially at dawn or dusk — is one of the delights of Provence. It takes about 1 hour to make the journey, the walk going over several gates, particularly on the seaward side, and past many towers. One of these is the Wick Tower, where a lamp burned, not, as might be supposed, as a beacon to ships, but as a constant source of fire for the lighting of powder in the cannon.

The ramparts at Aigues-Mortes

The Burgundian Tower has a much less attractive reason for its name. In the Hundred Years' War, the Burgundians held the town and sided with the English in the fight for the French crown. In 1418, the Gascons laid siege to Aigues-Mortes, eventually gaining secret access one night and slaughtering the garrison to a man. Needing a quick solution to the problem of a pile of dead Burgundians without polluting the near-stagnant waters around the town, the Gascons threw the corpses into this tower, pouring salt on to preserve them until they could arrange a more discreet burial.

Near the town's Old Port is the Constance Tower, separated from the main ramparts by a bridged moat. This massive structure, almost 55m (180ft) high, has been used as a prison on several occasions. A climb up the steps to the tower's top is rewarded by a fine view over the town.

North of Aigues-Mortes, the visitor is on the road to Nîmes. But before reaching that town, stop off at Teillan Castle, near **Marsillargues**. This fine Renaissance *château* is actually a converted monastery. The outbuildings include a pigeon loft with over 1,500 nest holes and a rotating nest ladder. It is also worth visiting the source and bottling plant of Perrier Water. Annual production of the naturally carbonated water now approaches 1,000 million bottles. Much of this output is exported, to the rest of Europe, North America, Australia and the Middle East.

Nîmes is the old Gaulish tribal capital of *Nemausus* — named after a local god said to live in a spring near the first town site. The town was taken early by the Romans and was soon important because of its position on the road to Spain. In medieval times, Nîmes was often in the wrong place or on the wrong side at crucial times and was looted and plundered on many occasions. Once, when it was free of the ravages of war for a time, the town was hit by the plague instead. Real stability did not arrive until the late eighteenth century, so that the town has much architecture of that period.

The prosperity of that time came partly from the production of a heavy blue serge cloth, later known as denim (from *de Nîmes*), which was exported to California for Levi Strauss. He rivetted the cloth together to form wear-resistant trousers for Gold Rush miners. Also from Nîmes was Jean Nicot, born in the town in 1650. In the late seventeenth century he introduced tobacco to France, and the drug isolated from its leaves was called nicotine.

It is, however, for the Roman remains that most visitors come. The Arena (Amphitheatre) is smaller than that at Arles, but in a better state of preservation. Built in the first century AD, it is 128m (420ft) long and 100m (330ft) across and could hold 20,000 people — and still does so for shows and bullfights. In medieval times, it served as a village, housing 2,000 people. As with Arles, the Arena bullfights are both Provençal and Spanish style.

Maison Carrée, the other important Roman monument, stands a little away from the Arena. The name means 'Square House', which shows a certain lack of geometric awareness concerning what is now believed to be the finest surviving Roman temple, built in Hellenic style in the first century BC. It was probably dedicated to Jupiter, Juno and Minerva. The sanctum of the temple is walled and is used for regular exhibitions of comtemporary art.

Close by is the Carré d'Art, a new building of stone, glass and steel designed by the British architect Norman Foster. The building opened in 1993 and houses a permanent gallery of contemporary art.

In the Fountain Gardens there are the ruins of a much less well-preserved Roman temple of Diana, together with the remains of the town's baths. Close by, the Magne Tower is of first century AD construction and is believed to have been part of the Roman town's defensive ramparts. Elsewhere, the *castellum* was the collecting basin for the water brought by aqueduct from Pont du Gard. The start of the ten canals that distributed the water can be seen at this most interesting site, the only other example of which is at Pompeii. Finally, Porte d'Auguste is the old gateway in the town walls and through it ran the Via Domitia.

Those with enough time, can find Alphonse Daudet's birthplace, the fine house at 20 Boulevard Gambetta, or visit one of the the town's museums. The Archaeology Museum, which houses the best of the excavated finds from the Roman period, occupies the ground floor of the old Jesuit College, the first floor being occupied by the natural history museum, which has an interesting collection of local prehistory and an ethnography section with collections from Africa and Asia. The Fine Arts Museum has a collection from many schools and periods, while the Museum of Old Nîmes, perhaps the best, has a collection of furniture and items on the history of bullfighting. The museum is housed in a fine seventeenth-century house that was once the Bishop's Palace.

Finally, Nîmes has an excellent planetarium, to the north of Porte d'Augustus on the flank of Mont Duplan and, for younger visitors, the Aquatropic, a water park with slides and a wave-making machine.

East from Nîmes, and reachable by going north from Arles, are the twin towns of Beaucaire and Tarascon, staring at each other from opposite sides of the Rhône.

Tarascon's massive, fifteenth-century moated castle, named after Good King René the most famous of Provençal rulers, is an outstanding example of medieval fortification and is very well-preserved. After it was built, it defied the castle of Beaucaire on the opposite bank — independent Provence confronting the Kingdom of France. Elegant upper rooms served as the apartments of royalty and were used for banquets when the nobles were entertained by strolling troubadours.

Close by is the restored twelfth-century church of Ste Marthe, which is said to contain her remains. Legend has it that the saint, coming from the Camargue, vanquished the *tarasque,* a monster which terrified the town and devoured its children. The saint pacified the monster by giving the sign of the Cross and, placing her girdle round its neck, led it to the Rhône, into which it vanished for ever. A festival, decreed by King René in 1496, has been kept alive on the last Sunday in June when a papier-mâché *tarasque* is paraded with much jollification — a symbol of Christianity's triumph over Paganism.

Northwest from the church, in Rue Proudhon is Musée Souleïado which explores the town's textile industry which brought prosperity a couple of hundred years ago. The curious name is Provençal for the sun seen through clouds and was used by a company which revived the industry earlier this century. The museum has a vast collection of old wood blocks and other items relating to the hand-printing of fabrics.

Northwest again is the Maison de Tartarin. Tartarin was the central character in one of Daudet's most famous books. Fat and bearded, and portrayed as a modern Don Quixote, Tartarin brought great fame to the town in the 1870s and in his honour the house — built at that time — has been furnished in authentic period style. Behind the house there is a small tropical garden with a conservatory housing a statue of the Tarasque beside a knight in the ar-

The Roman Amphi-
theatre, Nîmes

Maison Carrée,
Nîmes

Frédéric Mistral & the Langue d'Oc

In France two languages evolved after the Romans had withdrawn across the Alps. In the north the Oïl language (*lange d'Oïl*) was spoken, while in the south the Oc language (*lange d'Oc*) evolved, the names of the two derived from the words used for 'yes'. Oc was spoken throughout an area now called Occitania, encompassing Gascony, Roussillon/Catalonia, Provence and Savoy: the regional name Languedoc is a reminder of the Occitan past. Oc was the language of the troubadours, the minstrels of the southern French courts and became the language of romance and courtliness. But, in 1539 the Edict of Villers-Cotterêts decreed that French should be the countrywide language of administration and commerce. Thereafter Oc — now known by the more romantic name Provençal — was used only in villages and by the peasant folk, becoming the language of the unsophisticated. Nevertheless it survived and when, in the late seventeenth and early eighteenth century, southern France begun to awaken to its cultural heritage, interest in it revived. A group of writers formed the Félibrige (from the Provencal *félibre* — doctor) with the aim of re-establishing the language. Foremost of them was Frédéric Mistral who was born in 1830 in Maillane (north of Arles, near St Rémy-de-Provence). Mistral composed his great works *Mirèio* and *Calendau* in Provençal and collected examples of the language from all over the area to compile a dictionary and reference book that is still in use today. Mistral was awarded the Nobel Prize for Literature in 1904. He died at Maillane in 1914. Today, thanks to his efforts Provençal lives on, though this is mainly in literature rather than its spoken form.

mour of King René's time.

Beaucaire, on the far bank, has an equal amount to keep the visitor occupied. In contrast to Tarascon, the castle is disappointing, being largely ruinous. However, the castle's Tour Polygonale is interesting for its shape, for a small Romanesque chapel and the Musée Auguste Jacquet which houses an archaeological collection. The view from the castle ramparts is excellent and the gardens on its southern edge are equally good.

Close to the town, about 3km (2 miles) or so to the north-west, off the D986, lies the twelfth-century Abbaye de St Romain.

North of Tarascon, on the D35, is **Boulbon** which lies on the slopes of the Montagnette hills overlooking the River Rhône and the Vallabrègues Dam. Boulbon is a pleasant old *bourg* whose focal point is its ruined castle. Each first of June they hold the Procession of the Bottles (*Fioles*) and blessing of the wine at the Chapel of St Marcellin, the patron saint of wine.

Continuing northwards on the D81 and then bearing right, the visitor reaches the abbey of St Michel-de-Frigolet. This was named after the Provençal word for thyme, the building being set amid aromatic herbs of the *garrigue*, and was immortalised in Alphonse Daudet's story, 'The Elixir of the Reverend Father Gaucher' from the *Lettres de Mon Moulin*. The site museum has collections of Provençal furniture and ancient pharmacy jars.

North of the abbey is **Barbentane** with a *château* whose interior is almost a museum devoted to the furniture of the Louis XV and Louis XVI periods, though the room decoration shows a distinct Italian influence. There is also some fine porcelain and china. Alternatively, the traveller can turn east to reach **Maillane** where the great man of Provençal history, Frédéric Mistral, was born and lies buried. The house that he occupied for the last 40 years of his life is now a museum in his honour.

Close to Maillane is **Graveson** where a house that once belonged to the monks of St Michel de Frigolet Abbey is now a small museum of perfumes, with a collection of early copper stills and other equipment used in perfume making, and a collection of different essences.

Southward now is **St Rémy-de-Provence**, a popular centre for its choice of hotels, its setting close to the Alpilles Hills, and the fruit and market-gardens which surround it.

The most famous of all astrologers, Michel de Nostradamus (1503-66) was born here, though he chose to live in Salone-de-Provence. The Musée Alpilles Pierre de Brun, in a handsome sixteenth-century mansion, has some souvenirs of the man who became physician to Charles IX, and was struck off for keeping his remedies secret. Turning to astrology, he wrote his highly obscurantist *Centuries*, quatrains of predictions which impressed Catherine de Medici. These predictions made him rich and famous and still have their enthusiasts, who believe that Nostradamus foretold wars, the death of President Kennedy, and much more.

Another famous resident of St Rémy was Vincent van Gogh who was treated at a sanatorium in the converted monastery of St Paul-de-Mausole — to the south along the D5 towards *Glanum* and Les Baux. The monastery maintains a few reminders of his year-long stay. It was here that van Gogh painted *Starry Night* and *The Sower*, two of his distinctive works. Do not miss the twelfth-century cloisters with their richly carved capitals. Behind the monastery, the Mas de la Pyramide is a farm built into the rock of Les Alpilles, above which the Romans had their quarry for the construction of *Glanum*. The farm now houses a small museum of the old rural life. The farm's name derives from the 20m (66ft) pillar of rock left behind by the quarrymen.

Back in the town, the Hôtel Estrine, a fine eighteenth-century mansion in Rue Estrine, houses the Centre d'Art Présence van Gogh, with an audio-visual display and other items illustrating van Gogh's time at St Rémy and some of the local views he painted. There are also regular exhibitions of contemporary art. Close to the Centre — turn right on exiting to reach the street junction — is the Nostradamus Fountain, with a portrait of the astrologer.

The Hôtel de Sade, once the home of relatives of the notorious marquis, houses an archeological museum that should be looked at after a visit to the archaeological site of *Glanum*, as many items from there are shown in the museum.

However, before going to *Glanum*, it is worth going to see two Roman monuments whose grace will delight even those not interested in antiquities. Less than 2km (1¼ miles) south of St Rémy, on the right-hand side of the D5, they are unenclosed, surrounded by turf and trees. Their lightness and delicacy betray a Greek influence. One is the municipal arch of around 20BC, the oldest and smallest to survive in France. It stood at the entrance to the town of *Glanum* on the other side of the road, and the *Via Domitia* highway passed under it. The reliefs commemorate Julius Caesar's victories over the Gauls and Greeks of *Massalia* in 49BC, but there is also a Gaul being granted his freedom. Next to the arch is a mausoleum, the best preserved of any in the Roman world and one of the most beautiful. Apart from the finial — probably a pine cone — it is complete. Its reliefs and freezes depict battle and hunting scenes, the inscription suggesting it was raised in memory of two grandsons of the Emperor Augustus.

In *Glanum*, excavations have revealed the presence of Neolithic, Ligurian and Gaulish peoples who settled here before Phoenician traders named the place *Glanon*, a name that Caesar later Romanised to *Glanum*. Houses with fine mosaics, a forum, baths, temples and a *nymphaeum*, can be seen in this extensive open-air museum where much remains to be uncovered. The state of preservation of the site owes much to the history of the city. After it was abandoned, but before there had been much time for pillage, the waterways to the site became blocked with debris, and silt from the hills quickly built up, covering the site and hiding it from view.

The Chaîne des Alpilles, bare white limestone formations eroded into striking sculpted forms, dominate the otherwise flat, well-irrigated landscape to the south of St Rémy. They give an impression of height and grandeur, though nowhere do they reach 500m (1,640ft). A round tour of 80km (50 miles) re-

Roman remains at St Rémy-de-Provence

Evening sunshine on the Montagne du Défends, Chaîne des Alpilles

A Provençal vineyard, Les Alpilles

veals the loveliest parts; walkers can cross the chain on the GR6 pathway. This is one of the best walks in Provence, touching Eyguières, Aureille, Eygalières, the peak of La Caume, Les Baux-de-Provence and St Gabriel. If that is too far, then walkers should limit themselves to following the GR either from Eygalières to Les Baux — a distance of about 27km (17 miles),

Santons

During the Revolution, when churches were closed, Jean-Louis Lagnel, a Marseilles sculpture, started to make small figures that the locals, deprived of access to their nativities at Christmas, could use to create their own cribs. The figures, modelled in clay, fired and painted in bright colours, were called *santons*, 'little saints' in Provençal. Their appeal was immediate and santon cribs soon become an important feature of Provençal homes. When churchs re-opened, santon cribs were often set up within them, the santon makers turning their hands to more traditional figures — knife grinders, fishermen, milkmaids and so on. Today santon making is one fo the Provence's most traditional crafts, the figurines being one of the area's best loved souvenirs.

taking about 7½ hours — or from Les Baux to Tarascon — a distance of about 21km (13 miles) and taking around 6 hours. Each of these is a good day's outing by the time the bus has carried you back, but a day that does full justice to this fine, little hill range.

For most visitors **Les Baux-de-Provence** is the main objective. This extraordinary village is hardly distinguishable from the spur of naked rock in which it is set. Prehistoric man has left traces of his safe *oppidum*, but little is known about his occupation. More is known of the Lords of Les Baux who, from the eleventh to the fifteenth centuries, were powerful far beyond the confines of Provence. They have a history that is filled for the most part with brigandage except for the thirteenth century, when Les Baux was famous for its 'Courts of Love' and its troubadours.

In the seventeenth century, the town embraced Protestantism; Louis XIII and Richelieu had the castle and ramparts destroyed. A once populous town then began to crumble into decay. Today, the rituals of the sixteenth-century Midnight Mass (*pastrage*) — symbolic of pastoral Provence — are kept movingly alive each Christmas Eve in the church of St Vincent which is packed for the occasion. As part of the Mass, shepherds in traditional long cloaks escort a new-born lamb — seated in a cart pulled by a ram — to the altar.

Visitors enter the new village of Les Baux through Port Mage, cut in 1866. To the right is the seventeenth-century town hall which now houses a *santon* museum. At the road fork, the right branch can be followed to Porte Eyguirères, the old entrance. Continue along Rue de l'Église to reach the sixteenth century Hôtel des Porcelet which houses the Musée Yves Brayer, a collection of works by Brayer who settled in Les Baux after spending many years in Spain and Morocco.

At the Hôtel des Porcelet, Grande Rue — the left branch at the fork — rejoins. Grande Rue passes the Renaissance Hôtel Jean de Brion in which the engraver and painter Louis Jou lived. It houses an exhibition of his work. Also in Grande Rue are the Hôtel de Manville housing a gallery of contemporary art, and a sixteenth-century Protestant chapel. A side road, Rue de Trencat, to the left, is carved from the rock. It passes the old village bread oven and leads to the deserted village. From the junction of Grande Rue and the Rue de d'Église the twelfth-century church of St Vincent, with its beautiful campanile (the 'lantern of the dead'), is reached. Close to the church is the Chapelle des Pénitents Blancs, seventeenth century but restored in 1936 when the walls were frescoed by Yves Brayer. From the nearby viewpoint in Place St Vincent is a fine view over the Val d'Enfer (Valley of Hell), with its tortured rock formations. In the valley stands the Pavilion de la Reine Jeanne, an interesting Renaissance building erected in the late sixteenth century by a 'Queen' of Les Baux. The building was much loved by Mistral who had a copy made for his tomb.

The old, deserted, village is reached at the Hôtel du Brau in Rue Trencat. Here there is a small museum of excavated items and a fine model of how the village looked in medieval times. Inside the old site there are several old chapels, a Saracen Tower, the Paravelle Tower which offers a fine view of the old castle, the castle ruins themselves and a stone pigeon loft. Within St Blaise Chapel there is a small olive museum. There is also a monument to the local poet, Charloun Rieu of Paradou, who wrote the words for Nöel at Midnight Mass.

At the time of writing there is also a collection of ancient siege artillery built from original plans.

The deserted village, floodlit at night, is a real delight, but those with children or walking difficulties should be cautious. Some areas of the site have unprotected cliff edges and the ascent of the Saracen Tower is not for the faint-hearted.

Bauxite, discovered here in 1822 as a vital mineral from which aluminium is extracted, perpetuates the name of Les Baux, although the major bauxite quarries are elsewhere in central Provence. One cavern has been used to house the Cathédrale d'Images in which forty projectors are used to create huge murals thrown on giant white walls. The spectacular images include famous wall paintings — from neolithic caves and Egyptian tombs — as well as images of Provence. The cavern lies north of Les Baux: to the south is another unusual site, La Petite Provence, in the village of Pardou. Here over 300 *santons* have been used to recreate an old Provençal village.

An itinerary west of St Rémy is to follow the D99, turning off at St Etienne-du-Grés on to the D32. At the next crossroads, and set back on the hillside on the left, is the curious twelfth-century chapel of St Gabriel. The Auberge du Carrefour has the key. A mixture of antique Roman motifs, Romanesque, Oriental and Classical themes cover the façade. In contrast, the interior is severe and simple.

Now keep on the road signposted 'Fontvieille'. Outside the village is the **Moulin de Daudet**, a much-visited mill-museum because of its associations with Alphonse Daudet. His *Lettres de Mon Moulin* were not written here; Daudet did not write them entirely himself, and he hardly ever visited the mill. He was essentially a Parisian teller of elegantly turned tales borrowed from Provençal sources. Despite this, the windmill attracts the faithful. The views from it are stunning, embracing Les Alpilles and the Rhône Valley.

Beyond the mill is a remarkable Roman ruin at **Barbegal**. A fourth-century water-mill was fed by ingenious aqueducts whose ruined arches can be seen nearby. Two parallel series of shutes worked sixteen water-mills which ground the local wheat for Arles and Rome. Slots which held the grindstones, and the course of the mill-race, are still visible.

An itinerary east of St Rémy allows a delightful part of the Alpilles to be discovered. Take the D5 south and, for a panoramic view, turn left

Medieval war machine at Les Baux-de-Provence

Château de l'Empéri, Salon-de-Provence

after 4km (2½ miles) and go to the top of La Caume 387m (1,270ft) where a short walk reveals a view of the flatlands of Crau, the Camargue, lagoons, and the distant sea.

Continue on the D5 almost as far as Maussane where a left turn enters the peaceful valleys of the buckled, eroded flanks of the Alpilles. Follow the route through Le Destet, Mas-de-Montfort and Aureille to Eyguières, with its fountains. Turn left on to the Orgon road (D569), and left again where the Castelas de Roquemartine ruins overlook the road. Return to Mas-de-Montfort, and turn right to Eygalières. It is worth exploring here before continuing east to the twelfth-century chapel of St Sixte, which is on a slope bare except for some cypresses and is another of those unforgettable rural chapels.

To the south now is **Salon-de-Provence**, the olive oil capital of Provence. In the sixteenth century, the town was home to Adam de Craponne, a famous civil engineer, and Nostradamus, the much more famous astrologer. There is a museum to the latter in what was his house. Elsewhere in the town, the beautiful, if somewhat angular, Château de l'Empéri is well-worth visiting. It stands on top of the Puech Rock and dominates the town. Inside is one of the finest military museums in France, with a collection of more than 10,000 pieces covering the history of the French Army from the Middle Ages through to World War I. Students of the campaigns of Napoleon will be especially interested in the museum.

Also in the town are the Salon and Crau Museum, with a series of collections on Provençal furniture and wildlife, and some fine local landscape paintings, and the Grévin de Provence Museum which explores the history of the area through a series of paintings. Find time, too, to locate the Fontaine Moussue ('mossy fountain') in Place Crousillat, just beyond the Porte de l'Horloge, a remnant of the town's seventeenth-century ramparts. The fountain, which lives up to its name, is eighteenth century and quite charming.

From Salon, take the D572 eastwards towards Aix-en-Provence. Beyond Pélissanne, a left turn leads to **La Barben** where an ancient castle, built around 1000, was transformed into a fine mansion over a three-hundred-year period ending in the seventeenth century. The interior has beautiful ceilings and wall decorations, and some fine paintings. Of particular note is the reception hall, decorated with Cordoban leather made in the late seventeenth century by Avignon leather-masters. The castle stands in fine gardens, and the old outbuildings house an aviary, vivarium and aquarium, with collections from all over the world. Across the road from the castle is the La Barben Zoo, covering 40 hectares. The zoo has over 400 animals from around 120 different species.

Continuing eastwards along the D573, visitors reach **St Cannat** where children may be amused by the Village des Automates — just to the south, off the N7 — a series of outdoor tableau animated by automatons and marionettes. In the village, the Musée Suffren explores the life of Admiral Suffren, one of France's most successful admirals. He was born in what is now the town hall, which houses the museum.

South of Salon lies the Étang de Berre, a huge brackish lagoon covering some 150 sq km (60 sq miles) and with a depth that never exceeds 9m (30ft). Until 1920 the shores of the lagoon were largely uninhabited, but at that time it was developed into an oil port. Today it supports a huge oil and petro-chemical industry, and on its eastern shore lies the Marseille-Provence airport. Despite this industrialisation there are several interesting sites along its perimeter. Beside the airport is **Marignane** whose old castle is now the town hall, worth visiting for its decoration. The town church has excellent barrel-vaulting, and is intriguing for having no windows. The folklore and history of the town is explored in a small museum in Rue de la Cité.

Martigues, on the southern shore is still a name to conjure with from the days when artists such as Augustus John fell in love with the little fishing port. Today, the town — where the poet Roy Campbell also briefly made his home — still has some old houses lining the canals. In Ferrières, in the northern part of the town, is the Ziem Museum with paintings by the local landscape artist.

From Martigues, take the D5, turning off left along the D51 to the St Blaise archaeological site. The site here was inhabited as early as the seventh century BC and includes a near-perfect Greek rampart wall from that period. Though the site is chiefly for the specialist and enthusiast, the small museum, housing the best of excavated finds, is of more general interest.

Across the smaller *étangs* to the west of St Blaise lies the Fos petrochemical complex, centred on **Fos-sur-Mer**. A boat trip around Fos Bay has its merits, and the town museum, housed in an old chapel, explores the area's development.

North of St Blaise lies **Istres**, important for the military airbase which lies to the west. The museum here is very interesting for its section on underwater archaeology, one of several devoted to local history. There is also a good section on local wildlife.

Finally, head for the northern shore of the *étang* to visit the Roman Pont Flavien, built in the first century AD. The bridge crosses the River Touloubre and, to celebrate its own success, has triumphal arches — topped by lions — at each end.

To the south of the *étang* lie the arid hills of l'Estague, an area beloved of painters including Cézanne who occasionally left Aix and Ste Victoire to paint the hills and Marseille Bay. The southern edge of l'Estaque is a network of inlets on which sit small fishing villages. No one place stands out, but Carro, Sausset-les-Pins and Carry-le-Rouet are all worth a look.

To the west of the *étang* is the Plaine de la Crau, little-known and infrequently visited. Once the flood plain of the River Durance, the Crau is low and bleached, its rocks and pools an ideal habitat for reptiles. It is one of the last strongholds of the harmless Montpellier snake — Europe's longest, reaching 2.5m (over 8ft) — and is home to four other non-poisonous snakes, one a water snake. Insect life includes the praying mantis, while birds include Benelli's and short-toed eagles, Montagu's harrier, the calandra lark, black-eared wheatear, pin-tailed sandgrouse and the rare and beautiful cream-bibbed pratincole. The ecology of the area is explored in a fascinating museum at **St Martin-de-Crau**, just off the N113 that runs along the Crau's northern edge.

South of Arles, the Rhône bifurcates and makes a triangular delta bounded on the east by the Grand Rhône and the Petit Rhône to the west. Some 40km (25 miles) separates the two estuaries which empty into the Golfe du Lion. In this triangle is the Camargue.

The Camargue is a strange place. Flat, featureless, windswept, mosquito-ridden, flooded or dried out, its luminous melancholy is captivating. Shallow, brackish lagoons, salt marshes and salt-tolerating plants, sand spits, coastal dunes, stunted tamarisks, small black bulls, and white horses; all these make southern Camargue a unique experience.

Coming from the direction of Arles, a quick impression can be gained by taking the D36, which follows the Grand Rhône for a while. Turn right for Villeneuve, go right again to skirt the north shore of the Nature Reserve of Etang de Vaccarès and pass rice paddies, vines and other crops in the desalinated area.

When the D570 is reached, near **Albaron**, a right turn — towards Arles — leads through the village and on to the Musée Camarguais housed in the old sheepfold of the *mas* (farm) at Pont de Rousty. This fine museum traces the history of the area and illustrates life in a traditional *mas*. A footpath of about 4km (2½ miles) leads through the local marsh and farm land.

A left turn along the D570 leads towards Stes Maries-de-la-Mer, passing the Château d'Avignon, a huge mansion with some excellent tapestries. The gardens are delightful, and are traversed by a signed botanical footpath.

Single-storeyed thatched cottages, the dwellings of the cowboys (*gardians*) can be seen. They are blank on their north walls to keep out the *mistral* and are scattered about on the approaches to the only town of any size in the Camargue.

Before the town is reached, there are two more sites of great interest. The Information Centre at Ginès explores the flora, fauna and ecology of the Camargue, and has a viewing gallery from where there is a superb view across the Étang de Vaccares, the heartland of the Camargue. Birdwatchers will also want to visit nearby Pont de Gau. Here a trail leads through the marshland, with information boards on local species. Bulls can also be seen from the path.

Stes Maries-de-la-Mer is named after a Provençal legend that Mary,

The Camargue

Formed in the triangle between the Grand and Petit Rhône rivers and the sea, the Camargue is the finest wetland area remaining in Europe, its fragile and important ecology now protected by Camargue Regional Park. Formerly the area was truly wild, but with the increase in rice production during and after World War II, and the increase in salt extraction in the southeastern corner of the region, the 'natural' wetland is now that surrounding the central Étang de Vaccares, an area of about 825 square kilometres (330 square miles).

The area's most famous inhabitants are not birds or animals, but the cowboys and their horses and herds. The herds (*manades*) are of horses, sheep or bulls, the bulls — small, black and long-horned — being raised to fight in the *cocardes* at Arles, Nîmes and other places. In the *cocarde*, the Provençal style of bull-fighting, the bull is not killed, the aim of the bullfighter being to retrieve a rosette from the bull's horn.

Camargue horses are born brown, but gradually turn white, and are ridden by the *gardians*, who carry long tridents (*ferres* or *ficherouns*) used to 'encourage' lazy animals. In additon to stock raising, the Camargue dwellers fish using *trabaques*, nets arranged to drive the fish — chiefly eels and grey mullet — towards hooped nets called *coeurs*.

The other famous inhabitants of the area are its flamingoes, the sight of a flock of these graceful pink and white birds being one of the delights of a visit. Other interesting birds of the park include pratincoles, little egrets, bee-eaters, rollers, penduline tits, hoopoes, and black-winged stilts. The area's graudal change in salinity, from fresh to seawater, also supports a unique flora, one that was endangered in 1993 when the Grand Rhône burst its banks sending millions of gallons of freshwater into the brackish lagoons. It is to be hoped that the damage this caused, and the pressure of further development, can be resisted to maintain one of Europe's most important and interesting areas.

the mother of St James, Mary, the mother of St John, Mary Magdalene and others, including St Maximinus and Sarah, the two Marys' black servant, landed here after being put in a boat without sails or oars following the Crucifixion. Mary Magdalene went to Ste-Baume, but the other two Marys stayed, their tombs becoming a centre for pilgrimages.

The tomb of Sarah had a special interest for gipsies, as the legend had her descending from gipsy stock. Today the town is dominated by the fortress-church that holds the relics of the saints and an image of Sarah, the patron saint of gipsies in the crypt. Within the church, steps lead to a paved path around the roof from which there are fines views of the Camargue and the sea.

Huge and colourful gipsy celebrations take place in the town every 24-5 May, and again over the weekend nearest to 22 October. The images of Sarah and other saints are carried through the streets to the sea accompanied by gardians on horseback. Prayers and blessings taking place in the shallow waters themselves. Another colourful celebration is held on 26 May, Baroncelli Memorial Day, when traditional costumes are worn and there is danc-

The horses of the Camargue

ing, horse racing and bull running. The Marquis Falco de Baroncelli was responsible for reviving Camargue traditions in the first half of this century. The museum that bears his name is an excellent evocation of Camargue's wildlife, and also includes Provençal furniture and memorabilia of the Marquis.

At nearby **Boumain**, wax tableaux recreate the way of life in ancient Camargue.

On the Camargue's eastern side the D36 and smaller side roads explore the marshland. At **La Capelière**

on the edge of the Étang de Vaccares there is another information centre with footpaths and observation points. Southwards there are good facilities for the birdwatcher at **Salin-de-Bondon**, close to the only nesting site for the area's most famous birds, flamingoes.

On the D36 itself, there is a museum exploring the area's rice production just south of Le Sambuc and, near **Salin-de-Giraud**, a further information centre on the area's ecology at the Domaine de la Palissade.

ADDITIONAL INFORMATION

PLACES TO VISIT

Aigues-Mortes

**Constance Tower
& Town Ramparts**
Open: June to mid-September daily 9am-6pm; mid-September to May daily 9am-12noon, 2-5pm
Closed on official holidays
☎ 66 53 61 55, 66 53 79 98
or 66 53 73 00

Source Perrier
16km NE of Aigues-Mortes off D979
Open: all year Tuesday to Saturday tours at 9am, 10am, 1pm, 2.30pm and 3.30pm (also 5pm from June to September), Sunday and Monday tours at 9am and 10am
☎ 66 87 62 00 ext 3842

Château Teillan
10kms north of Aigues-Mortes, off the D265 near Marsillargues,
Open: Mid-June to mid-September daily except Monday 2-6pm
☎ 67 40 42 43

Arles

A combined ticket is available for the Amphitheatre, the Classical Theatre, Constantine's Palace, the Alyscamps, the St Trophime Cloisters, the Pagan and the Christian Art Museums, the Réattu Museum and the Arlaten Museum.

**Arènes (Roman Amphitheatre)
Théâtre Antique (Roman Theatre)
Allée des Sarcophages (Alyscamps)
St Trophime Church & Cloisters**
Open: June to September daily 8.30am-7pm; March to May and October daily 9am-12.30pm, 2-6.30pm; November daily 9am-12noon, 2-6pm; December to February daily 9am-12noon, 2-4.30pm
Closed on official holidays
☎ 90 96 93 37 (Amphitheatre)
☎ 90 96 93 30 (Theatre)
☎ 90 96 83 17 (Alyscamps)
☎ 90 49 36 36 (St Trophime)

Musée d'Art Paeïn
(Museum of Pagan Art)
Place de la République
Open: June to September daily
8.30am-7pm; May and October daily
9am-12noon, 2-6.30pm
☎ 90 49 36 36

Musée d'Art Chrétien
(Museum of Christian Art)
Rue Balze
Open: May to September daily 9am-
12.30pm, 2-7pm; March, April and
October daily 9am-12.30pm, 2-
6.30pm; November to February daily
9am-12noon, 2-4.30pm;
☎ 90 49 36 36

Musée Arlaten
Palais du Félibrige
29 Rue de la République
Open: June to August daily 9am-
12noon, 2-7pm; April, May and
September daily 2-6pm; October to
March daily 2-5pm
☎ 90 96 08 23

Musée Reattu
Rue du Grande Prieúre
Open: May to September daily 9am-
12.30pm, 2-7pm; October daily
10am-12.30pm, 2-6pm; November to
January daily 10am-12.30pm, 2-5pm;
February to April daily 10am-12.30pm,
2-5.30pm
☎ 90 49 38 34

Espace van Gogh
Rue de la République
Open: All year daily except Sunday
9am-7pm
☎ 90 49 36 72

Fondation Vincent van Gogh-Arles
Place des Arènes
Open: All year daily 10am-12.30pm, 2-7pm
☎ 90 49 94 04

L'Abbaye de Montmajour
On the D17 north-east of Arles
Open: April to September daily 9am-
7pm; October to March daily 9am-
12noon, 2-5pm
☎ 90 54 64 17

Beaucaire

Beaucaire Castle
Open: April-September daily except
Tuesday 9.30-11.30am, 2.15-6.45pm;
October-March daily except Tuesday
10.15am-12noon, 2-5.15pm
☎ 66 59 26 57

Musée Auguste Jacquet
Beaucaire Castle
Open: April-September daily except
Tuesday 9.30-11.30am, 2.15-6.45pm;
October-March daily except Tuesday
10.15am-12noon, 2-5.15pm
☎ 66 59 47 61

Abbaye de St Roman
5km north-west of Beaucaire, off the
D986
Open: July and August daily except
Monday 10am-7pm; April-June and
September Wednesday-Sunday
10am-7pm; October-March Saturday,
Sunday 2-5pm
☎ 66 59 26 57

Les Baux-de-Provence

Santon Museum
Old Town Hall
Place Louis Jou
Open: all year daily 9.30am-6pm
☎ 90 54 34 03

Fondation Louis Jou
Hôtel Jean de Brion
Open: April to October daily 10am-
1pm, 2-7pm
☎ 90 97 34 17

Musée Yves Brayer
Hôtel des Porcelets
Open: April to September daily 10am-
12noon, 2-6.30pm; October, November, mid-February to March daily
10am-12noon, 2-5.30pm
☎ 90 54 36 99

Gallery of Contemporary Art
Hôtel de Manville
Open: June to September daily 8.30am-
8pm; October to May daily 9am-5pm
☎ 90 54 34 03

Deserted Village
(including Hôtel de Brau Museum and
St Blaise Olive Museum)
Open: June to September daily 8.30am-
8pm; October to May daily 9am-5pm
☎ 90.543403
Combined ticket available for deserted
village and municipal museums.

La Petit Provence
(Santon Exhibition)
Paradou
5km south of Les Baux on the D17
Open: June to October daily 11am-
8pm; November to May daily 2-7pm
☎ 90 54 35 75

Cathédrale d'Images
On the D27, 500m north of the village
Open: mid-March to mid-December
daily 10am-7pm
☎ 90 54 38 65

Moulin de Daudet
15km south-west of Les Baux
Open: May to September 9am-
12noon, 2-7pm; October to December and February to April 10am-
12noon, 2-5pm
☎ 90 54 60 78

Camargue

Musée Camarguais
Albaron
At Mas de Pont Rousty, 8km south-
west of Arles on the D570
Open: July and August daily 9.15am-
6.45pm; April to June and September
daily 9.15am-5.45pm; October to March
daily except Tuesday 10.15am-
4.45pm
☎ 90 971082

Château d'Avignon
near Albaron
Open: April to October, guided tours
only, at 10am, 11am 12noon, 1.30pm,
2.30pm 3.30pm and 4.30pm
☎ 90 97 86 32

Musée de Cire
(Waxworks Museum)
Boumain
Open: April to November daily 10am-
12noon, 2-7pm
☎ 90 97 82 65

La Capelière Information Centre
Open: all year daily except Sunday
9am-12noon, 2-5pm
☎ 90 97 81 68

Information Centre
Ginès
Open: April to September daily 9am-
6pm; October to March daily except
Friday 9.30am-5pm
☎ 90 97 86 32

**Pont de Gau Ornithological
Centre**
Near Ginès
Open: Mid-April to September daily
9am-sunset; October to mid-April
daily 9.30am-sunset
☎ 90 97 82 62

Church
Stes Maries-de-la-Mer
Open: May to September daily 8am-
12noon, 2-7pm; March, April and
October daily 8am-7pm; November to
February daily 8am-6pm.
The paved roof path open: April to
June daily except Thursday 9.30am-
12noon, 2-6pm; July and August daily
10am-12noon, 2.30-7pm; September
to March Wednesday, Saturday and
Sunday 10am-12noon, 2-5pm
☎ 90 47 87 60

Baroncelli Museum
Ste Maries-de-la-Mer
Open: June to September daily 10am-
12noon, 2-6pm; October to May daily
except Tuesday 10am-12noon, 2-6pm
☎ 90 97 87 60

Salin-de-Badon Bird Observatories
Open: all year daily except Wednes-
day sunrise-10am, 4pm-sunset.
Permits must be obtained from La
Capelière.
☎ 90 97 81 68

Ecomuseum
Domaine de la Palissade
Salin-de-Giraud
Open: Mid-June to August daily 9am-5pm; September to mid-June Monday to Friday 9am-5pm
☎ 42 86 81 28

Musée du Riz
(Rice Museum)
near Le Sambuc
Open: all year daily 10am-12noon, 2-6pm
☎ 90 97 20 29

Istres

Town Museum
Place du Puits Neuf
Istres
Open: all year daily except Tuesday 3-7pm (6pm from October to May)
☎ 42 55 50 08

Martigues

Musée Ziem
Boulevard du 14 Juillet
Ferrières
Open: July and August daily except Tuesday 10am-12noon, 2.30-6.30pm; September to June Wednesday to Sunday 2.30-6.30pm
☎ 42 80 6606

St Blaise Archaeological Site & Museum
6km north-west of Martigues on the D51
Open: June to September daily 9am-12noon, 2-7pm; April and May daily 9-12noon, 2-6pm; October to March daily 9am-12noon, 2-5pm
☎ 42 80 30 72

Town Museum
Chapelle de Notre-Dame de la Mer
Fos-sur-Mer
12km west of Martigues on the N568
Open: July and August Saturday and Sunday 3-7pm
☎ 42 05 01 22

Town Museum
Rue de la Cité
Marignane
16km east of Martigues on the D9
Open: all year Wednesday and Saturday 2.30-5.30pm
☎ 42 88 95 36

Nîmes

Roman Monuments
(Arena, Maison Carree & Magne Tower)
Open: Mid-June to mid-September daily 9am-7pm; mid-September-mid-June daily 9am-12noon, 2-5pm.
The Arena is closed on the day of a bullfight or show. Guided tours in English available.
☎ 66 67 29 11

Archaeology Museum
13 bis Boulevard Amiral Courbet
Open: Mid-June-September daily Monday-Saturday 9.30am-6.30pm, sunday 2-6.30pm; October to mid-June Tuesday, Saturday 9.30am-12.30pm, 2-6pm
☎ 66 67 25 57

Natural History Museum
13 bis Boulevard Amiral Courbet
Open: Easter-August Tuesday-Saturday 9.30am-6pm, Monday 2-6pm
☎ 66 67 39 14

Musée de Vieux-Nîmes
Place aux Herbes
Open: all year daily 10am-6pm
☎ 66 36 00 64

Musée des Beaux-Arts
(Museum of Fine Arts)
Rue Cite-Foule
Open: Mid-June to September daily 9am-7pm; October to mid-June daily 9.30am-12.30pm, 2-6pm
☎ 66 67 38 21

Carré d'Art
near Maison Carrée
Open: all year Tuesday to Saturday 9.30am-12.30pm, 2-5pm
☎ 66 76 35 80

Planetarium
Mont Duplan
Times currently under review. Ask at Tourist Information Office for details or ☎ 66 67 60 94

Aquatropic
Chemin de l'Hostellerie
Open: all year Monday-Friday 9am-10pm, Saturday and Sunday 10am-7pm
☎ 66 38 31 00

St Gilles

St Gilles Abbey
Church open: July-September daily 9.30am-12.30pm, 2.30-7pm; October-June Monday-Saturday 9am-12noon, 2-5pm, Sunday 9am-12.30pm; Crypt and staircase: as church, but closed Sundays October to June
☎ 66 87 33 75

Maison Romane
Open: June to September daily 9am-12noon, 3-7pm; March-May, October-December daily except Sunday 9am-12noon, 2-5pm
☎ 66 87 40 42

St Martin-de-Crau

Le Crau Ecomuseum
Avenue de la Provence
Open: April to September daily except Monday 9am-12noon, 3-7pm; October to March daily except Monday 10am-12noon, 2-5pm
☎ 90 47 02 01

St Rémy-de-Provence

Musée des Alpilles Pierre-de-Brun
Place Flavier
Open: July and August daily 10am-12noon, 3-8pm; September to June daily 10am-12noon, 2-6pm
☎ 90 92 08 10

Centre d'Art Présence van Gogh
Hôtel Estrine, Rue Estrine

Open: March to November daily 10am-12noon, 3-7pm; December to February daily except Monday 10am-12noon, 2-6pm
☎ 90 92 34 72

Centre Archéologie
Hôtel de Sade
Rue du Parage
Open: all year daily 10am-12noon, 2-6pm. Guided tours at approximately hourly intervals
☎ 90 92 13 07

Glanum
3km south of St Rémy-de-Provence
Open: April to September daily 9am-7pm; October to March daily 9am-12noon, 2-5pm
☎ 90 92 23 79

Monastery of St Paul-de-Mausole
1km south of St Rémy
Open: all year daily 9am-12noon, 2-6pm
☎ 90 92 05 22 for information

Mas de la Pyramide
Behind Monastery of St Paul-de-Mausole
Open: all year daily 9am-12noon, 2-5pm
☎ 90 92 00 81

Salon-de-Provence

Château de l'Empéri
Place Farreyroux
Open: All year daily 10am-12noon, 2.30-6.30pm. Closed on Tuesday from January to April.
☎ 90 56 22 36

Musée de Salon et de la Crau
Avenue de Pivasis
Open: All year daily 10am-12noon, 2-6pm. Closed Tuesdays January-April.
☎ 90 56 28 37

Maison de Nostradamus
Rue de Nostradamus
Open: June to September daily 10am-10pm; October to May daily 10am-6pm
☎ 90 56 64 31

Musée Grevin de Provence
Place des Centuries
Open: June to September daily
10am-10pm; October to May daily
10am-6pm
☎ 90 56 36 30

Château La Barben
10km east of Salon-de-Provence, off
the D572
Open: all year daily except Tuesday
10am-12noon, 2-6pm
☎ 90 55 19 12

Aviary/Vivarium/Aquarium
& La Barben Zoo
Château La Barben
Open: all year daily 10am-6pm
☎ 90 55 19 12

Village of Automatons
St Cannat
16km east of Salon on the D572
Open: April to September daily 9am-
6pm; October to March Wednesday,
Saturday, Sunday and Holidays
(including school holidays 10am-5pm)
☎ 42 57 30 30

Musée Suffren
St Cannat
Open: all year first Sunday of each
month 10.30am-12noon, 2.30-6.30pm
☎ 42 57 20 01

Tarascon

Château du Roi Réne
Open: May to September daily 9am-
7pm; October to April daily 9am-
12noon, 2-5pm
☎ 90 91 01 93

Maison de Tartarin
55 Bis Boulevard Itam
Open: April to September daily
9.30am-12noon, 2-7pm; October to
March Monday to Saturday 9am-
12noon, 1.30pm-5pm
☎ 90 91 05 08

Musée Souleïado
39 Rue Prudhon
Open: all year Monday to Friday.
Guided tours by appointment only
☎ 90 91 08 80

L'Abbaye de St Michel-de-Frigolet
10km north-east of Tarascon off the
D35
Open: All year. Guided tours only,
Monday to Saturday at 2.30pm,
Sunday at 4pm.
Site museum open: daily 10am-5pm
☎ 90 95 70 07

Le Château
Barbentane
12km north-east of Tarascon on the
D35
Open: all year daily 10am-12noon, 2-
6pm. Closed Wednesdays November
to April
☎ 90 95 51 07

Musée Frédéric Mistral
11 Rue Lamartine
Maillane
12 km east of Tarascon off the D28
Open: June to September daily
except Monday 9am-12noon, 2-6pm
☎ 90 95 74 06

Musée des Arômes
et des Parfums
(Museum of Essences and Perfumes)
Le Chevêche
Petit Route du Grès
Graveson
12km east of Tarascon off the D28
Open: all year daily 10am-12noon, 2-
6pm
☎ 90 95 81 72

Central Provence 4

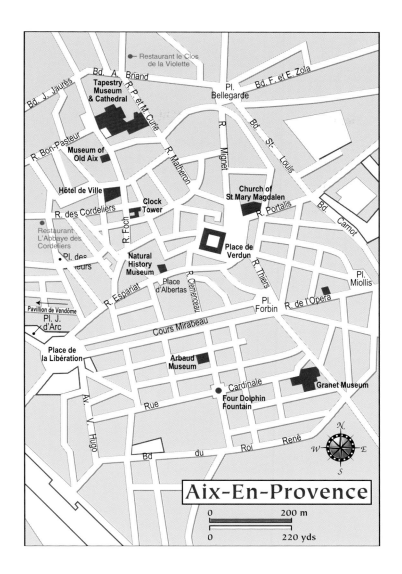

Aix-En-Provence

Restaurant le Clos de la Violette

Bd. A. Briand

Bd. J. Jaurès

R. P. et M. Curie

Tapestry Museum & Cathedral

Pl. Bellegarde

Bd. F. et E. Zola

R. Bon-Pasteur

Museum of Old Aix

R. Matheron

R. Mignet

Bd. St. Louis

Hôtel de Ville

Clock Tower

Church of St Mary Magdalen

R. Portalis

R. des Cordeliers

R. Foch

Bd. Carnot

Restaurant L'Abbaye des Cordeliers

Natural History Museum

Place de Verdun

Pl. des ...eurs

Place d'Albertas

R. Clemenceau

Pl. Miollis

R. Espariat

R. Thiers

Pavillion de Vendôme

Pl. Forbin

R. de l'Opera

Pl. J. d'Arc

Cours Mirabeau

Place de la Libération

Arbaud Museum

Granet Museum

Cardinale

Four Dolphin Fountain

Av. V. Hugo

Rue

René

Bd.

du

Roi

N
W · E
S

0   200 m

0   220 yds

Opposite: En route to St Mary
Magdelene's Cave, Ste Baume

Youthful vitality, as befits a university town; a character all its own; elegance inherited from its eighteenth-century past; these constitute some of the elements of **Aix-en-Provence**. In addition to these qualities, the town is full of shops, hotels and restaurants. It is a very attractive provincial city with a marvellous centre, built around Cours Mirabeau, one of the most elegant streets in southern France. There is much to see besides this street in a town that is an undisputed magnet.

Some people do not like staying in large towns, but there are also pleasant and quieter places in the vicinity, all with very acceptable hotels. These include Célony, Eguilles, Roquefavour, Beaureceuil and Vauvenargues. But a few days in the centre of Aix is a less tiring way of absorbing what it has to offer.

The Old City, surrounded by boulevards which radiate exits in all directions, exudes its seventeenth- and eighteenth-century personality. Aix really is very different from Avignon and Arles. It is best to begin an exploration with the Cours Mirabeau, named after the scandalous and outstanding orator of the French Revolution, who ably represented Aix in the Paris parliament. The Cours follows the line of the old town ramparts east and west and, having been planted with four rows of plane trees in 1830, it provides shade all summer long. With its trees, its wide pavements, elegant shop fronts and the fountains at its curve, the Cours is delightful, a place to linger. Of its three fountains, the one at the eastern end is a statue of ✳ the fifteenth-century ruler of Provence, 'Good' King René (King of Sicily only, in Provence he was 'just' a Duke). He was a scholar and patron of the arts and husbandry.

The Good King was also a friend of the countryside and an amiable host, altogether a man out of his time. The statue has him holding a bunch of muscat grapes, which he introduced (along with silkworms) into Provence. He may have been a politically incompetent ruler, but is viewed with affection in retrospect. As the visitor will notice, his name is used frequently by hotels, shops, cafés and little businesses.

In the centre of Cours Mirabeau is the moss-covered Fontaine Chaude, ✳ coming from the same hot springs tapped by the Romans when they founded Aquae *Sextiae Saluviorum* in 122BC. The water, mildly radioactive as well as containing a brew of minerals, reaches the surface at 36°C (97°F).

On the north side of the Cours are cafés, restaurants, bookshops and shops selling that speciality of Aix; *calissons*, delicate almond biscuits. On the south side are some seventeenth-century mansions (*hôtels*) whose handsome doors, caryatids and wrought ironwork characterise much of the old town. Beyond Cours Mirabeau, to the north as far as the cathedral, is Vieil Aix, the oldest part of the town. Some of the streets are pedestrian thoroughfares, lined with smart shops selling antiques or Provençal handicrafts.

To obtain the flavour of Vieil Aix

leave Cours Mirabeau along Rue Fabrot, close to King René's statue, noting No 55 where Cezanne's father opened his hat shop in 1825. Follow Rue Fabrot into Place St Honoré, bearing right there into Place de Verdun, passing the Palais de Justice. The Palais dates, in part, from the late eighteenth century but with later, post-Revolution, additions in a simpler style. Place des Prêcheurs is then reached, where a food market is held on Tuesday, Thursday and Saturday mornings.

In the square, the front of Ste Marie-Madeleine church is of little interest, but the interior has a masterly eighteenth-century marble 'Virgin' by the Avignonnais J. P. Chastel, and a fifteenth-century triptych of the *Annunciation*, full of mysterious symbols, perhaps painted by Jean Chapus. The church also contains works by such well-known artists as J. B. and Carle van Loo, Nicolas Mignard, Michel Serre, and there is a *Martyrdom of St Paul* attributed to Rubens.

Return to Place St Honoré and take Rue Espariat: at No 6, the Hôtel Boyer d'Eguilles contains the Natural History Museum with important collections of fish and plants. One noteable item is a unique display of dinosaurs' eggs, found embedded in Montagne Ste Victoire. Thousands of these eggs were unearthed. There are various theories as to why they remained unhatched. It may have been a sudden cooling of the subtropical climate which caused the dinosaurs to become extinct, millions of years ago.

Rue Espariat leads into the best of the many little squares dotted about Vieil Aix. This is Place d'Albertas, cobbled and with a fountain and terraced houses whose arches support the balconies of the upper windows.

From Rue Espariat, go northwards along Rue Aude into Place Richelme where a flower and vegetable market has been held for centuries. It is said that, at one time, poverty forced King René to sit at a stall and sell the produce of his own royal gardens. The former Corn Market, now a sub-post office, was strikingly decorated by Chastel, the Rhône and Durance Rivers being symbolised in the work by the mythological figure of Cybele.

Adjoining this is Place de l'Hôtel-de-Ville. Next to the town hall is a Flamboyant clock-tower of 1520. The lower, modern statues upon this — added in 1925 — represent Day and Night, while above there are wooden statuettes of the four seasons, each one visible for its three months. Higher still, there is an astronomical clock of 1661. The whole is capped by a Provençal bell-cage.

Continue northwards along Rue Gaston de Saporta — named after a nineteenth-century naturalist — which was once the Roman Via *Aurelia*. It is a street of elegant mansions and smart shops. Pierre Puget (1620-94) — Provence's greatest sculptor whose Baroque style was disliked by Louis XIV — is thought to have sculpted the façade of No17, which houses the Musée du Vieil Aix. It is full of things which illuminate the arts and crafts of the past:

Place Charles de Gaulle, Aix-en-Provence

Paul Cézanne

Paul Cézanne was born in Aix in 1839, the son of a properous hatter who, later, became a successful banker and property owner. This is in contrast with the early years of many painters: Cézanne did not starve in an attic, his family being able to keep him in comfort and to afford years of study. His schooling lasted until he was 20, Cézanne studying law and befriending Emile Zola, a fellow student. His requrest to be allowed to concentrate on painting was then granted by his father and he spent two years in Paris, returning disillusioned to Aix to join his father's bank.

Soon he returned to painting, and over the next 20 years he sought his own style, eventually rejecting Impressionism, though making many friends among its artists. By 1885 it seemed his career was over: Zola modelled one of his characters on Cézanne, portraying him as a washed-up has-been, a portrayal that ended their friendship. In 1886 Cézanne's father died, leaving him a wealthy man. Freed of the unsuccessful attempts to sell his work Cézanne finally found his style, using bright colours in exaggerated blocks and reliefs to form stunning landscapes. This new work brought him fame at last, and also increased his self-confidence. 'A painter like me — there is only one every century' he famously remarked. This apparent immodesty was nothing of the kind — Cézanne now knew his worth to the artistic world. Today he is recognised as a master, a pioneer and as the father of both Fauvism and Cubism. In October 1906, aged 67, he was caught in a storm. A week later he died of pneumonia.

Sadly there are no paintings by Cézanne at Aix, but as he spent virtually all his life in the town there are many spots where the lover of his work can feel in touch with the artist:

28 Rue de l'Opera: born in 1839

Eglise de la Madeleine: baptised in 1839

Rue des Epinaux: primary school 1844-49

14 Rue Matheron: family house

Rue Cardinale: Collège Bourbon (now Lycée Mignet), at school with Emile Zola 1852-8

Jas de Bouffan: estate acquired by father 1859. Now the site of the Vasarely Foundation, in Avenue Marcel Pagnol, 4km (2½ miles) to the south-west of the town.

44 Cours Mirabeau: site of Café Clem where he met friends.

Château Noir: on the D17. His favourite workplace where he rented a room.

23 Rue Boulegon: rented room 1899. Died 1906.

9 Avenue Paul Cézanne: studio 1902. Now a museum.

faïences from Moustiers; documents relating to Mirabeau; old prints of Aix; nativity cribs (*santons*); old costumes and furniture; paintings on velvet. A few paintings by J. A. Constantin (1756-1844) are interesting because he, even before John Constable, was painting from nature, a revolutionary practice.

Still further north is Place des Martyres-de-la-Résistance where the former Archbishop's Palace contains the Tapestry Museum, noted for eighteen Beauvais tapestries of the seventeenth and eighteenth centuries that include the *Life of Don Quixote*. During Aix's prestigious International Music Festival from mid-July to mid-August, the palace courtyard serves as an open-air theatre. In the nearby Place de l'Université, there is a bust of Fabri de Peiresc (1580-1637), a Provençal universal savant.

Beyond the bust is the cathedral of St Saveur, within which are some of the oldest remains in Aix. The fifth-century baptistry, with a full immersion pool, is supported by eight Roman columns and covered by a sixteenth-century cupola. Part of the church began as the nave of a twelfth-century church and the cloisters are also of this period. Later, that building was incorporated into the Gothic structure, a large part of which is in the sixteenth-century style known as Flamboyant Gothic.

Once in the church, the visitor should find the sacristan and ask him to allow access to that section of the nave where the splendid triptych, *The Burning Bush* is kept. Painted by Nicolas Froment of Uzès in 1476, it shows King René kneeling on the left; portly, double-chinned and earthy compared to the religious figures in the panels. The painting represents the Virginity of Mary, and the visitor can, perhaps, recognise the castles of Beaucaire and Tarascon on the side panels.

The visitor should also ask the sacristan to open the walnut panels of the west door on which the four prophets and twelve sybils are carved, work carried out in the sixteenth century. The south door leads to the Romanesque cloisters.

Although it lies just outside Vieil Aix, the Pavillon de Vendôme — at 34 Rue Célony, close to the thermal baths: there is a second entrance at 13 Rue de la Holle — is a charming seventeenth-century town house set in formal gardens. Built for the Cardinal Duke of Vendôme, it was later acquired by the influential Provençal painter, J. B. van Loo (1684-1745) who died here — there were eleven artists in this family of Dutch origin. A handsome double staircase, period furniture and paintings sustain the original atmosphere.

Turn now to the south side of Cours Mirabeau, the once aristocratic Mazarin Quarter, smaller than Vieil Aix, the façades of its *hôtels* more restrained.

Rue du 4 Septembre leads to the Paul Arbaud Museum, where there are pictures by locally important artists, together with sculptures, ceramics and old furniture. Further along the street is one of Aix's most

✳ popular fountains, that of the Four Dolphins, built in 1667 and standing in a *place* of the same name. In Rue Cardinale, which crosses the *place* at right angles to our approach, is Lycée Mignet, the school attended by Paul Cézanne, Emile Zola and the musician Darius Milhaud.

Go right into Rue Cardinale, at the end of which is the church of St Jean-de-Malte, the chapel to the former Priory of the Knights of St John of Malta, and the first Gothic church in Provence. Its interior is delightful for the purity of its proportions and the audacity of the lovely choir window. Its 67m (220ft) high belfry was built on the nave so that at street-level it is a chapel.

Almost next door is the former priory itself. In 1825 it was owned by the painter François Granet who willed it to the town of Aix, along with his collection. Since that time it has been known as the Granet Museum, despite its formal title of Musée des Beaux-Arts. Among the archaeological exhibits on the ground floor is a collection of Celto-Ligurian items removed from the *oppidum* of *Entremont* outside Aix. These are the oldest of all the pre-Roman sculptures discovered in France. There are primitive carvings of warriors' heads, death masks, a hand resting on a head whose eyes are closed and a bas-relief of a galloping horseman carrying a severed head on the neck of his mount.

The museum has many galleries filled with paintings of numerous schools and periods, but take a close look at the work of the Provençal *petits maîtres* whose interpretations of the landscapes around Aix give a profounder understanding of the elements in the Provence countryside. These artists include J. A. Constantin, the earliest; François Granet (see also Ingres' sumptuous portrait of him) Prosper Grésy; Paul Guigou, the finest Provençal landscape artist before Cézanne, who created jewel-like colours and great atmospheric depth; Emile Loubon, the pastoralist; and Auguste Chabaud, who was nearer our time.

Of Cézanne himself, there is virtually nothing. Aix awoke too late to his genius to have been able to afford anything of significance. The most intimate momento is his studio, preserved more or less as it was at the time of his death. It is at 9 Avenue Paul Cézanne — in his day known as Chemin des Lauves — north-west beyond Boulevard Jean Jaurès. He had it built in 1902, the workshop of a man who willed the landscape into the harmonious architectural planes and restrained colours which informed the paintings of his maturity and made him one of the most significant figures in the history of art.

The estate acquired by Cézanne's father in 1859 is now home to the Vasarely Foundation, a modern museum about 4km (2½ miles) southwest of the town. This large structure — looking like a thrown collection of dice, each with one large spot, rather than up to six small ones — is a study and information centre and also houses a large collection of the work of Victor Vasarely, the Hungarian-born geometric modernist.

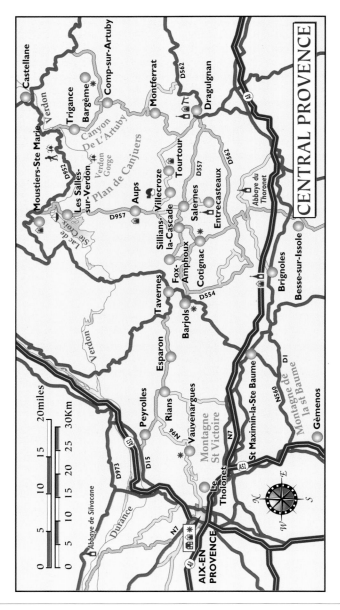

CENTRAL PROVENCE

Castellane
Trigance
Bargème
Comp-sur-Artuby
Montferrat
Draguignan
Verdon
Canyon De L'Artuby
Moustiers-Ste Marie
Les Salles-sur-Verdon
Verdon Gorge
Plan de Canjuers
Tourtour
Villecroze
Aups
Sillans-la-Cascade
Salernes
Entrecasteaux
Abbaye du Thoronet
D957
D557
D562
Lac de Ste Croix
Verdon
Fox-Amphoux
Cotignac
Brignoles
Besse-sur-Issole
Tavernes
Barjols
D554
Esparon
Peyrolles
Rians
Vauvenargues
Montagne St Victoire
St Maximin-la-Ste Baume
Montagne de la st Baume
Gémenos
N560
N7
A52
Verdon
Abbaye de Silvacane
Durance
D973
D15
N7
Le Tholonet
AIX-EN PROVENCE

0   5   10   15   20miles
0   5   10   15   20   25   30Km

N
E
S
W

Montagne Ste Victoire from the south east

Walking in the Massif de la Ste Baume

Another cultural centre southwest of Place Général de Gaulle, the superb *place* at the western end of Cours Mirabeau, is the Espace Méjanes, easily recognised by the huge books at its entrances. The centre houses the Méjanes Library, founded in 1787 by the Marquis de Méjanes, with 300,000 books and manuscripts, an invaluable source of reference for scholars. Also here are the Foundation St John Perse, a collection of memorabilia of this modern symbolist poet who won the Nobel Prize for Literature in 1960; the Historical Information Centre on Algeria; and a video library of music and opera.

On the opposite side of the town is *Entremont*, the excavated remains of the capital of the Saluvians, the local tribe crushed by the Romans in 123BC. The foundations of ramparts, towers and houses are all that can be seen. There are fine views from the site, especially of the Montagne Ste Victoire, Cézanne's inspiration.

To the west of Aix — follow the D64 for about 12km (7½ miles) — the visitor will find a visit to the modern Aqueduc de Roquefavour interesting, if only to see how the work of 1842 compares to that of Pont du Gard. The more recent aqueduct is the larger of the two. Still on the D64, the visitor can continue to **Venta-bren** where there is a ruined castle that offers fine views of the Chaîne de Vitrolles and the Etang de Berre.

Visitors going eastwards instead, can round Montagne Ste Victoire. The D10 is the best starting route; follow it as it heads east. At St Marc-Jaumegarde a turning to the right leads to the Barrage de Bimont (Bimont Dam), a new construction, beautifully set in a wooded valley.

From here the view of the Croix de Provence, at the western tip of Montagne Ste Victoire, is exceptional. The *Montagne* is an east-west running ridge presenting a high wall along its flanks. But viewed end on, it becomes a narrow, shapely peak.

The Croix de Provence (945m, 3,100 ft) is not the highest point, but is the most worthwhile for its views. To climb it, park at the farm of Les Cabassols and follow the GR9 to the summit. This is not an easy walk, the path rising about 550m (1,800ft) and the climb taking between 2½ and 3 hours, but it is well worthwhile. The walker passes the priory of Ste Victoire, which has fifth-century origins but is basically a restored seventeenth-century building, and reaches the top about 20 minutes later. The first cross on the summit was erected in the sixteenth century, but the present one — nearly 18m (60ft) high — is the third. The view from the top is superb, extending to Mont Ventoux and the Maures. On clear days, the Dauphiné can also be seen.

From the cross, the walk can be extended to almost any day-size length. To walk the ridge here is to understand the inspiration that Cézanne sought. It is an irony that the mountain's name derives from a victory the Romans gained at its foot over an invading Teuton horde. The Roman historians claimed that the barbarians lost 100,000 killed, with a further 100,000 captured.

Having considered the inspiration of Cézanne, we go further east to **Vauvenargues**, to see the *château* on a spur of the hill where Picasso spent his last years. The artist is buried in the parkland here, but the site is not open to the public. Beyond Vauvenargues, the road continues east. At the first chance, turn right to Pourrières, and go west there on the D57 and so back to Aix.

The traveller on the A8 Autoroute or the N7 reaches **St Maximin-la-Ste Baume** very soon after leaving Aix, as it is only 38km (24 miles) by these direct routes. The basilica in the town is the best example of Gothic architecture in Provence. Built on a sixth-century church, the basilica was started in 1295 as a resting-place, according to legend, for the remains of St Mary Magdalene (and later St Maximin).

The crypt still holds a cranium said to be that of St Mary Magdalene, now in a nineteenth-century reliquary.

The building was worked on intermittently until the sixteenth century, but no belfry was ever built, nor was the west front completed. Destined to be demolished during the French Revolution — when the town was renamed Marathon — good fortune found Napoleon's youngest brother Lucien (who called himself Brutus) turning the church into a storage depot. By having the *Marseillaise* played regularly on the very organ in use today, he saved both the building and its contents.

Inside the austere and finely proportioned basilica, the famous organ, built in 1773, can be seen. Wooden panels — twenty-two in number — painted by the Venetian François Ronzen in the sixteenth century, include the earliest known view of the Palace of the Popes at Avignon. Choirstalls, screen, gilded statues and pulpit are all carved to a high standard. Organ concerts of French music are given every summer on the church's instrument, while the adjacent former Royal Monastery, now the town's tourist office and cultural centre has evening music concerts each July. The monastery was built at the same time as the basilica and has elegant cloisters, made more so when the townsfolk dress in eighteenth-century costume for Sunday festivals which compliment the music concerts.

La Ste Baume, with which the church of St Maximin is associated, is a mountain 23km (14 miles) to the south-west. The most venerable of Provençal legends insists that St Mary Magdalene lived in solitary retreat in a cave on La Ste Baume for the last 30 years of her life, having spent 13 years with the Virgin Mary after Christ's crucifixion. Mary Magdelene, St Maximin, the Virgin's sister and Mary, the mother of James and John, were cast adrift from the Holy Land in an open boat with various other saints and the black servant, Sarah. They landed at Les-Stes-Maries-de-la-Mer, where they parted and set about evangelising Provence. Maximin went to Aix to become its first bishop. Mary Magdalene made her way to La Ste Baume.

From the fifth century onwards,

The western end of the Massif de la Ste Baume

Festival time at St Maxime-la-Ste Baume

pilgrims streamed to the sacred place, until the Saracen invasions interrupted them. In the eleventh century, the monks of Vézelay in Burgundy claimed to have acquired the saint's relics and pilgrims went to Vézelay for five centuries. St Mary Magdalene's remains were then discovered in the little Merovingian church at St Maximin. The basilica was erected, and the pilgrims returned.

On Ste Baume, the cave (Grotte de St Pilon) can be reached on foot either from the one-time Hôtellerie (hostel) or the Carrefour des Trois Chênes, both on the D80. There is little to choose between the routes, that from the Hôtellerie having the advantage of starting and ending at a café. The routes are very well marked and on broad paths through the excellent woodland of the Ste Baume forest. The walks end together, with a straightforward climb up a stairway hewn from the rock. The cave houses an altar, a shrine holding relics of St Mary Magdalene and a statue saint. Midnight Mass is celebrated on July 22.

From the cave, a short but steep climb reaches the summit of St Pilon, named after a column, long since gone, erected to commemorate the saint. Today a small chapel marks the top. A further legend has St Mary Magdalene being brought to this spot seven times each day by angels because it was the best place to listen to the music of Paradise. The panorama from the top is impressive, including the Luberon hills, Mont Ventoux, the Lure hills, Montagne St Victorie, the Alpilles and the coast near La Ciotat.

Nowhere is the contrast between the plant life of north and south slopes (in Provençal *hubacs* and *adrets* respectively) illustrated more clearly than in the Ste Baume range. South-facing slopes confront the full glare of heat and drought for which Mediterranean plants are adapted to survive. On the north slopes, which are shaded and moist, there is an extensive and remarkable forest. Beech, yew, maple, lime and privet — found hardly anywhere else in Provence — flourish in this grove once sacred to the Ligurians, and perhaps felled by Caesar as timber for his fleet. Royal decrees in the past and modern ideas on forest ecology have preserved the forest, a relic of distant times when the climate of Provence was more like Britain's.

Follow the D2 when a road branches off right towards Aurio, climbing to the Col de l'Espigoulier, from where the view of the Marseille and the coast is breathtaking. A short climb goes up the peak to the right, the path picking its way between blocks of glaring white limestone picked clean by wind, frost and rain so as to resemble the bones of some huge prehistoric animal. From the top of this shallow peak the view northwards, to Montagne Ste Victoire and Mont Ventoux, is even better.

Now take the winding descent of the D2. On the left is Parc de St Pons whose trees, springs, waterfall, Romanesque chapel and ruined abbey offer a romantic parkland in which to roam. At **Gémenos**, which has a

🏛 large eighteenth-century *château*, a left turn reaches Aubagne, explored in the next chapter. Here turn right and, in about 2km (1¼ miles), right

⛪ again to the chapel of St Jean-de Garguier. Its interest lies in the collection of some 200 ex-voto paintings completed between 1500 and 1914. They are religious works, executed by anonymous local artists or artisans on behalf of people wishing to give thanks for divine interventions: for the safe delivery of a child, recovery from severe illness, or for any miraculous escape from death. Ex-voti hang in many a Provençal church, but those at St Jean-de-Garguier compress 400 years of gratitude for survival.

An attractive route running through the length of central Provence is the road between Aix and Draguignan. The N96 northwards from Aix and then east as far as Peyrolles can be congested, but the D561 soon branches right and runs peacefully through open, wooded countryside. It links the widely differing villages of Jouques, Rians, Esparron, Varages and Tavernes to reach **Barjols.** This village has the

❋ largest plane tree in Provence, 12.5m (41ft) round its base, as well as a huge, moss-green fungal growth of a

❋ fountain (Fontaine de Champignon) that is nearly the largest in the region, and an enormous market-square.

This is truly a village of superlatives. In addition to the mushroom fountain there are twenty-seven others, and twelve ancient wash-houses. Look out for the Hôtel de Pontevés which has a fine Renaissance doorway. Each year, in January, the people of the village celebrate the day of their patron saint, St Marcel (whose remains were brought to Barjols in the Middle Ages) by parading a bust of the saint through the streets, the bust being followed by an ox that is led to the slaughterhouse. The ox is roasted on the following day while the villagers dance and sing, and, on the third day, the ox is eaten. It seems that the celebration is only religious in part, the arrival of the saint's remains having corresponded with an existing festivity that celebrated an earlier escape from a siege.

A deviation south from Barjols, along the D554, goes through Châteauvert and then follows the D45 along the Vallon Sourn, a narrow valley enclosing the River Argens whose spring can be visited, before the landscape opens out again at Correns, a quiet village that is relatively untouched by tourism.

After Barjols comes **Cotignac**, a picturesque village. An 80m (262ft) 🏛 high brown cliff of tufa rock, riddled with one-time rock-shelters and topped by ancient castle ruins rears behind it.

From Cotignac, a number of other charming villages, set in these wide valleys where evergreen oaks dominate the woodlands, repay a visit. These include perched Fox-Amphoux and walled **Sillans-la-Cascade**. The 🏛 waterfall of the name is reached by a short walk — no more than 1 hour for the return journey — which is signposted from the south side of the village. It is a fine waterfall, with the water cascading nearly 46m (150ft), but it is best to go in late spring, early summer or when there has been rain, because in long, dry summers the falls are reduced to a tap-like trickle. Also near Sillans are the Bresque Streams, one of which goes over the falls, where trout-fishermen meet. At nearby **Salernes**, where tiles are made, there are the ruins of a thirteenth-century castle.

Entrecasteaux, to the south of Salernes, is complete with a large *château* and gardens, a fortified Gothic church, a humpback bridge and medieval streets. The *château*, a disproportionately long and plain seventeenth-century building, was restored by Ian McGarnie-Munn, a Scottish artist. It is now a museum housing a collection of furniture and knick-knacks from around the time of its building, the best of which is some porcelain.

On higher ground to the north-east of Salernes is **Villecroze**. The medieval section of the village, especially Rue des Arceaux near the old clock tower, is a delight, as is the park — signed from the road to Aups. Here there is a lovely waterfall, 40m (130ft) high, and a once-fortified cave whose petrified columns and fifteenth-century windows can still be seen.

On the road to Tourtour be sure to stop at the *belvédère* where a panorama dial points out the main sites of a remarkable view over the central Provence plateau. **Tourtour**, set at 633m (2,080ft), has restored, honey-coloured stone houses, smart hotels

and two elm trees planted in 1638 to mark the birth of the future Sun King, Louis XIV. Today it is a fashionable holiday centre with uninterrupted views over the Maures Mountains. A small museum has a collection of locally-found fossils.

To the north is **Aups**, its name deriving from the Celto-Ligurian *alp* (hill pasture). The picturesque village basks in a wide valley and is backed by sheltering hills, whose honey has a local reputation. There is a small but interesting museum of modern art here, set in an old Ursuline convent.

Lorgues, to the south-east, is a small *bourg* surrounded by vineyards and olive groves, its plane-filled square lending impressive dignity. A marble fountain, eighteenth-century church, and fourteenth-century fortified gateways all make a visit worthwhile. About 2km (1¼ miles) west of Lorgues, along the narrow D50, is a remarkable little chapel. This is the simple sixteenth-century Notre Dame de Benva (Bon Voyage), partly built into the rock. From its façade an arch spans the narrow path — once the main highway — and contemporary murals are clearly visible on the inner faces of the arch: Virgin and Child, St Joseph, and St Christopher with the infant Jesus on his shoulder as he plunges a tree trunk into a stream. More murals can be found inside the chapel if the key is obtained from the presbytery in Lorgues.

Brignoles, a centre of bauxite-mining, marble-quarrying and wine production, is the next big town.

Once plum-growing was the major occupation, Brignoles plums — sugared as a dessert — being famous throughout France. Production ceased in the sixteenth century when the townspeople rose against their local lord and destroyed all the orchards. Brignoles plums can still be bought, but they now come from Digne, to the north. The town's old quarter, with covered streets and pretty, ancient houses is a delight and a visit should also be made to the Museum of Local History to see what is thought to be the oldest of all Gaulish Christian sarcophogi. Dating from the second or third centuries, its carved messages are beautifully preserved. It was retrieved from the tiny chapel of La Gayole, 10km (6 miles) west, on the estate of the St Julien farm.

To the east of the town, along the N7, is Parc Mini France, a floral park where some of France's better known sites — Loire *châteaux*, cathedrals distinctive villages — have been created in miniature.

South-west of Brignoles is Celle Abbey, built in the thirteenth century as a convent. It always attracted the daughters of noblemen, but it was said that by the Middle Ages the sisters could only be told apart from the other women of the area by their nun's habit and the fact that their lovers were of the better classes. Not surprisingly, this eventually caused a scandal and the house was closed on the orders of the local bishop. Part of the old convent has now be taken over as a hotel, but other parts — including the cloisters and chapter-

house — can be visited. The old abbey church can also be seen as it was used as the parish church.

South-west from the abbey, the visitor should go to Montagne de la Loube. Continue on the D405 to join the D5, and then take the narrow, marked road to the right. Drive as far as possible and then take the obvious track towards the mast. The climb — which will take about 1 hour to complete — becomes increasingly steep, finishing with a scramble up rocks to the summit. From here there is a good panorama over the local forests and northward to the hills of Haute-Provence.

South of the N7, along the D13, is yet another intriguing village, **Besse-sur-Issole** set close to one of the few natural lakes in Provence. Besse was the birthplace of Provence's eighteenth-century Robin Hood, Gaspard de Besse. He spent a life of romanticised brigandage before he was caught and sentenced by the judges of Aix to be broken at the wheel . His execution was a social event attended by high-born ladies who wept at the untimely death of so romantic a young man.

On the other side of the N7 from Besse lies the third, and many argue the finest, Cistercian monastery of the 'Three Sisters of Provence', the secluded abbey of Le Thoronet. It is set, like all Cistercian houses, in a wild hollow to express the order's humility. The abbey was founded in 1136, most of the buildings dating from a 30 year period ending in 1190. As with the other abbeys, after a period of prosperity its fortunes de-

The Verdon Gorge

Walking on the Sentier Martel in the Verdon Gorge

clined and it was abandoned in the late eighteenth century. It has now been restored to its former glories. The dry stone church and cloisters are quite beautiful, as is the chapterhouse, its capitals decorated with simple carvings of local plants.

Draguignan is not normally thought of as a tourist centre, but as a place where the knowledgeable come to buy quality food at sensible prices, which is recommendation enough. In fact, the town has considerable merits. There are modest but entirely adequate hotels and restaurants, it makes a good excursion centre, and the Old Town is excellent.

The town was a Roman settlement called *Antea*, the present name apparently deriving from the fifth century when the Christian bishop of Antibes arrived to convert the locals. They lived in fear of a nearby dragon that was making life a misery over a wide area. The bishop fearlessly tackled the dragon and killed it. In honour of this, the locals become Christians and named the town after the dragon, not Hermentarius, the dragon-slayer, as might be expected. The dragon is featured in the town's coat-of-arms.

The traffic-free town centre is dominated by the Tour d'Horloge, built in the seventeenth century on the site of the town's castle. The tower can be climbed for a fine view over both the town and the Maures Mountains. Near the clocktower, the streets and squares have evocative names: Place du Marché with its fountain; Rue des Marchands; Place aux Herbes, with a medieval gate-

way; Rue des Tanneurs and the old Porte Aiguière; and Rue de la Juiverie, with the façade of a thirteenth-century synagogue.

The town museum, at 9 Rue de la République, is housed in a seventeenth-century Ursuline convent which was later used as a summer palace by the bishops of Fréjus. It contains Gallo-Roman finds, coins, paintings, busts and natural history specimens, as well as some remarkable manuscripts in the large library. One is a fourteenth-century illuminated manuscript of the *Romance of the Rose*. Close by, in Rue Joseph-Roumanille, is a museum of crafts and traditions of the Draguignan area. Elsewhere, take a stroll among the six rows of plane trees that line the handsome Allées d'Azémar. The walk is flanked by gardens and mansions, and passes a bust of Georges Clemenceau who represented Draguignan in Parliament for 25 years.

To the east of Draguignan, on the D59, is an Allied Military Cemetery, where some of the men who were parachuted or landed in gliders near the area on 15 August 1944, are buried. The nearby military camp has a weapons museum which can be visited. It traces the development of artillery from the eighteenth century to the present day.

Less sombre than either is St Roseline's Chapel, reached by following the N555 south-eastward out of the town and then going right along the D91 towards Les Arcs. The chapel is the only part of an old abbey that is open to the public, and contains the body of the saint in a remarkable state of preservation considering its age — around 650 years. Elsewhere, the chapel is note-worthy for its Renaissance rood screen and a very good Baroque altarpiece.

North of the town — leave along Boulevard Joseph-Collomp — is the peak of Le Malmont, reachable by car and famous for its panorama over the Maures and Esterel Ranges, the Argens Valley and towards Toulon. If, instead of going north, the visitor goes north-west, along the D955, he or she soon reaches the Pierre de la Fée, (the Fairy's Stone). This is a superb Neolithic cromlech — or dolmen, as they are known in France — with a huge table stone supported delicately on three stone fingers, each about 2m (6ft) long. It is easy to see why such objects had an aura of the supernatural to later folk unaware of their significance and builders.

Beyond the stone, the visitor should continue on the D955 which goes through the Gorges de Château-double. This is a fine, verdant gorge, but is only a prelude to the main event further north.

Europe cannot match Arizona's Grand Canyon, but the Verdon Gorges which borrow the name, Grand Canyon du Verdon, are none-theless spectacular. Over countless years, the Verdon River, a tributary of the Durance, has cut into the lime-stone plateau over which it flowed. The production of such deep, clean cut gorges is not well-understood, as it requires a process that is at once both very rapid and very corrosive.

The best explanation proposes that the erosion occurred at times of a general local uplifting or, alterna-tively, when the sea level was falling so that the river's pressure head was vastly increased. It is thought that this, together with the natural rifting of limestone, would allow very rapid cutting. Whatever the process, the river is now hemmed in by nar-row cliffs which plunge 700m (2,300ft) amid wild scenery. The Verdon gets its name from its jade green waters which add to the beauty.

There are interesting villages close to the gorge. **Castellane**, at one end of the gorge's finest section, is a a market-town as well as tourist cen-tre and is dominated by a cube of rock 180m (590ft) high, topped by a seventeenth-century chapel. The chapel — unsurprisingly dedicated to Notre-Dame-de-Roc — is reached by a steep, narrow track marked by the Stations of the Cross. The view from the chapel makes the effort of the climb worthwhile. Being one of the main tourist centres for visitors to the Verdon Gorge, Castellane has good accomodation, ranging from camp sites to a cluster of excellent little hotels in Place Marcel-Sauv-oire. In nearby Rue Nationale, at No 34, Napoleon had lunch on his route from Antibes to Grenoble. In addi-tion to the gorge, Castellane is also close to the inter-connected artificial lakes of Chaudanne, Castillon and St André-les-Alpes.

Moustiers-Ste Marie is set at the other end of the gorge's Grand Can-yon, and is famous for its pottery —

The Verdon Gorge & Sentier Martel

Édouard-Alfred Martel was born in 1859. He was interested in both geology and geography from an early age, an interest which, in adult life, he applied to the study of caves. Martel was responsible for the exploration of almost all the great cave systems of France — including the fabulous show caves of the limestone *causses* of Languedoc — and also opened up caves in Spain, Austria and Britain. His scientific interest in cave formation and cave hydrology virtually founded the science of speleology.

The Verdon Gorge fascinated Martel, who was intrigued by both its formation and the fact that it was unexplored. In August 1905 he and three others became the first men to travel along its length, a journey which took almost four days. Today a footpath (*Sentier Martel*) named after the great man links La Malene, a hostel about half-way along the Route des Crêtes, with Point Sublime.

The walk takes a full, and hard, day. Walkers must be well-equipped. Boots with good support are essential as there is a risk of a turned ankle on the uneven ground. Warm and waterproof clothing are also essential as there is no escape once the route has been started. Food must be carried, because there are no shops; the same applies to water, especially in summer when the gorge is a sun trap and the river is too dangerous to

reputedly introduced to the town by a monk from Faenza in Italy in medieval times, but refined over many centuries by French artists and craftsmen. The town has many shops selling modern Moustiers-ware, but equally fascinating is the Musée de la Faïence (Pottery Museum) where the history and development of the local work is shown through numerous examples.

Moustiers is beautifully positioned at the base of a narrow ravine, its huge, almost vertical, walls dominating the main village square. From the square a steep path leads to the twelfth-century church of Notre-Dame du Beauvoir from where there are dramatic views of the village, the ravine and the Verdon Gorge. High above is a star suspended from a rusty chain strung across the ravine. The original is said to have been erected in the thirteenth century by Baron Blacas d'Auls, a local lord, to celebrate his release from captivity attempt to reach. Head torches must be carried as the route uses tunnels through the rock in several places.

A good guide and a map — these are available from *Fédération Française de Randonnée Pédestre* and IGN (*Institut Geographique National*) respectively — must be carried as some of the tunnels are not to be entered and it is important to know which ones. Finally, you **must** keep to the marked path, the river is part of a dam system and the opening of sluice gates upstream can cause very sudden rises in river level. If you are in an awkward position when this happens, it could be very unpleasant indeed, even fatal.

However, do not be put off by all these precautions. The walk is reasonable enough for the experienced walker and offers an unforgettable experience. The route starts with a straightforward, though occasionally steep and uneven, descent, almost reaching the river. The path reaches the river at Pré d'Issane, where bathing is possible. Ahead is the Cavaliers Gorge, a beautiful spot. The cliffs of the Brèche Imbart are negotiated by steep, exposed ladders, beyond which are the tunnels, one of which is many hundreds of metres long and has an uneven floor. Beyond, it is easy and breathtakingly beautiful walking to Point Sublime.

Once you have walked the gorge, you will want to get back to your starting point. There are no buses, so call a taxi on 92 74 44 50 or 92 83 65 38 from either the inn at Point Sublime or the chalet at La Maline; the service is reliable.

Those captivated by the Verdon might like to know that in addition to Sentier Martel, two alternative versions of GR4 include the gorge, as does Sentier de l'Imbut on the opposite side from the Martel route.

after one of the Crusades. The present star dates from 1957.

Closer to the gorge's western end (near Moustiers) is **Aiguines** where a small, but very good, craft museum is named after the local wood tuners, who used boxwood gathered from the gorge to produce kitchen items, chess sets and for decoration.

It is, however, the gorge which visitors come to see. Both the northern and southern edges can be followed. The Corniche Sublime (the D71) follows the south side, a road hewn from the rock in 1947. Going east from Aiguines, the Corniche enters the Grand Canyon at Illoire, soon reaching the Cirque de Vaumale, a hollowed-out section of the cliff face that allows the first, superb, view of the gorge. Further on, the road offers good views of the steepest section of the gorge before reaching the viewpoints of Falaise des Cavaliers (Cavaliers' Cliff). The cliff itself is vertical for 300m (almost

1,000ft). Beyond the viewpoints the road goes through tunnels to reach the balconies, or *belvédères,* of Mescla (Balcons de la Mescla). This is probably the best viewpoint on this southern side of the gorge, located above the point where the Artuby River reaches the Verdon.

Going west from Castellane the D952 reaches one of the finest viewpoints of the gorge, the Point Sublime. From the car park by the roadside inn take the marked path for a walk of about 10 minutes to a stupendous view straight down to the point where the Baou River meets the Verdon. The gorge here is 'only' 200m (650ft) deep. Back on the road, a left turn follows the near-circular Route des Crêtes (Crest Road), built in 1973, on which a succession of engineered viewpoints (*belvédères*) are passed. The first is Trescaïre, beyond which is L'Escalès, by common consent the finest of all. From the viewpoint, the visitor is looking straight down the full height of the gorge to the footpath. If you are lucky, and have a head for heights, there will be a few ant-like people on the path to give scale to your view.

Closer at hand there are likely to be climbers at work on the near-vertical gorge walls. Some of the climbs ascend the full height of the gorge, but mostly the climbers abseil down from the top and climb up the final 30-60m (100-200ft). After L'Escalès, there are fine viewpoints at Tilleul, Les Glacières and L'Im, before the main road, the D952, is reached again at La Palud. Turn left here to reach Moustiers.

To the south of Moustiers lies Lac de Ste-Croix, dammed to supply water to a hydro-electric power station. The lake is a favourite spot for watersports enthusiasts, especially those wanting to take canoes or rafts into the Verdon Gorge. At the Belvédère de Galetas, the first viewpoint on the D592 heading east from Moustiers, the visitor can see the craft passing under the picturesque bridge that takes the D957 over the Verdon river.

ADDITIONAL INFORMATION

PLACES TO VISIT

Aix-en-Provence

Musée du Vieil Aix
17 rue Gaston-de-Saporta
Open: April to September daily except Monday 10am-12noon, 2.30-6pm; October to March daily except Monday 10am-12noon, 2-5pm. Closed on official holidays
☎ 42 21 43 55

Musée de Tapisseries (Tapestry Museum)
L'Archevêche
Place de la Résistance
Open: all year daily except Tuesday 9.30am-12noon, 2-6.pm. Closed on official holidays
☎ 42 21 05 78

Musée Paul Arbaud
2a Rue du 4-Septembre
Open: all year daily except Sunday 2-5pm. Closed on official holidays
☎ 42 38 38 95

Musée Granet
Place de St Jean-de-Malte
Open: all year daily except Tuesday
10am-12noon, 2-6pm. Closed on
official holidays
☎ 42 38 14 70

L'Atelier Cezanne
  (Cezanne's Studio)
9 Avenue Paul Cezanne
Open: June to September daily except
Tuesday 10am-12noon, 2-6pm;
October to May daily except Tuesday
10am-12noon, 2-5pm
☎ 42 21 06 53

Musée d'Histoire Naturalle
  (Natural History Museum)
Hôtel Boyer d'Eguilles
6 Rue Espariat
Open: all year Monday to Saturday
10am-12noon, 2-6pm, Sunday 2-6pm.
Closed on official holidays
☎ 42 26 23 67

Le Pavillon Vendôme
34 rue Célony or
13 Rue de la Molle
Open: May to September daily except
Tuesday 10am-12noon, 2-6pm;
October to April daily except Tuesday
10am-12noon, 2-5pm
☎ 42 21 05 78

Fondation Vasarely
4km west of the town: follow Avenue
Marcel Pagnol
Open: all year daily except Tuesday
9.30am-12.30pm, 2 -5.30pm, open on
Tuesdays in July and August
☎ 42 21 01 09

Espace Méjanes
Avenue de l'Europe
Library, Fondation St John Perse &
Algeria Centre open: all year Tues-
day, Wednesday, Friday, Saturday 2-
6pm
Video Library open: all year Tuesday,
Wednesday, Friday 2-6pm, Saturday
3-6pm
☎ 42 25 98 85

Entremont
3km north of Aix off of the D14
Open: all year daily except Tuesday
9am-12noon, 2-6pm
☎ 42 23 35 73

Aups

Fondation Simon-Segal
  (Modern Art Museum)
Rue Albert I
Open: mid-June to mid-September
daily 10.30am-12noon, 3-6pm
☎ 94 70 12 98

Brignoles

Musée du Pays Brignolais,
Place du Palais des Comtes de
Provence
Open: April to September Wednesday to Saturday 9am-12noon, 2.30-
6pm, Sundays and Holidays 9am-
12noon, 3-6pm; October to March
Wednesday to Saturday 10am-
12noon, 2.30-5pm, Sundays and
holidays 10am-12noon, 3-5pm
☎ 94 69 45 18

L'Abbaye de la Celle
on the D405 4km south-west of
Brignoles
Open: all year Wednesday-Saturday
10am-12noon, 3-5pm, Tuesday
10am-12noon, Monday 3-5pm
☎ 94 69 09 04

Parc Mini France
8kms east of Brignoles on the N7
Open: March-October daily 10am-
dusk
In July and August the park is floodlit
and open until midnight
☎ 94 69 26 00

Draguignan

Town Museum
9 rue de la République
Open: all year Tuesday to Saturday
10am-12noon, 2-6pm, Monday 2-6pm
☎ 94 47 28 80

Musée des Arts et Traditions Populaires de Moyenne Provence
15 Rue Joseph-Roumanille
Open: all year Tuesday to Saturday
9am-12noon, 3-6pm
☎ 94 47 05 72

Tour de l'Horloge
Open: all year Monday to Saturday
9am-12noon, 2-6pm
Key from Tourist Office (☎ 94 68 63 30)

American Military Cemetery
3kms east of the town along the D59
Open: mid-April-September daily
8am-6pm; October-mid-April daily
9am-5pm
☎ 94 68 03 62

Musée du Canon et des Artilleurs (Artillery Museum)
At military camp 3km east of the town
along the D59
Open: mid-January-mid-December
Monday-Friday 8.30-11.30am, 2.30-
5pm. Closed on official holidays.
☎ 94 60 23 85 or 94 60 23 86

Chapelle Ste Roseline
5km south-east of the town, off the
N555
Open: March to December Wednes-
day and Sunday 2.30-6.30pm, also
Saturdays 2.30-6.30pm July and
August
☎ 94 73 37 30

Entrecasteaux

Le Château
Open: April to September daily 10am-
7pm; October-March daily 10am-6pm
☎ 94 04 43 95

Chapel of Notre-Dame de Benva
Near Lorgues, 15km east of Entrecasteaux on the D562
Open: all year any reasonable time,
ask at the presbytery in Lorgues for key
☎ 94 73 70 53

Abbaye du Thoronet
8km north-east of Cabasse, off the D79
Open: April to September Monday to
Friday 9am-7pm, Sunday and holidays 9am-12noon, 2-7pm; October to
March daily 9.30am-12.30pm, 2-5pm
☎ 94 60 43 90

Fossil Museum
Tourtour
3km east of Villecroze on the D51
Open: mid-June-mid-September daily
except Tuesday 2.30-7pm, also during
the Easter holiday, same times.
☎ 94 70 54 74

Show Cave
Municipal park
Villecroze, 10km north of Entrecasteaux on the D557
Open: July and August daily 10am-
12noon, 2.30-7pm; mid-May to June
daily 2-7pm; mid-April to mid-May
and first fortnight of September daily
2-6pm; March to mid-April and mid-
September to October Saturday,
Sunday 2-6pm
☎ 94 70 63 06

Verdon Gorge

Musée de la Faïence
Place du Presbytère
Moustiers-Ste Marie
Open: April to October daily except
Tuesday 9am-12noon, 2-6pm
☎ 94 74 61 64

Musée des Tourneurs
(Wood Turners Museum)
Rue Haute
Aiguines
Open: July and August daily 10am-
12noon, 2-6pm; September to June
by request only
☎ 94 70 21 75

Western Riviera

The French Riviera, from Marseille to Menton, the most renowned of all coasts, is the subject of this and the next chapter. Visions of sea and beaches spring to mind, so a few general comments about both are worthwhile.

Cliffs, rocks, inlets, small bays, ribbons of sand, pebble beaches; all these help make up the coast's profile. On many public beaches there are areas (*plages aménagés*) where concessionnaires provide refreshments, hire beach equipment (sunshades, sunbeds, etc), sail-boards and pedalos, and where there may also be swimming and windsurfing instructors. Larger resorts have many ancillary recreational facilities, such as yachting and water-skiing, while there are subaqua and marine archaeological clubs for specialists.

The nearly landlocked sea produces an inter-tidal zone that can be measured in centimetres. The width of beach varies imperceptibly. Intense evaporation creates high salinity and a buoyancy for swimmers and physically handicapped people alike. The famous intense Mediterranean blue, which is a delight to the eye, indicates a low level of planktonic life. Pressure in this particularly deep sea creates a constant annual temperature of 13°C (55°F) and gives a thermostatic effect; the coast is warmed in winter and cooled in summer. As the following figures show, inshore water is slow to cool in autumn. However, the statistics are a little deceptive. The *mistral* can play havoc with surface temperatures, especially between Marseille and St Tropez. It may not blow for long in summer but the water is made chill and rough, particularly along west-facing beaches. As the water calms, the sun's heat quickly raises the water temperature about 3°C to make the difference between brave and comfortable swimming.

Average Sea Temperatures

	Marseille-Toulon		Toulon-Menton	
	°C	°F	°C	°F
May	15	59	16	61
June	20	68	19	66
July	19	66	21	70
August	21	70	23	73
September	17	63	23	73
October	18	64	19	66

Marseille is the major port of the Mediterranean — the oldest and second largest city in France. It is a commercial, industrial and university city, volatile, energetic, raw-humoured, chaotic at rush-hours; its Levantine origins seem never to be far from the surface.

The city has a reputation for being aggressive and a little shady, characteristics seen in part as due to its cosmopolitan mix of peoples: Marseille is where Africa, the Middle East and Europe meet. Ignore such dubious ideas, which derive more from western snobbery and prejudice than from reality. Marseille's cultural mix adds to its vibrancy.

Visitors should, of course, be cautious, particularly after dark — but this advice should be heeded in any European city the size of Marseille.

Marseille is no place for the casual driver: a car is only an encumbrance; use the city and suburban buses, trolley-buses, taxis or the underground (*Métro*). There is no shortage of hotels: impersonal, international hotels, a few elegant converted residences or adequate modest places, either in the centre of the city or along the Corniche Président Kennedy. There is an equally wide range of restaurants; some have a Michelin rosette. Many will offer that distinctive Provençal dish, *bouillabaisse*, for which everybody claims to have the only authentic recipe. As a general rule; if it is genuine, it must be expensive.

Marseille is large enough to have a book all to itself, so this will necessarily be a brief introduction, with an attempt to point out the things that are worth seeing in the town, both in a cultural and a more general sense.

The city was founded here, on the eastern edge of the Rhône Delta by Greek settlers in the seventh century BC, and was called *Massalia*. It was primarily a trading port, with trade both along the coast and inland with the Ligurians. The coming of the Romans, whose first settlement was at Aix, just inland from Marseille, had little immediate effect on the city. However, the feud between Julius Caesar and Pompey was critical because the town chose the wrong side — that of Pompey. It was captured and had its defences destroyed. For some time after that, the town played a supporting role to the Roman town of Arles.

With the departure of the Romans, the town was passed from one ruler to another as the power pendulum swung in the south of France, a swing that reached its low point in the tenth century when it was destroyed by the Saracens. After being rebuilt, it was at first a free city, then under the rule of the House of Anjou, until 1481 when it was finally made part of France. Its importance as a harbour grew quickly in the early Middle Ages when it was the chief port of embarkation for the Crusades. Much of the defensive work that can be seen today, particularly in the area of the Old Port, and including Château d'If, dates from this period.

At the time of the Revolution, the city had its own 'reign of terror' with the guillotine, installed on La Canebière, working long and bloody hours. To support the Revolution, the city sent 500 volunteers to Paris. As they marched they practised a new song, recently composed by Rouget de Lisle, an army sapper, in Strasbourg. The song was the *Chant de guerre de l'Armée du Rhin* — the war song of the Rhine Army. By the time the Marseille volunteers reached Paris the song had been taken up as the anthem of the Revolution, and in honour of the city's 'choir', been renamed *La Marseillaise*.

Since that time, both the port and the city have expanded, with Marseille playing a leading role in the economic life of France.

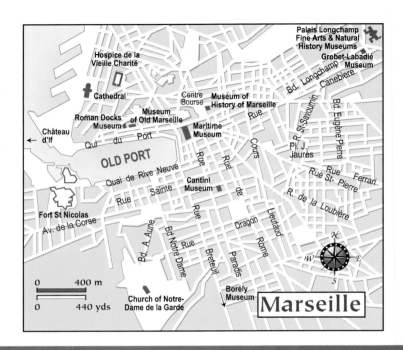

Palais Longchamp
Fine Arts & Natural
History Museums

Hospice de la
Vieille Charité

Grobet-Labadié
Museum

Bd. Longchamp

Canebière

Cathedral

Centre
Bourse

Museum of
History of Marseille

Bd. Eugène Pierre

R. St-Savournin

Roman Docks
Museum

Museum
of Old Marseille

Rue

Château
d'If

Maritime
Museum

Pl. J.
Jaurès

Quai du Port

OLD PORT

Rue

Rue

Cours

Rue St-Pierre

Rue Ferrari

Quai de Rive Neuve

Cantini
Museum

de

R. de la Loubière

Rue

Sainte

Rue

Lieutaud

Fort St Nicolas

Av. de la Corse

Bd. A. Aune

Bd Notre-Dame

Rue
Breteuil

Rue
Paradis

Dragon

Rome

N

W   E

S

0   400 m

0   440 yds

Church of Notre-
Dame de la Garde

Borély
Museum

Marseille

A trip around the cultural high spots of Marseille is not easily accomplished as the town, unlike many capitals — Paris, to name the prime example — does not have a compact, harmonious centre. We will start, however, near the heart of the old town, at the archaeological site near the Centre Bourse, not far from the Old Port. There, in addition to a pleasant garden, which is actually situated above an underground car park that is very handy for the visitor, are the remains of the ramparts of Old Marseille. Nearby are the History of Marseille Museum, which includes the best finds from excavations of the old town, and the Maritime and Commerical Museum, housed in the old *Bourse* (Stock Exchange), which traces the history of Marseille as a port and town from the late Middle Ages to the present day.

Those interested in the port's earlier history should follow the northern edge of the Old Port, passing the town hall to reach the Roman Docks Museum where there is an interesting collection of ancient maritime items, including a model of how the Roman Port would have looked. Next to the museum is another, that of Old Marseille. This is housed in a fine sixteenth-century house known as Maison Diamentée because of the stones used to build it. The museum behind the jewelled walls concentrates on Provençal life of the eight-

eenth and nineteenth centuries, with collections of furniture and kitchen ware, together with some interesting prints of Old Marseille. There is also a fascinating collection on the history and manufacture of playing cards donated by a local company.

To the north-west of this clutch of museums are the old and new cathedrals. The old cathedral, almost destroyed in the last century but now partially restored, is one of the most beautiful examples of Romanesque architecture in Provence and dates from the twelfth century. By contrast, the new cathedral is as recent as the late nineteenth century. It is huge — the largest cathedral built in France for several hundred years — and was built in a style that can be most accurately described as eclectic. It looks best when viewed from a boat entering the Old Port. Close to the cathedrals is a fine old hospice from the seventeenth century.

The hospice now houses the Museum of Mediterrenean Archaeology with a fine collection of Egyptian antiquities and an equally good Celtic (Ligurian) section, and the Museum of African, Polynesian and American Indian Arts, collections from the three areas donated by individuals and old colonial museums. The masks and sculptures are interesting, but by far the most bizarre items are the shrunken heads and carved skulls from the South Seas.

Back at the Old Port's northern quay a ferry will take the visitor across the harbour from the town hall to the southern quay, offering a good view of the boats and of Notre-

Opposite: a replica galleon in the old port at Marseilles

Dame de la Garde on its hill to the south. On landing, a right turn leads past the Théâtre de la Criée: bear left to reach the Basilica of St Victor. The basilica, seemingly more castle than church, stands on the site of a fifth century church built to honour St Victor, the patron saint of sailors and millstones. St Victor was martyred in the third century by being ground between two millstones.

Ahead now, beyond the offices of the Foreign Legion and Fort St Nicolas, is the Parc du Pharo. The old palace here was once the home of the Empress Eugénie, wife of Napoleon III. From the park drivers can follow the Corniche Président J F Kennedy along the coast, a delightful road which ends at La Pointe Rouge where the corniche meets Avenue du Prado. Here, rather incongruously, stands a copy of Michelangelo's *David*. Nearby, the Plage du Prado is Marseille's best beach, a huge expanse with a park and pool. Just beyond the roundabout is the Parc Borély. Here the annual Provençal Boules Competition is held in late July/early August. At the centre of the park is Château Borély, a late eighteenth-century mansion decorated and finished in period style. The *château* houses the museum of decorative arts. East of the *château* are the park's botanical gardens.

The visitor can follow Avenue du Prado to the Rond Point du Prado. To the right here, in Boulevard Michelet, stands Corbusier's *Cité Radieuse*, built in 1952 as a prototype for 'vertical living'.

Turn left at the Rond Point du Prado to head back into the city. The road is a continuation of the Avenue du Prado, wide and spacious, the epitome of modern Marseille. To the left of the next roundabout (Place Castellane) the visitor can climb to Notre-Dame de la Garde, the tall, finger-like basilica that dominates most views of Marseille. The basilica, built in the mid-nineteenth century, stands on a 160m (530 ft) hill and is 60m (197 ft) from base to the top of the gilded Madonna on the belfry. Inside, the multicoloured marble is particularly impressive, while the view to the city and the sea from the site is magnificent.

Continuing towards the city from Place Castellane, the visitor can soon turn left to reach the Cantini Museum, which has arguably the finest collection of Marseille and Moustiers pottery in France. There is also a superb art gallery with works by Miró, Max Ernst, Picasso and Matisse, together with an excellent collection of the work of contemporary artists, including Balthus, Bacon and Adami.

From the Cantini, continue southwards to the main quay of the old port. The area close to this quay is the heart of the city, and shows Marseille at its best. On the quay there are *ad hoc* fish stalls when the boats arrive, and in the surrounding streets there are pavement cafés to make the best of the lively scene. Ending at the port is La Canebrière which, with Rue de Rome, Rue St Férréal and the Centre Bourse offer the best shopping in the city. La Canebière is named from the Provençal *canébe*, hemp, the street once having been the rope-making heart of the old port. Today it is *the* place to go for shops, cafés and restaurants, and with its wide pavements, noise and bustle, is every bit as joyous and interesting as it is famous.

Walk away from the sea along La Canebière, then contine north-eastwards along Boulevard Longchamp, to Palais Longchamp, a baroque mansion with two wings linked by a semi-circular colonnade that faces a superb fountain. The *palais* houses the Fine Arts Museum which has some interesting paintings, including a collection of the work of the artist Pierre Puget, a seventeenth-century Marseille painter and sculptor. Also here is the Natural History Museum with dispays on the wildlife of Provence. Close to the *palais* is the Grobet-Labadié Museum housed in the late nineteenth century mansion of Alexandre Labadié, a local merchant. The museum has a collection of French tapestries and porcelain, together with musical instruments from the collection of the musician Louis Grobet.

The nearest island to Marseille's harbour is Château d'If, reached by a regular boat service from the old port. The castle on this small rocky inlet was built in the remarkably short time of 4 years from 1524 to 1528 — though the curtain wall was added later — in order to protect the entrance to Marseille harbour. It is an interesting building and offers splendid views of the nearby islands of Ratonneau and Pomègues, and of Marseille. The *château* might just be famous for its view, but Alexander Dumas chose it as the prison for two of the characters in *The Count of Monte Cristo*. As a result, most visitors now make literary pilgrimages.

Another fine excursion from the city heads north-east towards the Chaine de l'Etoile, a wild ridge of hills, to reach **Château-Gambert**, a hamlet that is now virtually a part of Marseille. The shady main square has a fine seventeenth-century church and an equally good mansion which houses the Musée des Arts et Traditions Populaires du Terroir Marseillais — ie, the arts and traditions of the local area. The museum has collections of costumes, tools, ceramics etc. Nearby are the large Loubière show caves with some interesting stalagmites and stalactites.

To head east, take the D559 southwards from Marseille, towards Cassis. On this road, stop at Col de la Gineste. Inland is a view of the denuded white limestone Chaîne de St Cyr. Seawards is the inlet of Cassis and, beyond this, the towering Cap Canaille, the highest cliff in France at 399m (1,310ft). Sometimes, on a September evening, the panorama is suffused with intense purple light.

Cassis is a cheerful, busy little port, visited in numbers by the Marseillais. It has a recent casino and holds regattas and watersports events in summer. There is also a small museum of folklore.

South-west of Cassis are the Calanques, deep, fjord-like inlets formed by sheer limestone cliffs. The inlets, formed by the valleys of the hills to the west of Cassis continuing beneath the sea, are stunningly

153

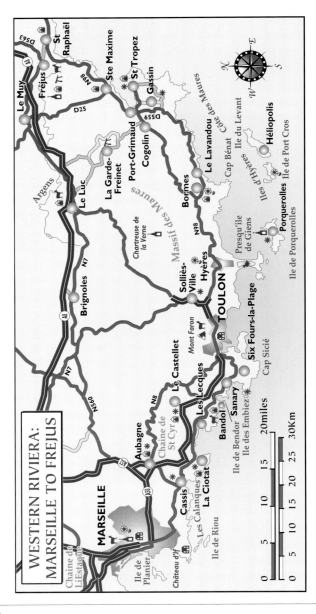

WESTERN RIVIERA: MARSEILLE TO FREJUS

MARSEILLE

Chaine de L'Estaque

Ile de Planier

Château d'If

Ile de Riou

Cassis

Les Calanques

La Ciotat

Aubagne

Chaine de St Cyr

Le Castellet

Les Lecques

Bandol

Sanary

Ile de Bendor

Ile des Embiez

Six Fours-la-Plage

Cap Sicié

TOULON

Mont Faron

Sollies-Ville

Hyères

Presqu'île de Giens

Cap Bénat

Massif des Maures

Chartreuse de la Verne

Brignoles

Le Luc

La Garde-Freinet

Port-Grimaud

Cogolin

Bormes

Le Lavandou

Côte des Maures

Iles d'Hyères

Ile du Levant

Ile de Port Cros

Héliopolis

Porquerolles

Ile de Porquerolles

Gassin

St Tropez

Ste Maxime

Le Muy

Fréjus

St Raphaël

Argens

N7

N8

N560

A50

A57

A8

N7

D25

D559

N98

N98

D563

0   5   10   15   20miles

0   5   10   15   20   25   30Km

The harbour and beach at Cassis

Calanque de Port-Miou (left) and Calaques En Vau (right)

beautiful — dazzling white cliffs rising from the clear blue water. Parking close to the Calanques is not easy (unless you are early or lucky), a visit inevitably requiring some walking. The first inlet is Calanque de Port-Miou, the longest and, with its collection of yachts, one of the most picturesque. Calanque de Port-Pin and Calanque En Vau can only be reached on foot — follow the path on the inland side of Port-Miou. Port-Pin has a small beach shaded by pines. En Vau is the most spectacular of the three, with huge cliffs and rock towers rising from the sea. The 1-1½ hour walk to reach it keeps it free of huge crowds, the visitor usually sharing the inlet with a couple of yachts, a handful of skilled rock climbers and other kindred spirits.

Inland from Cassis is **Aubagne** which has a museum that is a must for anyone with even a passing interest in that most romantic of organisations, the French Foreign Legion. The Legion, founded in 1831, was originally housed in Algeria but it moved here in 1962 when the African colony gained its independence. The history of the Legion is explained in a museum near the HQ. Although it is well-known that there was little glamour in the Legion, the legend of men who joined to escape or to forget a lost love is too strong to resist.

Elsewhere in the town the visitor can enjoy the *santon* workshops *Santon* making has been traditional in Aubagne for many yars, the workshops having tableaux displays as well as figures for sale. Several of the workshops exhibit scenes from the works of Marcel Pagnol (1895-1974) who was born in the town, at 16 Cours Barthêlemy. The excellent films made recently of Pagnol's most famous works, *Jean de Florette* and *Manon des Sources*, have brought the writer to new prominence, Aubagne responding by designating two Pagnol walks which visit some of his favourite places. Details of the both *santon* workshops and the walks can be obtained from the Tourist Office in Esplanade Charles-de-Gaulle (☎ 42 03 49 98).

A very different kind of entertainment is available at the Parc d'Attractions OK Corral, about 15kms (10 miles) east of the town along the N8. The park includes a number of white-knuckle rides, including a loop-the-loop roller coaster, a variety of other attractions guaranteed to thrill younger visitors and a satisfying array of bars, creperies and restaurants. Recognising its clientele, the park's entrance fee is height-dependent: under 1m (3ft 3in) tall, entrance free; under 1.4m (4ft 7in), 20 per cent discount!

Eastwards from Cassis, the Corniche des Crêtes goes over the Pas de la Colle and Cap Canaille. This is a wonderful drive, the view to the Calanques from Cap Canaille being magnificent, particularly at sunset. But be cautious, the headland is largely unguarded and the cliffs, the tallest in France, very steep. Further along the road there is another fine view from the lighthouse — reached by a short detour to the right — near the Grande Tête. The main road now descends to La Ciotat, with splendid views over the Rocher d'Aigle (Eagle's Rock) and across the bay to Pointe Grenier.

La Ciotat was a Roman port, an important port during medieval times and a shipbuilding centre in modern times. The virtual collapse of shipbuilding in recent years has dealt a heavy blow to the town's economy, though there are signs that the worst has been overcome. The town's sea-based history is explored at the Musée Ciotaden in Rue des Poilus, near the old port.

It was at La Ciotat that the Lumière brothers had the first private showing, in September 1895, of the moving picture film that was to cause a sensation a few weeks later in Paris.

Just south of the town — follow the seaside road towards the Calanque de Figurerolles, another fine rocky inlet — is Mugel Park, a lovely area with marked paths through the gardens and impressive views. There is also a small information centre on marine ecology.

Beyond La Ciotat is **Les Lecques,** whose good, sandy beach makes it popular. At La Madrague is the Tauroentum Museum with Gallo-Roman mosaics and relics, built on the foundations of a Roman villa near the sea.

Bandol, one of the more sophisticated coastal resorts, has bars and discos, as well as a Jardin Exotique et Parc Zoologique, on the way to Sanary-sur-Mer. Pleasant grounds laid out with exotic trees give shelter to a variety of small animals and birds. It also has a superb Romanesque chapel to Notre Dame-du-Bausset-Vieux which contains some fine paintings. Boat trips run to the Ile de Bendor, just off-shore. Here there is a recreated Provençal village of craft shops and art galleries, and a centre running courses on arts and crafts. There is also an exhibition of wine and spirits with over 7,000 bottles from around fifty countries.

The whole hinterland here is attractive for touring. It is worth visiting the picturesque villages of **La Cadière-d'Azur** and **Le Castellet** and, just off the N8, motoring enthusiasts will find the Paul Ricard motor racing circuit.

Next along the coast is **Sanary-sur-Mer**, a pleasant resort in a well-protected bay. From it, a road with fine views follows the blunt headland south. Off-shore of the Petit Gaou, at the headland's first 'corner' is the Ile des Embiez. The island, reached from the Port du Brusc, close to Petit Gaou, has become well-known through the marine research work conducted there by the biologist Alain Bombard, funded by Paul Ricard's Fondation Océanographique. As well as an aquarium and museum, the island has a marina, shipyards and hotel.

From Sanary-sur-Mer there is a fine trip inland, following the D11 to Ollioules and then going north, still on the D11 at first, but joining the N8, through the twisting Ollioules Gorge to Ste Anne-d'Evenos. There, go right and follow a narrow road to reach the viewpoint of Mont Caume where a brisk walk up the final few metres reaches a splendid panoramic view both inland and out to sea. On your return, go right on the D20 after leaving Ollioules to reach the Gros Cerveau, a fine piece of cultivated hillside that also offers extensive views from its high point.

Back in Sanary-sur-Mer, take the coast road beyond Le Brusc and make for Notre-Dame du Mai, an early seventeenth-century pilgrimage chapel, built on the high point of Cap Sicié and commanding extensive views over the Calanques and the islands off Hyères. To the east, reached via the elegantly named Six-Fours-les-Plages, is Toulon.

Like Marseille, the great naval base of **Toulon** is not usually visualised as a holiday centre. However, it does have things of interest in addition to its dramatic setting at the foot of Mont Faron and Mont Caume, both of which are surmounted by forts. In Roman times, local shells were boiled to produce the dye for Imperial purple, though the town is more famous for having been taken from the British in 1793, chiefly as a result of the bravery of Napoleon Bonaparte, a young Corsican officer in the French army. Equally famous in the annals of warfare is the scuttling of the French fleet in the harbour in 1942.

Make a point of seeing the Naval Museum at the western end of Quai Stalingrad. Beyond the impressive doorway the visitor will be amazed by the artwork on display. The decoration of French naval ships — figureheads, carvings etc. — was under the control of the king from the mid-seventeenth century, Louis XIV, the Sun King, encouraging an era of extravagant sculpture and painting. The master of the workshops, appointed in 1668, was Pierre Puget, some of whose fine work can be seen in the museum.Tthe huge fresco of old Toulon is by Joseph Vernet, a later artist. Sadly, but not surprisingly, the idea of elaborately carved warships did not long outlive Puget or Louis.

Two of Puget's most famous works are the caryatids that supprt the town hall balcony, eastwards along Quai Stalingrad. These, depicting *Force* and *Fatigue*, are said to have been modelled on local dockworkers. Also on Quai Stalingrad is the *Genius of Navigation*, a statue by the local sculptor Daumas. The pointing figure, naked apart from his unravelling loincloth, is supposed to represent the high ideals of seafaring. The locals maintain that it is a sailor leaving the local red-light area in disarray and agonisingly indicating his ship as it heads for the horizon.

Quai Stalingrad, with its shops and cafés, is the place to go if the visitor has little time to spare. From it the Old Town, which miraculously escaped the Allied bombing of the port, is reached by heading away from the sea along Rue d'Algar, to the west of the town hall, or Rue Méridienne, to its east. Rue Méridienne leads — by way of Rue a l'Huile (Oyster Street), to the right — to the cathedral, which houses several fine pieces by Pierre Puget. Close by is the Museum of Old Toulon with col-

The Allied Landings in 1944

Many visitors do not realise that the Allied armies invaded southern France after the invasion of Normandy, yet the Provence landings were critical to the long term strategy of freeing mainland Europe. On the night of 14/15 August 1944 American troops landed on the Hyères islands of Port-Cros and Levant to silence gun battereis that would have threatened landing craft and support ships. Then, on the morning of the 15 August, British and American airborne troops parachuted into Le Muy, to the north-west of Fréjus, while French commandos went ashore at Cap Negre near Le Lavandou and at Pointe de l'Esquillon on the Esterel coast. With an advance bridgehead and the flanks secured, the main invasion took place at 8am, American troops landing on the broad front between St Tropez and Esterel.

On 16 August French troops landed at St Tropez to continue the advance. Toulon was attacked on 21 August, Marseille on the 23rd, though the cities did not fall until the 26th and 28th respectively. The Americans advanced northwards at speed, reaching Grenoble on 22 August with the intention of turning west to block the Rhône Valley, cutting off the German line of retreat. Meanwhile, to the east the Americans attacked Nice on 21 August, taking it on the 30th. In fifteen days Provence had been liberated, the Allied troops sweeping northwards to join their colleagues in northern France.

lections on Bonaparte and other personalities and incidents in the town's history.

Rue Alger, a pedestrian-only street, leads to Rue Hoche and Place Puget, dominated by the Three Dolphins' Fountain. The dolphins of the name are almost completely obscured by the jungle-like plant life growing on the lime deposits of ages. Nearby is Toulon's Opera House, a very elegant building with splendid interior decoration.

The Naval Museum stands close to the entrance to the Naval Arsenal home of the Mediterranean fleet. The arsenal covers 240 hectares (about 500 acres) and employs some 10,000 people. North of the museum is the park of Place d'Armes: northwest now, across the main road which cleaves the town as it links the

A50 to the A57, is the Jardin Alexandre I, a fine park, with a bust of Puget. At the park's edge is the Municipal Museum. Here are the natural history museum and art gallery, notable chiefly for its collection of the works of nineteenth-century Provençal painters.

From Quai Stalingrad, motorboat trips go round the inner roadstead (Petite Rade) on a trip that includes the arsenal and dry docks. Les Sablettes, St Mandrier and the Iles d'Hyères make short boat excursions while Corsica can be visited between June and September. The inner roadstead is a good tour on dry land too, visiting Fort Balaguier. This was built in the sixteenth century to protect the harbour on its western side, and now contains some items from the Naval Museum, chiefly those from the Napoleonic era. The eastern side of the harbour was protected by the Royal Tower which can also be visited. It is 'royal' because it was constructed by Louis XII, at the same time as Fort Balaguier, and certainly deserves its alternative name of Great Tower, the walls being more than 6m (20ft) thick.

North of the town, the visitor can use a cable car to reach Mont Faron where there are marvellous views along the coast, a small zoo and the national memorial to the Allied Landings of 1944. The memorial, built around an old fort, is a fine one, impressive yet dignified. The small site museum uses audio-visual techniques to bring the landings to life.

One final excursion from Toulon takes the visitor north-eastwards to **Solliès-Ville** — take the A57 and exit at La Farlède. The old town lies on the hillside above the newer Solliès-Pont, a market town for the cherry orchards of the Gapeau Valley. From the old castle in Solliès-Ville the view of the valley is superb. Look, too, for the church, built in a mix of Romanesque and Gothic styles, which has two very fine altarpieces. Nearby, Maison Aicard, the house of the poet and dramatist Jean Aicard, has been turned into a museum in his honour.

To the east of Toulon, about 20km (12½ miles) by way of the coast road, lies **Hyères**, the oldest resort on the Riviera. First admired in the sixteenth century by Catherine de Medici, who thought of building a royal villa here, and patronised three centuries later by Queen Victoria and Robert Louis Stevenson, its exposed position in winter made it fall out of favour. It lies between the limestone ranges to the west and the Maures Mountains to the east.

It is worth strolling about the Old Town, which is huddled round the hilltop castle ruins. A medieval flavour hangs about the streets, particularly Rue Paradis and Place Massillon where markets are held on weekdays. In Place Massillon — named after one of France's greatest preacher's who was born in Hyères in 1663 — is Tour St Blaise, the last remnant of a fortress of the Knights Templar.

South of the Old Town, broad avenues lined with palms give the new town a sub-tropical look. The town museum is interesting for its items from the original Greek settlement of *Olbia*. Some Saracen pottery has also been found at the site, and the lighthouse that stands there today is called L'Almanarre, which is descended from the Arab *Al Manar* (a lighthouse).

The town is also worth visiting for its gardens, especially St Bernard Park, above the Old Town, which has many tropical plants and several fine viewpoints, and the Olbius-Riquier Gardens, in the lower town, which also has a large collection of tropical plants and cacti.

The beaches are further south, close to the neck of a 7km (4½ miles) long peninsula, the Presqu'île de Giens, on whose western side are the Presquier saltmarshes and a lagoon where flamingoes are frequently seen. On west side of the Presqu'île (the 'nearly island', a very apt description) there is a continuous beach beside the causeway road.

At the peninsula's tip is Tour Fondue from which boats take 15 minutes to reach the island of **Porquerolles**. Porquerolles (*Prote* or 'first' to the Greeks) is the largest of the group of islands known as the Iles d'Hyères or, more romantically, Les Iles d'Or (the Golden Isles). From the miniscule port of Porquerolles — where bicycles can be hired — paths go in various directions through lush vegetation and vineyards. The cyclist or walker can visit the lighthouse and old fort.

Port Cros can be reached in about 90 minutes by motorboats from Port de la Plage d'Hyères. It was called *Mese* or 'middle' by the Greeks, and is more rugged than Porquerolles. The whole of this tranquil, hilly island, and its Mediterranean fringe, has been made a national park, one of only six in France and the only one not associated with a mountain range. The park protects the island's flora and fauna, the latter including the Tyrrehenian Painted Frog, which is not found on mainland Europe. The park also protects the marine life of the island's fringe. The park can be explored along numerous paths, and tours of the island and the underwater margins are escorted by guides: useful booklets explaining the island's natural history can be bought.

The third island, **Ile du Levant**, is reached from Le Lavandou and Cavalaire. Most of it is occupied by the French Navy: only the western tip and the naturist village of Héliopolis can be visited.

East of Hyères, beyond **La Londe** where there is a tropical bird garden set in a large park of pine and eucalyptus, is the Côte des Maures, the 'new' Riviera, which was discovered as a summer pleasure-ground in the inter-war years. Backing the coast is the Massif des Maures (from the Greek *amauros* and Provençal *maouro*, both meaning sombre, a reference to the dark colour of the pine trees). Stretching some 60km (37 miles) between Hyères and Fréjus, the Maures are rounded by erosion and thickly forested with pines (these are prone to forest fires), cork-oaks and Spanish chestnuts. The crystalline rock contains mica-schist which glints like gold in the sun.

The Port Cros National Park

The Port Cros National Park, created in 1963 is the strangest of France's six parks. It is the only one not to cover a mountain area and includes not only the island, but a section of the sea surrounding it.

The park was created to preserve the vegetation of both the island and the sea bed. On the island botanists identify four distinct regions of vegetation: the costal belt, the valleys, the upland slopes and the high peaks. Though the latter rise only to 199m (650ft), the burning effect of the sun and wind has created an amazing micro-culture. The island's woodlands consist of holm oak, myrtle and strawberry tree. The vegetation at all levels also supports a good range of butterflies, some of them quite rare.

Beneath the sea there is a remnant of original Mediterranean sea-kelp forest and areas of posidonia 'grassland' formed from Neptune grass. On the rocks there are sponges and sea urchins, while the marine life includes octopus, moray eel and a range of beautifully coloured fish including cardinal, sea peacock and black-faced blenny.

The island is also home to the Tyrrehenian Painted Frog one of Europe's rarest frogs which occurs only here, on Corsica and Sardinia. The frog is about 7cm (3in) long, and sage green with darker blotches.

A very good round trip is to take the coast road to St Tropez, and to return over the hills. Just after the coast road, the D559, has turned seaward off the N98, a left turn reaches **Bormes-les-Mimosas**.

Bormes is an old, exquisitely sited, hill village. In that sense it is like many other Provençal villages, and would probably have remained a place for the connoisseur had it not been 'adopted' by artists and holiday-home owners. Careful restoration of the houses, the planting of the mimosas of the name — together with oleander, bougainvillaea, camomile and eucalyptus — and the tending of window boxes and giant pots, have turned Bormes into a showpiece village. The change of name, reflecting the coming of age of the tourist and floral village, occured in 1968. Some visitors may find the affect of it a bit overpowering, but for most Bormes will be as beautiful as its setting.

Returning from the wine shop at
Bormes-les-Mimosas

St Tropez harbour — ideal for
people watching

Within the village it is best to
wander at leisure. Art and craft
shops abound, but there are a few
gems that should not be missed.
Place St Francois has a statue of St
Francis de Paolo, who saved the village from plague in 1481, and a
chapel dedicated to the saint. The
village church, St Trophyme, is
eighteenth century and has a series
of paintings — by Alain Nonn in
1980 — illustrating the path to the
Cross. Of the old streets, be sure to
find Rue Rompi-Cuou. The name of
this very steep, shaded — and therefore damp — street is Provençal and
reflects its slippery, hazardous nature. In polite company it is best to
translate it as 'bottom breaker'.

Finally, the town museum, in Rue
Carnot, is worth visiting. Its history
collection explores the evolution of
Bormes and the Chartreuse de la
Verne, to the north, while its art collection reflects the work of local artists, particularly Jean-Charles Cazin.

Beyond Bormes the road reaches
Le Lavandou, an underrated resort
with a fine beach, a delightful central
square, laid out as a garden, and fine
views to Port Cros Island. On again,
the road passes through a string of
small resorts, each with its individual character: St Clair, La Fos-
sette, Aiguebelle, Cavalière. Ahead
now is La Croix-Valmer. A right turn
here follows the D93 around the
Ramateulle headland, crossing the

Col de Collebasse. Beyond the col a left turn through Ramateulle visits the Moulin de Paillas, three ruined windmills close to which is a viewpoint offering a magnificent panorama of the Esterel hills beyond the Golfe de St Tropez.

But whether the visitor takes the D93 or stays on the more rapid D559, the next stop is **St Tropez**. The French — and most visitors — call the port St Trop: an endearing nickname, but it is as well to remember that *trop* in French means 'too much'. There is excess in St Tropez, the shops and restaurant are often too expensive, there are always too many cars, usually too many people. But once the yachts, aspirants to stardom or notoriety, naturists and the crowds who want to share in the dream-world have left, St Tropez reveals itself to be as endearingly attractive as it was when Matisse painted it long ago. Matisse followed Paul Signac whose boat was forced into the port by bad weather. Signac liked St Tropez so much that he built a villa and stayed. He also spread word of the town's charms: soon Matisse, Derain, Braque, Marquet, Bonnard, Dufy and other artists fell under the spell of the light and immortalised St Tropez in paint, as did Colette in literature.

The work of some of these turn-of-the century masters is housed in the Annunciation Museum housed in the sixteenth-century chapel of Notre-Dame d'Annonciade. The chapel stands in Place Georges Grammont, named after the benefactor whose gift of around 100 canvases set the museum up in 1937. Today it is one of the finest galleries in France covering the work of artists active in the period 1890 to 1940.

The other museum in the town is the Maritime Museum in the citadel, the sixteenth-century fortress dominating the hill at the eastern edge of the town. The museum has a collection of old engravings of the town, information on the Allied landings in 1944 and various other sea-based collections. The view from the citadel alone is worth the journey, covering the Golfe de St Tropez and the Maures and Esterel hills.

The town is named after St Torpes, a Roman centurion beheaded (on Nero's orders) in Pisa for his faith. Legend has it that St Torpes' body and head were set adrift in a boat together with a dog and a cockerel who, it was anticpated, would eat the remains as a final humiliation. When the boat washed up here, the remains were miraculously intact. St Torpes is commemorated in one of two venerable processions that take place every year. These are the *bravades* (*bravados* or defiance). The first takes place between 16 and 18 May. The gilded bust of St Torpes is carried round the town by a corps of a hundred *bravadeurs* dressed in eighteenth-century costume making a thunderous noise with muskets, blank cartridges and music. By-standers join in the fun and, on the last day, the procession makes its way to the pretty sixteenth-century chapel of Ste Anne, on a rock just south of the town. The second *bravade* is on 15 June. This *Fête des Espagnols* honours the putting to flight of the Spanish fleet by valiant Tropéziens in 1637 during the Thirty Years' War.

At times other than *bravades*, the procession through the streets comprises the curious and the would-be stars. Ever since bikini-clad Brigitte Bardot appeared here in 1956, St Tropez has had a reputation for glitter. Bardot was promoting *And God Created Woman*, Roger Vadin's seminal film, but she stayed on in the town, buying a villa and opening a boutique (now-closed). But though many visitors are drawn by this reputation, they are held by the undoubted charms of the port. Along Quai d'Épi on the western (car park) side of the old port's basin, artists show their paintings and work on their latest masterpieces aware that many visitors have whetted their appetites for art at the nearby Annunciation Museum. From the Quai, the view across the basin is superb, the expensive boats backed by the warm coloured houses of Quai Suffren and Quai Jean Jaures with the Italianate bell tower of the town church peeping above them.

The Old Town with its exclusive boutiques lies close to the church, but for many the Quais are the essence of St Tropez. From them, in summer there are boat trips around the Gulf of St Tropez or further afield. On Quai Suffren stands a statue of the Bailli de Suffren (1729-88), the admiral who, with only five ships under his command, harrassed the English fleets from the West Indies to the Indian Ocean. Château Suffren, the family home, is in the

Old Town, near the town hall.

After St Tropez, it would be a pity not to see **Port Grimaud**. You must park at the entrance to the village, for it can be visited only on foot or by boat. It is an elegant, modern holiday village designed by François Spoerry and built out into the Golfe de St Tropez. It was designed for the yachting community: each front door has its own mooring. In imitation of a Provençal fishing village it has harmonious colours and graceful bridges over canals from one walkway to another. Shops, banks, cafés, church and post-office are grouped around a square which is decked with flowers. Self-drive boats can be hired to tour the canals, and there are sightseeing cruises.

A tour of the Massif de Maures begins at **Cogolin** to see the work- shops of the local carpet and fabric industry, where hand-weaving is still carried out. Carpet making is only one of several local industries, along with cork making and the manufacture of musical instruments and furniture from locally grown canes. The local cinema also houses the Espace Raimu, a collection of memorabilia of the comedy actor Jules A. C. Muraire whose stage name was Raimu.

North of Cogolin, beyond Grimaud, is **La Garde-Freinet,** with the interesting remains of a sixteenth-century castle reputedly built on the foundations of a Saracen fortress. North again — and out of the Maures — is **Le Luc**, where the historian will find much of interest in a museum in the old chapel of St Anne, while the

St Tropez, immortalised by painters for over a century

Port Grimaud

philatelist will be rewarded by a visit to the Stamp Museum.

Back in the Maures proper, it is best to follow the narrow road from La Garde Freinet to the Col du Fourches. The GR9 comes this way too, and at several of the high points it is worth leaving the car and following the waymarked trail for a short distance to savour the seclusion of the forest and the occasional surprising viewpoint. To the north of the col, head west along the D75 from Gonfaron, to the Village de Tortues (Tortoise Village) where the rare Hermann's tortoise is bred in captivity. The Maures is the only site in France where the tortoise now lives (though it is found elsewhere in Europe). The centre also has a breeding collection of European terrapins.

Eastwards from the col is the hermitage church of Notre-Dame des Anges occupying a site that is believed to have been a pagan site before the first, Merovingian, Christian building was erected. The view from the church is stunning.

After crossing the col, the road drops down to Collobrières, a centre for the making of *marrons glacés*. From here, there is a road which can only be found by using a local map; any attempt at directions is almost bound to fail. It leads towards the Chartreuse de la Verne, all that remains of a Carthusian monastery, beautifully situated in the middle of the Maures Forest. The charterhouse was founded in 1170 but has been abandoned, re-occupied and rebuilt several times. It has been occupied by the Order of Bethlehem since 1983. The charterhouse is worth visiting for its peace and solitude, and also for the beautiful view across the chestnut and holm oak forests of the Maures. Visitors should remember that the charterhouse is a religious building and dress appropriately.

South from Collobrières, the road goes to Bormes, passing some excellent viewpoints. Just before Bormes is reached, a left turn on to the N98 allows a drive through the Môle Valley, a mixture of forests and vines. Towards the valley's eastern end, take the D27 over the Col du Canadel, another fine viewpoint, and follow it as it winds back through the forest to Bormes.

Back on the coast, the next town is **Ste Maxime**; a fashionable and lively resort which is sheltered, unlike St Tropez across the bay, from the *mistral*. Fine beaches — especially at La Nartelle — entertainment at night, and plenty of hotels and restaurants make it very popular. The town has a small local history museum housed in the Dames Tower, built in the sixteenth century to defend the town, and an extraordinary museum of mechanical music with a collection of old gramophones, musical boxes and barrel organs. From Ste Maxime, the D25 leads inland towards Le Muy and Draguignan. Side roads, especially those between Col de Gratteloup on the D25, Plan-de-la-Tour on the D44 and Vidauban on N7, provide quiet round trips among the lower Maures hills.

The N98 continues to follow the coast. **Cap des Sardinaux** is another stopping-place for exhilarating views:

beyond it, tiny resorts are hidden among trees — Val d'Esquières, San Peire-sur-Mer, Les Issambres, and **St Aygulf**, widely known for its excellent camping facilities and separated from Fréjus-Plage by the mouth of the River Argens. A tour of the Argens Valley is well-worthwhile. It takes in **Roquebrune-sur-Argens** with its picturesque, arcaded houses and a walk to the chapel of Notre-Dame-de-Roquette, set among trees with fine views over the valley.

Fréjus-Plage has extensive sands which are 1.5km (1 mile) south-east of **Fréjus**. The town is far enough inland not to be a resort, its chief attractions being its Roman and medieval past. Guided tours of espiscopal Fréjus, which is concentrated at Place Formigé in the town's centre, are organised throughout the year by the Tourist Office.

The espiscopal area, or Cathedral Close, includes the cathedral, cloisters, baptistery and bishop's palace, the whole being fortified. The austere, early Provençal Gothic cathedral is thirteenth century. When you enter, it is clear that it is powerful rather than graceful (Provençal architects had not yet mastered the subtlety of Gothic art). Make a point of seeing a retable on wood by the Nice painter Jacques Durandi (1450), and the fifteenth-century chancel choirstalls. Close by is a fourth- or fifth-century baptistry, octagonal inside, and one of the oldest in France. In the restored thirteenth-century cloisters, a garden and ancient well are surrounded by delicate, twin-columned marble pillars; the beams of the arcades were painted in the fourteenth and fifteenth centuries with innumerable creatures and grotesques illustrating the Apocalypse. Adjoining the cloisters is the Archaeological Museum with items from Roman Fréjus.

Two thousand years ago, Fréjus was on the sea and Julius Caesar created a trading post here, *Forum Julii*, on the Aurelian Way, in 49BC. A little later, Octavius, the future Emperor Augustus, developed the place into a major naval base and settlement for his retired soldiers. For two centuries the large harbour was kept dredged but then its importance diminished, the River Argens silted it up, and Fréjus became surrounded by malarial marshes.

While the mind's eye may be able to reconstruct the layout of *Forum Julii* from the widely scattered remnants about the modern town, the remnants themselves are mostly disappointing, with the exception of the Arena. To visit this, park the car in Place Agricola, Rue Général de Gaulle. Fragments of Roman wall support the terrace of the *place*, and one tower of the Porte des Gaules survives, as does a small paved section of Via Aurelia. The Arena, the oldest in Gaul, is 300m (980ft) west along Rue Henri Vadon. Its dilapidation through the centuries of pillage was hastened by Roman jerry-building and cheese-paring. Here, there was none of the refinement lavished on other buildings in Roman Provence. The seating has been restored — bullfights and concerts are held in the amphitheatre in summer.

Students of history will seek out the traces of the only surviving example in France of a Roman naval and civil base. It includes a small theatre, aqueduct, citadel (the *Plate-Forme*), Porte d'Italie, Porte d'Orée (the arch attached to the baths), laundry, and the Lanterne d'Auguste (a medieval harbour landmark built on the foundations of a Roman lighthouse). The railway runs over what was the 54-acre harbour.

The artistically minded should visit the Le Capitou industrial estate where a recently renovated warehouse is now an art centre displaying contemporary works. The more militarily minded can go north-east of the town to the Marine Corps Museum that displays the history of the French Marines from their inception in 1622 to the present day. In the same direction, there is a surprising Buddhist pagoda, built by the Vietnamese to honour their dead of World War I. About 3km (2 miles) from here, in the grounds of the La Tour de Mare estate, there is a chapel decorated by Jean Cocteau. Nearby is Esterel Safari Park which has free-roving animals that can be viewed from the car, as well as caged species.

St Raphaël is the beach-half of Fréjus, though to say so in the town would be to risk permanent injury. The town's sedate air attracts the epithet 'the Bournemough of the Riviera', but that is not fair, as its marina and casino testify. Like Fréjus, St Raphaël is of Roman origin, though it is better known for being at the heart of two incidents in the life of Napoleon. In 1799 Bona-

parte landed here on his return from Egypt. Fifteen years later he departed from here on his way to exile on Elba. A pyramid in Cours Commandant Guilbaud, near the port, commemorates the earlier event. Nothing remembers the later one.

Scuba-divers have helped fill the town's Museum of Archaeology in Place de la Vieille Église with amphorae and other finds; there is also a display on the techniques of underwater archaeology. The 'old church' of the square's name is twelfth-century and fortress-like, having been built to protect the townsfolk from sea-borne marauders.

Beyond St Raphaël the N98 winds between the sea and the Massif de l'Esterel. The Esterel is an ancient and eroded range whose highest peak, Mont Vinaigre, rises to only 628m (2,060ft). It comprises volcanic porphyry, whose jagged, rust-red rocks plunge dramatically into the ultramarine sea. Esterel is the most colourful part of the Riviera coast, less wooded than the Maures hills, but with areas of *maquis*, a dense, shrubby undergrowth comprising gorse, lavender, cistus and heather. Esterel is a place for the walker, few roads penetrating its high heartland and those being unmetalled and often strewn with landslide debris. Those who do venture into the area are assured of a wild country and excellent views: that from the top of the Pic de l'Ours (reached by a 1 hour walk from the car park of Col Notre-Dame) stretches from the Riviera coast to the Alps.

Mont Vinaigre is reached by a

shorter walk (about 30 minutes from the lodge at Le Malpey) and offers views almost as good. To the north-west is the N7 road, passes through the Esterel Gap once the notorious haunt of highwaymen.

The N98, called the Corniche d'Or, passes through the small resorts of Agay, Anthéor and Le Trayas, then crosses the administrative border that separates Provence from the Côte d'Azur.

ADDITIONAL INFORMATION

Places to Visit

Aubagne

La Légion Etrangère
(Foreign Legion Museum)
1km east of the town on the D44a off the D2
Open: June to September daily except Monday 10am-12noon, 3-7pm; October to May Wednesday, Saturday and Sunday 10am-12noon, 2-6pm. Open on official holidays
☎ 43 03 03 20

Parc d'Attractions OK Corral
15km east of Aubagne on the N8
Open: June to August daily 10am-7pm; April, May and September Wednesday, Saturday and Sunday 10am-6pm; March and October Sunday 10am-5pm
☎ 42 73 80 05

Bandol

Wine & Spirit Exhibition
Ile de Bendor
Open: All year daily except Wednesday 10am-12noon, 2-6pm
☎ 94 29 44 34

From June to September boats run to the island every 30 minutes from 9am to 8pm, and every hour from 9am to 7pm from October to May
☎ 94 29 41 35

Zoo-Jardin Exotique
Sanary-Bandol
3km north of Bandol on the D559

Open: April to September daily 8am-12noon, 2-6pm (7pm in July and August); October to March Monday to Friday 8am-12noon, 2-6pm Sunday 2-6pm
☎ 94 29 40 38

Chapelle Notre Dame-du-Bausset-Vieux
8km north of Bandol, off the N8
Open: all year Tuesday, Wednesday and Thursday 10am-6.30pm, Saturday and Sunday 2-6pm
☎ 94 29 41 35

Bormes-les-Mimosas

Musée Arts et Histoire,
65 Rue Carnot
Open: July to September Monday, Tuesday and Thursday 10am-12noon, 2-6pm, Wednesday, Friday and Saturday 9-11am, 2-6pm, Sunday 10am-12noon; October to June Wednesday 10am-12noon, 3-5pm, Sunday 10am-12noon
☎ 94 71 15 17

Cassis

Musée Municipal des Arts et des Traditions Populaires
Rue Xavier d'Authier
Open: April to September Wednesday, Thursday and Saturday 3.30-6.30pm; October to March Wednesday, Thursday and Saturday 3.30-5.30pm. At other times by appointment
☎ 42 01 88 66

La Ciotat

Musée Ciotaden
51 Rue de Poilus
Open: Mid-June to mid-September
Monday, Wednesday, Friday and
Saturday 4-7pm, Sunday 10am-
12noon; mid-September to mid-June
Monday, Wednesday, Friday and
Saturday 3-5pm
☎ 42 71 54 27

Mugel Park
Open: April to September daily 8am-
8pm; October to March daily 9am-6pm
☎ 42 08 07 67

Musée de Tauroentum
Route de la Madrague
Les Lecques/St Cyr-sur-Mer
Open: July to September daily except
Tuesday 3-7pm; October to June
Saturday,Sunday 2-5pm
☎ 94 26 30 46

Cogolin

Les Tapis et Tissues de Cogolin
(Carpets and Fabrics Workshop)
10 Boulevard Louis-Blanc
Open: all year Monday to Friday
8.30am-12noon, 2-6pm. Closed on
official holidays
☎ 94 54 66 17

Espace Raimu
10 Avenue Georges Clemenceau
Open: mid-March to mid-September
Monday-Saturday 10am-12noon, 2-5pm.
☎ 94 54 18 00

Ile des Embiez

Ricard Oceanographic Foundation
Open: July and August Daily10am-
12.30pm, 1-6.30pm; September,
October and April-June daily 10am-
12noon, 1-5.45pm; November to March
Thursday-Tuesday 10am-12noon,
1-5.45pm, Wednesday 1-5.45pm
☎ 94 34 02 49

Boats to the island run daily 9am-9pm
(8pm September to June)

Fréjus

Le Groupe Episcopal
(Cathedral Close)
Open: April to September daily
except Tuesday 9am-7pm; October to
March daily except Tuesday 9am-
12noon, 2-5pm. A single ticket (from
the cloister) covers the cathedral,
bapistry, cloister and museum.
☎ 94 51 26 30

Capitou Contemporary Art Centre
132 ZI du Capitou
Open: April to September daily
except Monday 2-7pm; October to
March Monday-Friday 2-6pm
☎ 93 40 76 30

L'Amphithéâtre (Roman Arena)
Open: April to September 9.30-
11.45am, 2-6.15pm; October to
March 9am-12noon, 2-4.30pm
☎ 94 51 34 31

La Pagode Bouddhique
Follow Avenue du XVe Corps (N7) for
2km north of Fréjus
Open: June to August daily 3-5pm.
At other times by appointment.
☎ 94 53 25 29 or 94 81 30 22

Safari de l'Estérel et Parc Zoo-
logique de Fréjus
5kms west of Fréjus on theN7
Open: May to September daily
9.30am-6pm (park open until 7pm);
October to April daily 10am-5pm
(park open until 6pm)
☎ 94 40 70 65

Musée des Troupes de Marine,
(Marine Corps Museum)
5km north of the town on the D4
Open: June to September daily except
Tuesday 10am-12noon, 2-5.30pm;
October to May daily except Tuesday
2-5.30pm
☎ 94 40 81 75

La Chartreuse de la Verne
In the Maures Mountains 20km south-
west of Fréjus. Follow D558 and D14,
leaving the latter to reach the site.

Open: March to September daily
except Tuesday 11am-6pm; October
and December to February daily
except Tuesday 10am-5pm
☎ 94 54 86 22

Hyères
Musée Municipale
Place Théodore-Lefébvre
Open: All year Monday, Wednesday
to Friday 10am-12noon, 3-6pm.
Closed on official holidays
☎ 94 35 90 42 or 94 65 39 67

Exposition Florale du Parc St-Bernard
Open: May to September daily 8am-8pm; October to April daily 8am-5pm
☎ 94 65 18 55

Jardin d'Acclimatation Olbius-Riquier
Avenue Ambroise-Thomas
Open: May to September daily 8am-8pm; October to April daily 8am-5pm
☎ 94.651855

Jardin d'Oiseaux Tropicaux
(Tropical Bird Garden)
Vogel Park, Route de Valcros
La Londe
6kms east of Hyères, off the N98
Open: June to September daily 9.30am-7.30pm; October to May daily 2-6pm
☎ 94 35 02 15

Lighthouse
Ile de Porquerolles
Open: Easter to September daily
11am-6pm
☎ 94 58 30 78

Fort St Agathe
Ile de Porquerolles
Open: June to September daily
11am-6pm
☎ 94 05 90 17

Le Luc

Musée Historique du Centre Var
(Museum of the History of Central Var)
24 Rue Victor Hugo
Open: July and August Wednesday to
Sunday 10am-12noon, 3.30-7pm,

Tuesday 10am-12noon; September,
October and March to June Wednesday, Saturday and Sunday 10am-12noon, 2.30-5pm.
☎ 94 60 90 70

Musée Régional du Timbre et de la Philatélie (Stamp Museum)
Place de la Convention
Open: all year except September,
Monday, Wednesday to Friday 2.30-5.30pm (6pm in July,August), Saturday and Sunday 10am-12noon, 2.30-5.30pm (6pm in July,August)
☎ 94 47 96 16

Village de Tortues de Gonfaron
(Gonfaron Tortoise Village)
On the D75 2kms east of Gonfaron
Open: March-November daily 9am-7pm
☎ 94 78 26 41

Marseille

Centre de la Vieille-Charité
(Museum of Mediterranean Archaeology and Museum of African, Polynesian and American Indian Arts)
2 rue de la Charité
Open: June to September daily except
Monday 11am-6pm; October to May
daily except Monday 10am-5pm
☎ 9156 28 38

Musée Cantini
19 rue Grignan
Open: June to September daily
except Monday 11am-6pm; October-May daily except Monday 10am-5pm
☎ 91 54 77 75

Musée des Beaux-Arts
Palais Longchamp
Open: June to September daily except
Monday 11am-6pm; October to May
daily except Monday 10am-5pm
☎ 91 62 21 17

Musée d'Histoire de Marseille
Centre Bourse
Open: all year Monday to Saturday
12noon-7pm
☎ 91 90 42 22

Musée du Vieux-Marseille
Rue de la Prison
June to September daily except
Monday 11am-6pm; October to May
daily except Monday 10am-5pm
☎ 91 55 10 19

Musée d'Histoire Naturelle
Palais Longchamp
Open: all year daily except Tuesday
10am-5pm
☎ 91 62 30 78

Château Borély
Avenue Clot-Bey
Open: June to September daily except
Monday 11am-6pm; October to May
daily except Monday 10am-5pm
☎ 91 79 29 10

Musée de la Marine et de l'Economie de Marseille
Palais de la Bourse
Open: all year daily except Tuesday
10am-12noon, 2-6pm
☎ 91 39 33 33

Musée des Arts et Traditions Populaires du Terroir Marseillais
Château-Gombert
Open: all year daily except Tuesday
2.30-6.30pm
☎ 91 68 14 38

Musée Grobet-Labadié
140 Boulevard Longchamp
Open: June to September daily except
Monday 11am-6pm; October to May
daily except Monday 10am-5pm
☎ 91 62 21 82

Musée des Docks Roman
Place Vivaux
Open: June to September daily except
Monday 11am-6pm; October to May
daily except Monday 10am-5pm
☎ 91 91 24 62

Les Grottes Loubière
500m from Château-Gombert
Open: May to October daily except
Tuesday 10am-5pm
☎ 91 68 15 02

Château d'If
Reached by boat from Marseille
Times of boats vary, but they generally run daily 9am-7pm during the
summer (May to September) and
9.30am-1pm, 2-5pm in winter.
☎ 91 55 50 09

Port Cros National Park
Port Cros National Park Information Centre
Castel Ste Claire, Hyères
Open: all year Monday-Saturday
9am-12noon, 2-5pm
☎ 94 65 32 98

There is also an Information Centre
on the island, near the landing stage,
open daily June to September
☎ 94 05 90 17

No camping, fires or mountain bikes
are allowed on the island. Fishing, from
shore or underwater is forbidden.

Guided tours of the underwater trail
open June to September, daily 10am-
5pm. Own diving gear recommended.
Unaccompaned dives must be cleared
with the park authorities in advance.

Ste Maxime
Musée des Traditions Locales
Tour Carrée des Dames
Place Aliziers
Open: April to September daily except
Tuesday 10am-12noon, 3-6.30pm (4-
7pm in July and August); October to
March daily except Tuesday 3-6pm
☎ 94 96 70 30

Musée du Phonographer et de la Musique Mécanique
Parc de St Donat
8 km north of Ste Maxime, on the D25
Open: Easter to September Wednesday to Sunday 10am-12noon, 2.30-
6.30pm
☎ 94 96 50 42

St Raphaël

Musée Archéologique
Place de la Vielle Église
Open: mid-June to mid-September
daily except Tuesday 10am-12noon,
3-6pm; mid-September to mid-June
daily except Sunday 10am-12noon,
2-5pm
☎ 94 82 15 00

St Tropez

L'Annonciade
Rue de la Nouvelle Poste
Open: June to September daily except
Tuesday 10am-12noon, 4-8pm;
October, December to May daily
except Tuesday 10am-12noon, 3-6pm.
Closed on official holidays
☎ 94 97 04 01

Musée de la Marine
Citadelle
Open: Mid-June to mid-September
daily except Tuesday 10am-6pm;
Mid-September to mid-November
daily except Tuesday 10am-5pm;
Mid-December to mid-June daily
except Tuesday 10am-5pm
☎ 94 97 06 53

Solliès-Ville

Jean Aicard's House
Place Eugéne Sylvain
Open: All Year except October, daily
except Wednesday 10am-12noon, 3-
6pm
☎ 94 33 72 02

Toulon

Musée du Vieux Toulon
69 Cours LaFayette
Open: All year daily except Sunday 2-
6pm. Closed on official holidays
☎ 94 92 29 23

Musée Naval
Place Monsenergue
Open: July and August daily 10am-
12noon, 2.30-7pm; September to
June daily except Tuesday 10am-
12noon, 1.30-6pm
☎ 94 02 02 01

Museum of Natural History
113 Boulevard Maréchal LeClerc
Open: all year daily 9.30am-12noon,
2-6pm. Closed on official holidays
☎ 94 93 15 54

Art Gallery
113 Boulevard Maréchal Leclerc
Open: all year daily 1-7pm. Closed on
official holidays
☎ 94 93 15 54

La Tour Royale (Royal Tower)
5km south of the town, along Avenue
de l'Infanterie de Marine
Open: July and August daily 10am-
12noon, 2.30-7pm; September to
June daily except Tuesday 10am-
12noon, 1.30-6pm
☎ 94 02 10 61 or 94 25 90 00

Musée Mémorial du Débarquement en Provence
(National Memorial to the Provençal
Landing)
Mont Faron. By road — go north of
the town along Avenue de Valbourdin
— or by *téléphérique* from Boulevard
Amiral de Vence.
Open: all year daily except Monday
9.30-11.30am, 2.30-4.30pm
☎ 94 93 41 01

Parc Zoologique
Mont Faron. By road — go north of
the town along Avenue de Valbourdin
— or by *téléphérique* from Boulevard
Amiral de Vence.
Open: June to September daily 10am-
7pm; October to May daily 2-5pm
☎ 94 88 07 89

Fort de Balaguier
West of the town on the N559
Open: all year daily 10am-12noon, 2-
6pm (3-7pm in July, August)
☎ 94 94 84 72

Côte d'Azur

Stephen Liégard coined the name 'Côte d'Azur' in a poem of 1887, for the French Riviera between Cannes and Menton. As with all such contrived names — particularly those attached to tourist spots — it has its detractors, but the name does seem to be appropriate. In the strong, overhead sun of the Mediterranean coast, the sea really is azure blue.

The Riviera coast is a fabled land of celebrities, parties and fun. All of that is true, the visitor being virtually assured of a hot sun shining down from a blue sky and of almost limitless potential for entertainment. But in addition to this paradise of warm sea, sand and sun there is a history of art that is virtually unrivalled: every major artist of the first half of the twentieth century, the golden age of 'modern' art, came to the Riviera, each leaving his own contribution. That, together with picturesque hill villages, grand architecture and the scenic beauties of the Mercantour National Park, make the Côte d'Azur one of the finest holiday areas in Europe.

Now the gently folded east-west ranges which give Provence its 'classical' ambience begin to be replaced by narrow Alpine valleys running north to south, valleys which run down from the 3,000m (9,800ft) peaks of the Alpes-Maritimes. These mountains protect the coast, so that places like Beaulieu (often referred to as *Petit Afrique*) and Menton, where the average winter temperature is 9.6°C (50°F), experience fog, ice or snow as sensational rarities. However, these same mountains confine the warmth, voluptuous colours and exotic plants to a coastal ribbon.

Ironically, most of the eye-catching trees, shrubs and flowers are imported: Bougainvillaea, prickly pear, loquat, mimosa, bananas, oranges, lemons and many other varieties of citrus fruits, as well as begonias, palms, aloe, agave and mesembryanthemum. Even the olive tree, which attains its most majestic proportions here, is not strictly indigenous, as it was probably planted by the Greeks in the sixth century BC.

The visitor will also notice a cultural difference between the Côte d'Azur and Provence. The former is Italianate, reflecting the long periods in which the County of Nice was part of Italy. Whole streets and squares in Menton, Nice and Villefranche are architecturally Italian. The traditional Nissard cuisine is also orientated towards Italy, and Italian-sounding surnames abound.

A short distance inland, the ground rises quickly and the landscape becomes Alpine; the only thing the area seems to have in common with the Mediterranean is a limpid light. In winter or spring it is possible to bask in warm coastal sunshine, and ski an hour or so later on deep soft snows at Peïra-Cava, Col de Turini, Gréolières-les-Neiges, La Colmiane, La Foux-d'Allos, or at the three major resorts of the Alpes-Maritimes; Valberg, Auron and Isola 2,000

Previous page: Château Grimaldi, Antibes

which have extensive *pistes*, lifts, ski schools and equipment for hire. This rapid and dramatic contrast between coast and hinterland lends exhilaration to an exploration of the region in summer and winter.

Densely populated, the Côte d'Azur is almost a conurbation between Cannes and Menton with driving and parking presenting familiar difficulties.

This tour of the region starts on the N98, the road between Esterel and the sea. Beyond the border of Côte d'Azur and Var there are little bays below the road, some rocky, some sandy. These can be reached by steep paths from roadside car parks. Facilities are limited, the clientele being those seeking a quieter day away from the Riviera's bustle. So quiet in fact that in addition to going without cafés and boutiques, many visitors also go without clothes.

La Napoule, with three beaches, a marina and an 18-hole golf course, as well as a massive medieval castle, is at the eastern end of the Esterel Range, and is the gateway to the Côte d'Azur proper. Be sure to visit the castle, of which only two huge fourteenth-century towers remain. Inland from La Napoule is the town of **Mandelieu**, reached by a road that goes around the 'Golf' roundabout with its amusing metal figures. Mandelieu has a pleasant array of shops, but is memorable to most visitors only for its exit/entrance to the A8 *autoroute*.

On the N98 coast road, **Cannes** is soon reached from La Napoule. The original fishing port here was called *Canois,* after the reeds that grew in the harbour, and was no more than a fishing village until 1834, when cholera in Nice caused the English Lord Chancellor, Lord Brougham, to stop there rather than to continue to his chosen destination. He liked the village, built a villa, spread the word back in England, and the resort was born.

The Tour Le Suquet in the Old Town is the beacon which identifies it from a distance. Not surprisingly, there is a fine view from the top for all who climb the 21m (70ft) Chevalier Tower though the view from the nearby terrace is almost as good. The tower is on the west side of Cannes where the Old Town occupies gently rising ground above the port and the Municipal Casino. Near the tower, which houses temporary photographic exhibitions during the summer months, is the Musée Le Castre, with fine collections of antiquities from all over the world, including the Mediterranean.

To the east of the Old Town are the sandy beaches and the glittering Boulevard de la Croisette — which no one should miss — with hotels, shops, cafés and marinas. At the western, Old Town, end of the Croisette (as the sea-front boulevard is known locally) is the Palais des Festivals et des Congrès, a 1982 creation, its square-slab lines earning it the affectionate name of The Bunker. The great Cannes Film Festival is held here, those visitors not invited to the showings (and that means almost everybody) being able to come close to the stars by exploring the

Tourism & The Riviera

Travel to the south of France began before the Revolution, Tobias Smollett writing about one such journey in 1763, but it was not until after the Napoleonic Wars that significant numbers of tourists began to arrive. These, mainly British, headed for Nice, Monaco and Menton. In 1834 Lord Brougham, British Lord Chancellor, was prevented from crossing from French Provence into the Kingdom of Sardinia's town of Nice because there was a cholera epidemic on the French side. He returned to Cannes, then a small fishing port, loved it, built a villa and added a new resort.

The coming of the railways revolutionised travel to the Riviera. Cannes was reached in 1863, Nice — by then a part of France — in 1864 and Monaco/Menton in 1868. In 1882 Queen Victoria used the railways for her first visit, a visit that added the Riviera to winter's social scene. By 1887 there was an English newspaper, a cricket club in Cannes and expensive hotels were springing up in all the resort towns. The English almost took over the Riviera in winter — Queen Victoria would receive visits from European aristocracy while in residence, just as she did back in England; on one occasion she even received the French President!

Soon, the British were joined by the Russians — dukes, grand dukes

and those with ever grander titles, whose wealth created renewed prosperity and whose eccentricity even outdid the British. With them came the cream of the Russian art world. Stravinsky, Pavlova and Nijinsky came to join Diaghilev in Monaco, making it (briefly) the world centre for ballet.

After the 1920s insecticides eliminated the mosquitoes and refrigeration cooled the drinks so that summer on the coast was possible. The new summer visitors were Americans. Frank Jay Gould converted Juan-les-Pins from a non-descript village into a famous playground for sun worshippers. Soon Cole Porter, Isadora Duncan, Dorothy Parker, Gertrude Stein, and Scott and Zelda Fitzgerald were enlivening the scene. Fitzgerald's *Tender is the Night* immortalises the Jazz Age on the Riviera.

The World War II brought a temporary halt, until Brigitte Bardot appeared at St Tropez in the 1950s. Today the rich and famous still come — to Cannes for the Film Festival, to Monaco for the Grand Prix — and many of the famous sites still retain their aura of wealth and sophistication. Perhaps the most famous of all is Monte Carlo's Casino. Created by François Blanc, the Casino has been a source of legend for over a century: a British Prime Minster was refused entry as he did not have his passport; one man put his life savings on the number of the last hymn at the Principality's church — and won a fortune. But the only real winner is the house: in François Blanc's day it was said that on the roulette wheel the win was sometimes *rouge* and sometimes *noir*, but it was always *Blanc*.

hand prints set in cement that form a trail around the paved Allée des Stars in front of the Palais. Cannes' old port lies beside the Palais. It is fronted by La Pantiéro which also encloses one side of the Allées de la Liberte, a popular tree-shaded open area. Here each morning is a flower market, and boule players can be found most times of day, all watched over by a statue of Lord Brougham raised by a grateful population.

To the east of the Palais there is another fine open area, the Esplanade Pompidou. Here old and young alike meet to sit, talk and watch the pram-pushers and roller-skaters.

The Croisette is the essence of the Riviera: beach and sea on one side, classy shops and hotels on the other, the promenade alive with purposeful walkers and strolling on-lookers. No 47 La Malmaison, once the annexe of the Grand Hotel, is now an art gallery with regular exhibitions of contemporary art. Look out, too, for the Carlton Hotel. This was built in 1912 by the Swiss hotelier Henri Rubl. He was captivated by Caroline

Opposite: the beach at Cannes

179

Otéro, a beautiful half-gypsy/half-French girl who made a small living as an actress and a very much larger one as a 'paramour' (to use the expression of the time). Having failed to persuade her to become a hotelier's wife, Rubl modelled the hotel's cupolas on La Beller Otéro's most prominent features! The hotel's fine restaurant is today called La Belle Otéro.

At the Croisette's extreme eastern end is the Pointe de la Croisette. At the tip is the Palm-Beach Casino with restaurant, cabaret, disco and swimming-pool under the same roof. In Rue des Belges is the Casino des Fleurs. However, you will need to find Rue d'Antibes for smart shops and discos, while Rue Meynadier has food shops. There are morning markets in Rue Louis Blanc, and the sweet tooth of many a visitor has been satisfied by a visit to the working Confiserie Blachère.

On the heights above the Pointe is the observatory of La Californie. Lifts will take you to the top of the tower for one of the finest coastal views in Europe. See the sun setting behind the Esterel and you will understand why Kipling said this was the most beautiful coast in the world.

From Cannes, boats go to the Iles de Lérins reaching Ile Ste Marguerite in 15 minutes and Ile St Honorat in half an hour. Sightseeing of the historical buildings on the two islands combines with walks through pine and eucalyptus woodlands to make this an attractive half-day excursion. The monastery of St Honorat on the island of the same name is worth visiting to see the fortifications necessary to protect churches in the tenth century; the marine museum on the larger island is interesting for its Roman items, and for the Man in the Iron Mask's cell. The mask was velvet not iron, but that has not diminished the romantic legend of the man imprisoned on the island from 1687 to 1698, and then in the Bastille until his death in 1703. The rightful king of France, brother of the king, illegitimate son of the king, even the great-grandfather of Napoleon — all these and more have been suggested as possible identities for the prisoner, but the story remains a pleasing enigma.

North of Cannes' old port is **Le Cannet**, now a suburb of the larger town, but famous as the home of the painter Pierre Bonnard. The St Saveur Chapel, in the road of the same name, has been redecorated by the artist Tobiasse, and is worth visiting for its wooden panelling, stained glass windows and the Murano enamel mosaic on the external façade. The latter illustrates the Creation of the World. In the same road (Rue St-Saveur), at No 190 is another external artwork, a fresco of the famous lovers of Raymond Peynet.

Finally, head north-eastwards from the centre of Cannes, taking the Avenue de Vallauris to reach the Chapelle Bellini, set in the Fiorentina Park. The Florentine-Baroque Chapel was built in the 1880s, then used by the artist E. Bellini as a studio. Bellini worked in Murano glass and made jewellery as well as painting. The studio is now used by his daughter, also an artist.

Continuing along the coast road, the visitor passes through **Golfe-Juan**, where Napoleon landed after his escape from Elba. Napoleon ate at a local inn while his lieutenants negotiated with the Antibes garrison. The negotiations failed and the Emperor marched towards Cannes: despite this inauspicious start Napoleon reached Paris in triumph, though the triumph was to be short-lived.

Juan-les-Pins, beyond Golfe-Juan, started life in the 1920s so has little history, but it is blessed with fine silver sands and has maintained some of the elegance of its early days. In keeping with its discovery by Americans during the Jazz Age, Juan is now the summer venue of an international Jazz Festival, one of the world's finest and best known. Many of the concerts are given outdoors among the pine trees that give the resort the addition to its name. During the festival, indeed during most of the summer, Juan, a resort for the young, is a lively noisy place, falling quiet only in the small hours and when the season ends.

For a contrast with youthful Juan, walk along the sea walls of **Antibes** and about the Old Town's narrow and bustling streets. This is a town with a very ancient history, having been the Greek port of *Antipolis*. In his early years as a general, Napoleon defended the Mediterranean coast from the town so it must have come as something of a surprise when he received a hostile reception on his return from Elba. This hostility has not prevented the town from exploiting the association, as a museum at Cap d'Antibes includes memorabilia of the emperor.

In the Old Town — an area of tightly packed, narrow streets which make driving difficult and parking almost impossible — is Château Grimaldi built in the twelfth century on Roman foundations. The castle houses an archaeological collection of locally found Roman remains, but is chiefly memorable for its Picasso Museum. Picasso spent six months working at the castle in 1946, donating the phenomenal output of work produced to the town. The collection is fantastic, truly illustrating Picasso's genius. Everyone will have a favourite work, but by common consent *La Joie de Vivre* ('The Joy of Life'), a vast work on asbestos-cement, is one of his masterpieces. The castle also houses the Nicholas de Staël collection, the tortured canvases of the Russian artist, born in St Petersburg in 19145, who committed suicide in Antibes in 1955. There is also a collection of work of contemporary artists, including some surprising and amusing sculptures, on a terrace above the sea.

Elsewhere in Antibes there are other museums. The St André Bastion, part of Vauban's defensive works, houses another archaeological museum with items from the Greek and Roman periods, while the Musée de la Tour investiages local traditions, with collections of furniture, costumes and art. There are also some oddities including the first

Juan-les-Pins (left) has a world-renowned jazz festival (right)

Antibes: the fort and marina (left) and a café near the old sea gate (right)

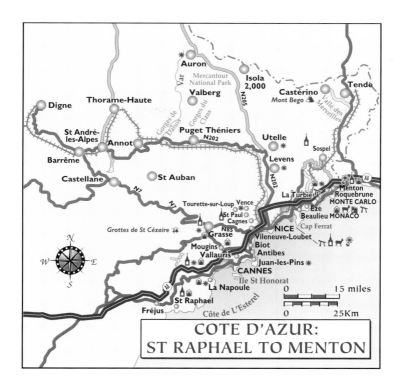

COTE D'AZUR:
ST RAPHAEL TO MENTON

pair of water skis ever used at Juan-les-Pin's, reputed birthplace of the sport. Finally, in Place Nationale, there is a museum devoted to the curious drawings of Raymond Peynet, the French creator of the *Lovers* series of sentimental pictures.

There is a short-cut from Juan-les-Pins to Antibes, but the best road is that around the Cap d'Antibes. That road soon reaches the Naval and Napoleonic Museum in the Le Grillon battery. The Napoleonic memorabilia includes his autograph, several proclamations, model soldiers from the Grand Army and a bust by Canova. The naval section includes many fine model ships. Beyond the museum a turn left reaches Jardin Thuret, a large botanical garden named after its creator, Gustave Thuret. In the mid-nineteenth century he imported plants from tropical climates, including the first eucalyptus from Australia, to study plant acclimatisation. The garden now has over 3,000 species of plants and trees, and is still a research centre. To the east of the garden is the Plateau de la Garoupe. Here stand a lighthouse with one of the most powerful beams on the Riviera coast, carrying over 60 kms (40 miles), and a church well-known for its collection of sailors' ex-voti. The most famous piece is the Notre-Dame de Bon Port, Our Lady of Safe Homecoming, a gilded wooden statue of the patron saint of sailors. Back on the coast road Pointe Bacon, a fine viewpoint, is passed before Antibes is reached.

A complete contrast to the art and history of the Antibes sites is Marineland to the north of the town. This, Europe's first marine zoo, has dolphins, orca (killer whale), penguins, seals and sea lions. The site includes a small marine museum, one item of which is a model of Columbus' *Santa Maria* constructed from 1½ million matchsticks. Close to the site are several amusement parks — as listed in the section on entertainments.

West of Antibes, at **Vallauris**, is the National Picasso Museum, built around his *War and Peace*, housed in the Romanesque chapel that is all that remains of a priory that originally stood on the site now occupied by the fine Renaissance castle. Picasso's mural, covering 125 square metres, was painted on plywood between 1952 and 1959. With its echoes of *Guernica*, its images re-state the horrors of war.

The castle, one of the few examples of Renaissance architecture in Provence, also houses a gallery of modern and contemporary art, the collections including two rooms of ceramics by Picasso and many works by the Florentine artist Alberto Magnelli. The ceramics are especially appropriate as Vallauris was once a major pottery centre. Picasso's work revitalised the industry which is now flourishing again, with several workshops operating in the town. The Pottery Museum in Rue Sicard, in a still-functioning workshop, explores the trade's history and techniques.

North-west of Vallauris, and north of the A8, is **Mougins**, where a photographic museum consists of portraits of Picasso by the world's leading portraitists. There are frequent exhibitions of the work of leading photographers. There is also a motor museum — which, appropriately, can also be entered from a service area on the A8 itself (either eastbound or westbound) — with a collection of over 200 cars.

North of Antibes, the coast road is dominated by the Marina Baie des Anges at Villeneuve-Loubet-Plage. The four triangular blocks, each a gentle S bend, were designed by André Minangoy and are one of the most distinctive structures on the Riviera. The blocks have lovers and loathers: such is their dominance it is difficult to be neutral about them.

Before the blocks are reached, a left turn heads inland to **Biot**, a town surrounded by acres of carnations and roses destined for the Riviera flower markets. The ubiquitous and handsome terracotta vases that adorn many gardens once formed the main industry of Biot. Today the visitor can watch glass-making in the village, the factory being famous for Biot bubble glass.

Outside the village is the Fernand Léger Museum; its huge, garish mosaic façade looking a little out of place in this setting. Works by this robust northern artist (1881-1955), interpreter-in-chief of the factory age, fill the museum built by his widow. The town's other museum, which is of local life, includes a restored kitchen and a collection of locally made ceramics.

Back on the coast road, the next major town is **Cagnes-sur-Mer**, though its centre is inland. Cagnes is a sprawling mass which has engulfed the chic racecourse, l'Hippodrome de la Côte d'Azur. In Cagnes-Ville is the Renoir Museum, Avenue des Collettes, the house and garden where Renoir (1841-1919) spent the last 12 years of his life. The overall impression is that everything has been left much as it was. There are the tools of his trade in the studio, a painting, some drawings and sculptings, correspondence, photographs and momentos. Saddest of the items is the great man's wheelchair. Outside stands the *Venus Victrix*, the large bronze that is Renoir's most famous sculpture. It overlooks a beautiful garden, well laid out with olive, lemon and orange trees. The museum is a moving tribute to an artist who expressed his love for the freshness of life.

At Haut-de-Cagnes, which is the prettiest part of the town, the handsome Château-Musée houses an exhibition devoted to the olive tree, that veritable symbol of Provence. Also in the *château* is a museum of modern Mediterranean art, including works by some of the many painters who have been profoundly influenced by the light of this coast which is often called the 'Mecca of Modern Art'. During the summer the castle houses an exhibition of contemporary art.

Close to Cagnes is **Villeneuve-Loubet**, with an excellent culinary art museum housed in the home of the Escoffiers, the most famous family in the history of 'cooking-as-art'. There are all the things you would imagine in the world's most famous kitchen, together with exhibitions of sugar and chocolate work. There is also a military museum devoted to the great wars of the twentieth century.

Inland from here are the twin towns of St Paul and Vence. **St Paul** has always been a little too far from the sea to share in much of the general prosperity, but it was discovered by artists in the 1920s and has been an artistic, rather than jet-set, centre ever since, that rebirth accounting for the huge number of art galleries in the village. For further proof, the visitor need look no further than the Maeght Foundation, a modern art museum set in a suitably designed building constructed in 1964. Some of the art on view is pleasantly displayed outdoors. Artists represented in the museum include Braque, Miro, Chagall and Kandinsky, and the work includes not only paintings, but sculptures and stained glass as well. In the village there are fine views from the old ramparts, and the church is worth visiting for a fine painting of St

Art & the Riviera

The brilliance of the light, the clearness of the air and the climate, which allows the artist to take advantage of the first two qualities, have attracted artists to southern France for centuries. It is, however, for twentieth century art that the area is most famed. Whereas Arles is associated with Van Gogh and Aix-en-Provence with Cézanne, the Riviera is not associated with one artist (though Picasso's admirers might dispute that) but with the development of art during the century.

The century began with Impressionism. Monet, the father of the movement, painted in Antibes, but Renoir, who transformed the idea from landscape to any real-life scene, is celebrated at Cagnes-sur-Mer where his studio is a poignant memorial to him. Pointillism was created by Seurat, but Signac, working in St Tropez, extended the techniques When Fauvism was born as a reaction to Impressionism, Matisse and Dufy, both living in Nice, were the leading lights. Today they lie in the same cemetery at Cimiez.

Cubism evolved from Cézanne's work, its masters, Braque and Picasso, both working on the Riviera. Picasso spent the last years of his life here, creating works, some of the best of which can be seen in Antibes. He too is buried in the area. Léger, another Cubist, one who sought to marry art and architecture, has a museum at Biot.

Following Picasso and his disciples, the Modernists arrived. Cocteau worked on the marriage hall at Menton, de Staël painted at Antibes and Chagall created his *Biblical Message* in Nice. Today new movements are at work, the visitor having an almost limitless choice of small galleries or temporary exhibitions, evidence that the qualities that tempted the great artist of yesterday to the area are still exercising the same pull.

Catherine of Alexandria attributed to Tintoretto. The museum of local history in the Place de la Castre explores facets of St Paul's history in eight diaramas.

Vence also has much to occupy the visitor. Though originally a Ligurian town, Vence was important in Roman times, and equally impor-

tant in the early years of Christian France. In the Wars of Religion, the town was besieged by Huguenots but did not fall, a fact commemorated each Easter with a festival. The visitor should definitely not miss the Old Town, which still has part of the original defensive wall and the old castle. The castle — built by the Bar-

The Renoir Museum at Cagnes-sur-Mer

The fountain in Place de Peyra, Vence

The famous Fragonard perfumery at Grasse

ons of Villeneuve whose conflicts with the Bishops of Vence enrich the town's medieval history — houses the Fondation Emile Hugues, named after a former town mayor. There is a permanent art collection, but the Foundation chiefly exists to promote contemporary art by way of an annual series of exhibitions. The castle stands in Place du Frêne, named after the huge ash-tree that dominates it. The tree is said to have been planted to commemorate the visit of François I and Pope Paul III to town. Close by is the old cathedral, on the site of a Roman temple to Mars and an early, Merovingian, church. The cathedral is in fine Romanesque style.

Elsewhere, the Old Town is a delight, helped by the exclusion of cars — neatly tucked away in a car park beneath the Place du Grand Jardin. Place de Peyra, near the Porte de Peyra, has a fine fountain and many other little squares and alleys are equally delightful. It is no surprise to discover that Vence has attracted many artists and writers over the years. Dufy, André Gide and D. H. Lawrence all spent time here, the latter dying in Vence, of TB, in 1930.

Henri Matisse also came to Vence, in 1941, but became very ill. He was nursed back to health by the local Dominican sisters and in gratitude he designed and decorated, between 1947 and 1951, the Chapelle du Rosaire, north-west of the Old Town. 'Despite its imperfections, I think it is my masterpiece' he said of the chapel, adding that it was the culmination of 'a lifetime devoted to the search for truth'.

The chapel is a simple, square, white building, the only clues to Matisse's work being the figures above the door, the white and blue tiled roof and the delicate wrought-iron cross that surmounts it. Inside, the simplicity is maintained, the murals being in black lines on white walls, the only colour coming from the sun through the stained glass windows. Of the murals, that depicting the Stations of the Cross is the most moving. Matisse is now considered to be one of the finest artists of the twentieth century, so the chapel should be high on the list of all visitors.

To the west of Vence — take the D2210 towards Grasse — lies the Château Notre-Dame des Fleurs, a nineteenth-century castle built on the site of a Benedictine monastery. The name reflected the fact that the owner's wealth derived from the perfume industry, and the castle now houses a Museum of Perfume and Liqueur, with items from the old methods of perfume making. From the *château* the view of the coast, from Cap Ferrat to Esteral, is superb.

Westward again is **Tourette-sur-Loup**, at the start of the Loup Valley. Tourettes has a long history, being a Ligurean settlement before the Romans named it — for an observation post (*turres altae*) they maintained to keep an eye an the hill tribes. After the Revolution it gradually emptied of people, but was re-discovered by artists after World War II. Today it is a flourishing art and craft village, almost every house given over to artwork, from hand-painted T-shirts to sculpture.

The Loup valley itself is definitely worth time spent away from the coast, its collection of picturesque villages being a delight. Of these, **Gourdon** is the most worthwhile, for the views from the square beside the church (of the Esterel in the distance and the Loup Gorge below) and the old castle. The castle, built in the thirteenth century on the ruins of a Saracen fortress and newly restored, includes a history and art museum. The history section includes a good collection of weapons, armour and sixteenth-century furniture, and a self-portrait by Rembrandt. The art collection, of naïve work from the period 1925-70, is one of the best in southern France.

Westwards from Tourettes, a right turn at Pont-du-Loup reaches the Loup Gorge, an impressive, tight gorge, its road narrow enough to cause the driver problems on busy days. Not far along the gorge is the 40m (130ft) Courmes waterfall — drive past, through the tunnel and park tidily on the roadside beyond. In summer there are often children here, playing in the pool below the fall, which cascades away from the overhanging rock. Further on, at an incongruous bar/café/kiosk, you can see (for a small fee) the Saut du Loup, a huge pothole scraped out by glacial and river action.

South-westward from Pont-du-Loup is **Grasse**, a town of great charm, spreading out over shallow hills as though relaxing in the sun or, perhaps, to make it easier to guard the perfume meadows that have made it famous.

In the very early Middle Ages the town was a republic, despite its size, with links to the Italian city-state of Pisa, but the bigger state of Provence soon put an end to this independence. The city is also famous as the home of the great Provençal artist, Fragonard, and for having been virtually on Napoleon's route north after his landing at Antibes. The Emperor, fearful of the reception he might receive, went round the town, only staying locally for an hour to rest his men on what is now known as Napoleon's Plateau.

Since the start of perfume-making as an industry rather than a small time job for a few locals, Grasse has been a leading perfume town. Fields of perfume-bearing flowers lie all around, and the visitor can watch the process of manufacture in several perfumeries in the town.

The best place to start exploring is Place du Cours, a terraced promenade set above the underground car park that is most convenient for visitors. From the Place there are fine views over the Old Town, to the east. The fountain dates from the time of the Revolution, while a statue commemorates the artist Jean-Honoré Fragonard who was born in the town in 1732. The artist's name lives on in one of the two biggest perfumeries, that originally set up in his villa.

At the eastern (town) end of Place du Cours steps lead down: bear slightly left to reach the International Perfume Museum with its collection of items on the history of the

Perfume Making

To create a perfume it is first necessary to extract an essence. Chiefly, and always in the early days, these are derived from flowers. Initially the extraction was by placing the flowers individually on blocks of animal fat, the fat absorbing the essence over a period of weeks and then giving it up when the fat was combined with the fixing agents. Today, steam extraction is used to reduce the time and expense of the process. It takes 300kg of lavender to produce 1kg of pure lavender essence, rising to 600kg for rose and to 1,000kg for some of the more exotic essences.

The next stage is for the factory's 'nose' to blend the essences to form a unique aroma. The factories in Grasse work for the big perfume houses of Paris and elsewhere. The houses specify the type of perfume they wish to have created — a lively one for the young, an exciting fragrance for evening wear and so on — and the 'nose' creates the aroma for them. The 'noses' cannot smoke or eat spicy food and must drink alcohol in moderation or their skill — for which they are very well paid — will be destroyed. A 'nose' must be able to distinguish at least 500 individual essences, and the very best can easily distinguish as many as 4,500.

Once the fragrance has been agreed, it is distilled into alcohol. *Eau de Parfum* contains 20 per cent essence in alcohol. For an *Eau de Toilette*, the ingredients are 10 per cent essence, 10 per cent distilled water and 80 per cent alcohol.

The best, and most expensive, fragrances are actually a mixture of aromas. The essences are very volatile and as they disappear the fragrance changes subtly. In general, the very best perfumes will have three distinct aromas, the first lasting around an hour, the second about 6 hours and the last as long as 24 hours. In the trade these are known as the head, the heart and the body.

At the *parfumeries* of Grasse visitors are shown the process and also allowed to buy fragrances which have been manufactured for the big perfume houses. The essence itself is not copyright, but the name is. So visitors can buy top name fragrances, but with names no one recognises.

Fragrances kept in glass lose their aroma in time as the essence reacts with the glass. The big perfume houses always use glass because more attractive containers can be made with it. For the very best long-term storage it is essential to use aluminium containers which are non-reacting. The *parfumeries* of Grasse invariably sell in aluminium.

industry. The collection of perfume bottles and flasks is especially interesting. Almost next door is the Ma-rine Museum. This seems an odd choice for a landlocked town, but is actually a commemoration of the life of Admiral de Grasse who was born at nearby Le Bar-sup-Loup. The admiral achieved fame during the American War of Independence and has a vessel of the Frency Navy named for him. The museum includes a fine collection of model ships of the admiral's time.

To the right from the bottom of Place du Cours steps is the Fragonard Perfumery Museum. The museum has six rooms dedicated to the history of the industry set above one of the company's perfume factories. Guided tours of the factory explain the perfume-making process and conclude with the obligatory visit to the site shop. For copyright reasons Fragonard (or the similar factories of Molinard and Galimard) cannot sell the product of the big perfume houses by name — but offer the same perfume under a different name, and at a lower price.

The Fragonard Museum stands at the corner of Rue Mirabeau. Turn down this to reach the Provençal Art and History Museum, with its collection of furniture, ceramics (including Moustiers ware), coins and

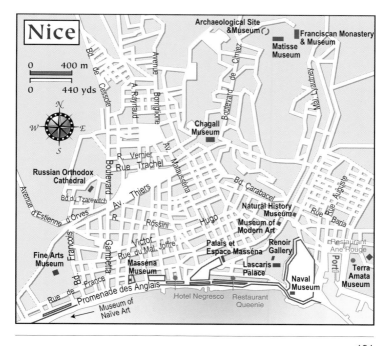

items of local archaeology. Bear left at the bottom of Rue Mirabeau to reach the Tour de Guet, once the Bishop's Palace and now the town hall, the name deriving from the huge, twelfth-century square tower. Close by is the cathedral, remodelled in the seventeenth century. Inside are three paintings by Rubens. To the north of the cathedral is the Old Town, an area of tight streets and alleys.

Other perfumeries offering tours to visitors are Molinard in Boulevard Victor Hugo (the road to Draguignan, close to Place du Cours), Molinard on the Route de Cannes (the old road to Cannes, not the new Voie Express which links Grasse to the A8) and another Fragonard factory, also on the Route de Cannes.

To the west of Grasse — follow the D562 towards Draguignan, turning right along the D11 towards Cabris, then left along the D13 — are the excellent St Cézaire show caves. The cave's stalagmites and stalactites are stained red by iron oxide and are quite beautiful. There are more caves to the north, near St Vallier de Thiey. The Audides caves are small, but were inhabited for many centuries during the Old and New Stone Ages: visitors can tour the cave, and see excavated remains and reconstructions of ancient life. Quite different is the model railway exhibition which lies 4km (2½ miles) south of Grasse near the N88. The models, steam and electric, are of railways from all over the world and run through delightfully created landscapes.

Also south of Grasse, in **Mouans-Sartoux**, the old castle has been turned into a museum of local traditions and modern decorative arts. East of Mouans is the Valbonne plateau, a beautiful area of holm oak and pine woods. **Valbonne**, the main village, is a straggling place, its museum exploring the plateau's arts and traditions.

And so to the 'Queen of the Riviera', as **Nice** styles itself. There is some justification for this claim, even though its enormous beach is exposed and a bit pebbly. Like Cannes and Menton, Nice used to be something of an English preserve. Until World War II, that purely English seaside phenomenon, the pier, had an example, complete with a casino at the end of it, suspended over the Mediterranean. Now, the Promenade des Anglais — named, in gratitude, by the city fathers — is the reminder of that *Belle Epoque*.

Nice was originally a Ligurian settlement, but was named (from *Nikaîa* — victory or, more likely, *Nîkaia* — water sprite) by the Greeks. The Romans had a settlement at Cimiez, at the northern end of the city, but that was destroyed by seaborne marauders after the legions had retreated over the Alps. Later, Nice was incorporated into Savoy, as a result of which it was, technically, Italian when Napoleon's campaigns against the Austrians in northern Italy and Garibaldi's invasion of Sicily and southern Italy brought the new kingdom into existence. However, an agreement struck before Napoleon's campaign led eventually to a plebiscite in 1860 when the people of Nice and its hinterland voted to join France. The vote was overwhelming: 25,743 to 260, but the transfer disgusted Garibaldi, a native of (Italian) Nice.

Today Nice is ebullient and noisy; it does not depend solely on tourism, having a richly varied life of its own. The visitor can take part in the exhibitions, fêtes, galas, concerts. Of all the annual festivities held in Nice, the Carnival, started in 1878, is the most hilarious. For a fortnight before Lent, King Carnival appears, followed by costumed processions, floats, grotesque masks, confetti showers and fireworks. King Carnival (called *Caramantran* or *Mardi Gras*) is burned in effigy on Shrove Tuesday. On Ash Wednesday there is the frenetic Battle of Flowers.

For many, a walk along the Promenade des Anglais is entertainment enough. The walk passes the Masséna Museum, housed in a nineteenth-century Ialianate mansion. The mansion was built by the great-grandson of Marshal Masséna, another son of Nice, said by Wellington to have been second only to Napoleon in military genius. The museum has a bust of the Marshal by Canova. There is also a great collection of local artwork and of religious items including a silver and enamel reliquary and an early stone Virgin. Further on is the Edwardian 'museum', Hôtel Negresco, whose public rooms contain works of art and whose lavatories are more lavishly ornamented than many other hotel lounges.

And all the while on the seaward side, the sun-seekers are out in force. Sections of the beach have been taken over by entrepreneurs offering food and drink, sunbeds and sunshades, and the promise of unhindered relaxation. Less relaxed are the parasailing sites where the intrepid can enjoy aerial views of Nice for a few minutes, suspended from a parachute towed by a speedboat. The take-off is sudden, the landing invariably wet, but the ride sensational.

Promenade des Anglais leads into Quai des États-Unis. Here the Gallery-Museum Raoul Dufy houses a collection of paintings, drawings, engravings and ceramics by this important artist. Nearby, the Gallery-Museum Mossa has collections of work by Alexis Mossa and his son Gustav-Adolf, the former an artist in the classical style, specialising in landscapes and carnival scenes, the latter in similar style at first, but developing a symbolic art with surrealist overtones.

Red stucco arcaded buildings line one side of the harbour, Port Lympia ('port of limpid waters') from which the boats for Corsica leave. The place where Garibaldi was born (in 1807) is marked by a plaque on the house at the corner of Quai Papacino. On the far side of the port the Terra Amata Museum has a model of a fossil beach uncovered 25m (85ft) above sea-level on nearby Mont Boron. The Palaeolithic finds uncovered at the same time are some of the earliest human remains discovered so far in Europe.

Young Visitors & the Riviera

Visitors seeking art and architecture, sun and sea, sports by the hundred — from a relaxing game of golf to the more hazardous pursuits of rock climbing and diving — are well served by the Riviera. Younger visitors may enjoy these too, but may also be interested in the following places which are more specifically aimed at them. Opening time are for the summer.

The Marineland Complex on the N7 between Antibes and Villeneuve-Loubet-Plage includes:

Marineland, with orca, dolphins, penguins and seals.

La Petite Ferme, a farm with goats, rabbits, horses, cows, chickens etc. There are pony tours on the farm, a nursery, mini-golf and a face-painting studio.

La Jungle des Papillons, a tropical house with over 150 species of exotic butterflies, together with spiders (some huge and hairy) and turtles.

Adventure Golf, the ultimate in crazy golf. Three courses of varying length and absurdity.

Aqua-Splash, an array of pools and water slides.

All the facilities are open from 10am daily. ☎ 93 33 49 49

Old Nice lies between the sea, Boulevard Jean Jaurès and the 'Castle' — as the hill just west of the port is known, even though the castle was blown up in 1706. There is a lift to the top from where the view of the city is exceptional. Close to the lift's bottom station is the Naval Museum housed in the sixteenth-century Bellanda Tower. Berlioz once lived here, though the collections are exclusively marine-based, with model ships, naval weaponry and interest-ing displays on modern racing and pleasure craft.

There is also plenty of sightseeing to do in this area, including the town hall, Baroque church of St François-de-Paul, opera house, cathedral of Ste Réparate, and the Chapellé de la Miséricorde of 1736; the latter has an outstanding retable painted by Jean Miralhet early in the fifteenth century. In addition to the shops and bistros which give an Italian vivacity to the Old Town, there are also a

Close to the Marineland complex is **Antibes Land**, a large amusement park with roller coaster, bungy jumping, water and many other rides. Open daily from 10am. ☎ 93 33 44 79

At Juan-les-Pins the **Visiobulle** operates from the Courbet quay. This large glass-bottomed boat explores the coast of Cap d'Antibes offering a glimpse of the underwater world normally seen only by divers. The hull shape means that you can, if you wish, sit under the water. Trips daily from 9.30am to 6pm. ☎ 93 67 02 11.

At Villeneuve-Loubet there is **Kindia Park** with tramolines, paint balls, go-karts, a bouncy castle and some more adventurous rope swings for older children. Open daily from 9am. ☎ 93 65 61 92

In Nice, the **Parc des Miniatures** in Boulevard Imperatrice Eugenie, at the western end of the town, has scale models of famous landmarks of France, some animated. Open daily from 9am. ☎ 93 44 67 74.

Nearby is a **Model Railway Exhibition**, open daily from 9am. ☎ 93 18 03 33.

There is also a **Model Railway Exhibition** on the N85 4kms south of Grasse, open daily from 9.30am. ☎ 93 77 97 97.

Just outside the Riviera area is **Luna Park**, near the junction of the N98 and D559, near Port Grimaud. This has typical fairground attractions. It opens evenings only, but that does have the advantage of big-wheel rides at night. Open daily from 8.30pm. ☎ 94 56 35 64.

Finally, there are zoos at Fréjus, Cap Ferrat and Monaco.

 number of Genoese buildings, the best of which is the Lascaris Palace in Rue Droite. Built in 1650 by the Count of Ventimiglia, the palace is beautifully decorated in period style: the tapestries and *trompe-l'oeil* ceilings are masterpieces. On the ground floor an eighteenth-century pharmacy from Besançon has been reconstructed.

South of the Palace is Cours Salega, famous for its flower markets (go in the mornings, Tuesday to Sunday). Here there is also the remarkable Malacology Museum, an annexe of the Natural History Museum, with a collection of shells from all over the world. Some the shells are very rare, the collection being one of the best in Europe. There are also Mediterranean fish in aquaria.

North of the Lascaris Palace is Place Garibaldi dominated by a statue of the Great Man. Close by is the Barla Museum of Natural History, with excellent displays on fungi and geology. However, the view from the *place* is dominated by the Museum of Modern and Contemporary Art, a vast array of square blocks and linking passageways, the work of Yves Bayard and Henri Vidal. Entry is by way of a huge piazza, the collections including a fine group of works by Yves Klein and by artists of the Pop Art movement.

Between the new museum and the sea is Place and Espace Masséna, the hub of modern Nice, an airy park with wonderful fountains and shady walkways, but enclosed by elegant shops and cafés.

At the western end of Promenade des Anglais, just north of the seafront in the area known as Les Baumettes, is the Musée des Beaux Arts with some good early works, a few by J. H. Fragonard, and a good collection of canvases by the Impressionists with whom the south of France is so readily associated — Signac, Dufy, Bonnard, Vuillard etc. Further west, towards the Nice-Côte d'Azur airport, is the Gallery of Naïve Art, its collection a bequest by Anatole Jakovsky. The collection comprises some works of Jakovsky himself, and some 600 works by lesser known artists from all over the world. North of the Jakovsky collection is the Parc des Miniatures. Here 1:25 scale models, some of them animated, explore the history and architecture of the Côte d'Azur. On the same site there is a museum of miniature trains, with models covering the history of European railways.

Further west, directly opposite the airport, is the Phoenix Parc Floral, a phenomenal garden park. The external areas of garden, with lake, rockeries and numerous delightful features, are excellent, but the truly remarkable feature is the Astronomical Garden, the largest plant house in the world. This conical greenhouse is divided into seven sections each of which has its climate automatically controlled so as to simulate one of the world's tropical areas. As a consequence the visitor can wander through areas of tree ferns or among exotic orchids. The house also has collections of appropriate birds and insects, the butterfly's alone making a visit worthwhile.

North of the Musée des Beaux Arts, the visitor will be surprised by the onion domes of the Russian Orthodox Cathedral. This magnificent red brick and grey marble building was built in the early years of this century and is brilliantly set off by the six domes, each covered with coloured ceramic tiles. North again, in the St Barthélemy area, is the Prieure du Vieux Logis, a priory created from a sixteenth-century oil mill and housing some excellent medieval furniture and artwork.

The northern district of Nice is called Cimiez, the name of the earliest Roman settlement. A visit to this area is a must, and should start with the Marc Chagall Museum or the National Biblical Message as it is more correctly known. Chagall was born to a poor Jewish family in Russia in 1887, moving to Paris and then to southern France when he followed his vocation as a painter. He died in St Paul in 1985. His art is usually categorised as primitive, but such groupings are not always helpful. It is better, to see Chagall as having maintained a child-like wonder for scenes and events, portraying them in an equally child-like way, both in form and in colour, the latter usually being very vivid. During the years from 1954 to 1967, Chagall painted the seventeen huge canvases that form the basis of the museum, these depicting scenes from the Books of Genesis and Exodus, and the Song of Songs. It is interesting to note that Chagall has included many Christian symbols in these essentially Jewish stories. The whole — canvases, setting and the somewhat severe building — represent a remarkable artistic statement of faith.

Northwards from the Chagall Museum, follow Boulevard de Cimiez, bearing right at the huge Hôpital de Cimiez. This was originally the Regina Hotel, so-called because it was built to accommodate Queen Victoria, was converted to a hospital and is now private apartments. Interestingly, Henri Matisse once live in one of the apartments, creating a mural on one wall which was removed when he left!

Bearing right at the old Regina leads to the Matisse Museum, a combination of a vividly red villa — though all is not quite as it seems, some of the apparent decoration being *trompe l'oeil* — and a new building beneath it.

Henri Matisse was born in 1869 and became the leading member of *Les Fauves*, the savages, who transformed art in the early years of this century. Matisse's real talent was in decorative art and the blend of this form with the 'new' art which disregarded natural forms. Picasso, the other great artist of the twentieth century, extended the work of Cézanne, developing it into Cubism and beyond. Matisse pursued a different route, his art developing into even more decorative forms, as exemplified by the famous blue paper cutout pictures. The visitor is greeted by one of Matisse's largest works, a paper cut-out maquette decorating the museum's entrance area. Beyond it are around seventy paintings and cut-outs, several hundred drawings and engravings and some artwork from Matisse's personal collection.

Beside the Matisse Museum's villa are the excavated remains of Roman *Cemenelum* (Cimiez), the better finds from the site being housed in the archaeological museum close to the Matisse building.

Also nearby is the Franciscan monastery of Notre-Dame de l'Assumption, founded in the ninth century by Benedictine monks, and taken over and restored by the Franciscans some 400 years ago. Within the abbey church are three superb works by Louis Bréa all dated to around 1475 — a Crucifixion, Deposition and Pietà. The monastery's museum explores the history of the Franciscans in Nice. Beside the monastery is a very quiet garden from which a cemetery is reached. Here lie Raoul Dufy, close to the

The beach at Nice

The Nice carnival

Peillan, a perched hill village close to Nice

entrance, and Henri Matisse, whose tomb is more difficult to locate, being at the lower level.

From Nice, several journeys northwards enter the fine country of Haute-Provence. Perched villages, characteristic of Provence, are even more spectacular above the Côte d'Azur. At a distance they look grey, aloof, even distrustful; they were built for protection against incessant invasion. Their thick walls, narrow, steep, twisting cobbled and arcaded streets, their tiny squares and fountains, clustering towards an ancient church, are a delight to explore. Many houses are now workshops for artist and artisans where paintings, ceramics, woven cloths, jewellery or olivewood carvings can be bought. One of the best perched villages lies very close to Nice. To reach **Peillon**, take the D2204 northwards towards L'Escarène, turning right, then right again towards the village. The road to the village offers superb views towards it (and rather pleasant smells from the Geriko coffee plant), but parking is very limited at its end — there is no car park and minimum roadside parking. The residents hope that an increase in tourism will be catered for by a shuttle bus up the hill. The village itself is so picturesque that words can barely do it justice — wander at will and be enchanted.

There is too much country to the north of Nice to cover each village, so a small number of excellent itineraries are suggested here.

Our first trip will be by the justly famous autorail scenic journey by the Chemins de Fer de la Provence from Gare de Provence in Nice, Place de la Libération. It takes in the Valleys of the Var, Vaïre, Verdon and Asse, and goes to the stations of Puget-Théniers, Entrevaux, Annot, Thorame-Haute, St André-les-Alpes and Digne. It covers 151km (94 miles) and takes 3hr 20min in each direction; the return can be made on the same day.

The second itinerary visits Levens and the Vésubie Valley. Take the N202 northwards, through pretty country, to Plan-du-Var, turning right there to drive through the beautiful Gorges de la Vesubie to reach St-Jean-la-Rivière. A right turn here leads to Duranus and the Saut de Français, a vertical drop where a group of soldiers were thrown to their deaths after being captured by local bandits. Ahead now is **Levens**, a beautiful village with an array of terraced gardens. The entomology museum here has live as well as mounted specimens, its aim being to educate children about insects. Equally interesting is the Maison du Portal which houses a permanent collection of the work of the sculptor Jean-Pierre Augier. The house is built beside a gateway that is all that remains of the medieval Grimaldi castle. Legend has it that the village folk, tired of their tyrant overlord threw him out one day and destroyed the castle. Just one stone, the *boutau*, remains and a procession to it is made every year on St Antonin's day.

A left turn at St-Jean-la-Rivière leads to the sanctuary of **Madonna**

d'Utelle, built in 1806 on the site of an earlier church. The view of the Maritime Alps from the church is one of the best on the Côte d'Azur.

Northwards the beautiful Vésubie Valley can be followed to Roquebillière. Just beyond the village the road forks: go right to follow the Vallon de la Gordolasque, a very picturesque valley, into the Mercantour National Park, passing the Cascade du Ray, a delightful pair of waterfalls. A left turn at the fork leads to **St Martin-Vésubie**, a starting point for climbers and walkers visiting the Maritime Alps. The pedestrian-only Rue du Docteur Cagnoli, leading to the church, is well worth exploring: set among its Gothic houses is the Chapel of the White Penitents with a bulb-shaped bell-tower.

St Martin is a cool alternative to the coast, but is almost at the limit of day trip exploration. Those with more time can go west to **St Saveur-sur-Tinée**, another picturesque village. North now are the ski resort of Isola 2000 (named after its height: 2000m — 6,560ft) and Auron from where a funivia takes the visitor to the 2,474m (8,115ft) peak of Las Donnas, a memorable viewpoint. From St Saveur, a fine return to the coast is to go westwards to Beuil and south from there, through the beautiful Gorges du Cians.

The final itinerary from Nice follows the D2204 past the turn to Peillon to reach Centes and L'Escarène. Northwards now, along the D2566, is **Lucéram**, notable for the altarpieces and treasury in its church. The altarpieces are by Louis Bréa and pupils of his school. Lucéram had been a major centre from which the poor, itinerant artists, commissioned by Penitent Brotherhoods and overshadowed by Italian Renaissance artists, carried their paints and brushes over mountain tracks from church to church. The treasury includes a beautiful fifteenth-century silver statnette and several excellent reliquaries. North again lies **Pierre Plate** another fine viewpoint.

East from Nice, there is a choice of four roads: the A8 *autoroute*, and the three famous Corniche roads. The Grande Corniche (D2564), built by Napoleon, is the 31km (19 mile) high route between Nice and Menton. Use this road for the impressive views and for visiting the majestic Roman Trophy of the Alps at La Turbie. It also offers fine views from Hotel Vistaëro and at Roquebrune. The Moyenne Corniche (N7) also provides viewing lay-bys; it is the direct route to Eze. The Corniche Inférieure (N98) winds along the coast to go through Villefranche, Beaulieu, Eze-Bord-de-Mer, Cap d'Ail, Monaco, Cap Martin and Menton. Side roads connect all three Corniches.

The old section of **La Turbie** is worth visiting for its picturesque houses, but it is the vast remains of the Alpine Trophy that draws the eye and the visitor. The trophy commemorates the defeat of the Alpine tribes of Gaul by the Emperor Augustus and was erected in about 10BC. When complete — as shown in the site museum — the trophy stood 50m (165ft) tall, a conical top held aloft by a circle of columns standing on a square plinth. What remains is a section 35m (115ft) high including part of the columned circle. The trophy can be climbed, the ascent giving a real feel for its engineering brilliance and majesty. One of the few sections of the original to remain complete (though this has been restored) is the inscription listing the titles of Augustus noting his subjugation of, and listing, the forty-five Alpine tribes. Some historians claim that this inscription is the first paragraph of the history of France.

From La Turbie it is a short distance, going beneath the A8, to **Laghet**, where the sanctuary church of Notre-Dame de Laghet, an old pilgrimage church, still attracts votive offerings from Italy as well as France. A small museum in Place du Sanctuaire has a collection of the best of those offerings.

Eze, on the Moyenne Carniche, is a hill village perched on a rocky spire that offers excellent views towards the coast. Near the car park, just off the main road, are the perfumeries of both Fragonard and Galimard. From them, or the car park, the visitor must walk steeply up to the village. The village is no less steep, any exploration involving climbing. The effort is worthwhile, the old houses — many now art or craft shops — being very picturesque. Finally, at the summit of the rock spire, is the Jardin Exotique, a stunning array of cacti and succulents. The spire is topped by the ruins of a fourteenth-century castle dismantled on the orders of Louis XIV. From the ruins, on

clear mornings, Corsica can be seen. Finally, visitors with time to spare can follow the Sentier Frédéric Nietzsche which descends from the village, through pines and olives, to Eze-Bord-de-Mer. The old mule track is named for Nietzsche because he is said to have thought through the final section of *Thus Spoke Zarathustra* while walking it. Bear in mind that such thoughts are not guaranteed, and that the only way back to the village is along the same track — uphill all the way. If you do decide to try, allow two hours for the return journey.

On the Lower Corniche, the visitor soon reaches **Villefranche-sur-Mer** whose excellent roadstead was recognised as soon as men started sailing the Mediterrenean, though the name reflects its fourteenth-century refounding as a 'free town'. A later event still causes amusement in the town: in 1538 a peace conference in Nice, with the Pope as mediator, was seeking to reconcile King François I of France and Emperor Charles V of the Holy Roman Empire. The emperor was staying in his ship moored here at Villefranche and was visited by his sister (François' wife) and other local lords of high office. As the party made their way up the gangplank from the quay, the walkway collapsed, dumping the whole party into the sea. No one was hurt, but dignities were waterlogged and egos bruised.

The Old Town — north of the sixteenth-century citadel — is well worth exploring: take time to visit the Chapelle de St Pierre which was

The Jardin Exotique, Eze

Eze from the Jardin Exotique

Villefranche-sur-Mer from Cap Ferrat

Villa Ephrussi at St Jean-Cap-Ferrat

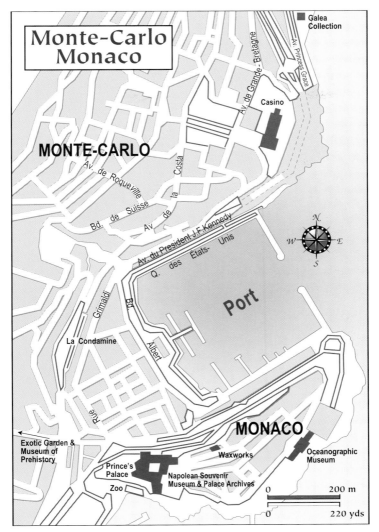

Galea
Collection

Av. de Grande - Bretagne

Av. Princess Grace

Casino

Monte-Carlo
Monaco

MONTE-CARLO

Av. de Roqueville

Av. de la Costa

Bd. de Suisse

Av. de

Av. du Président J.F. Kennedy

Q. des États- Unis

N
W · E
S

Grimaldi Bd.

Port

La Condamine

Albert

Rue

MONACO

Exotic Garden &
Museum of
Prehistory

Waxworks

Oceanographic
Museum

Prince's
Palace

Zoo

Napolean Souvenir
Museum & Palace Archives

0   200 m

0   220 yds

decorated in 1957 by Jean Cocteau.
Cocteau sought to retell the life of the
fisherman disciple, relating it to the
lives of the town's fisherfolk. Close

to the citadel are two museums
housing three collections. In the first
is a collection of work of the local
sculptor Volti. The second building

houses the Goetz-Boumeester collection of work by those artists, a husband and wife active in the first half of this century, together with souvenir works by artists such as Picasso and Mirò; and the Roux collection of ceramic figures illustrating life in medieval Villefranche.

Turn off at Villefranche to drive around **St Jean-Cap-Ferrat**. Soon you will reach the Villa Ephrussi de Rothschild, the finest villa on the Riviera, in a setting that defies description. The villa, a symbol of the *Belle Epoque*, was built in the early 1900s to house the antique furniture and art collection of Baroness Ephrussi de Rothschild. In glorious Italian style, its pink walls and white windows, columns and balconies making it look even more fantastical, the villa is a marvellous setting for the collections. The furniture, some of which belonged to Marie Antoinette, is set off by rich carpets and tapestries.

Outside, the 7 hectares (17 acres) of gardens are formally laid out with a large pond complete with fountain, and a double channel waterfall. With dragonflies darting over the ponds, the views of the house and the romantic setting beside the turquoise sea, it is difficult to imagine a more perfect site.

Beyond the villa, bear right to reach the coast, passing a zoo which, despite its relatively small size, boasts over 300 species of animals. On again is the lighthouse at the very tip of Cap Ferrat. From its top the view includes the Esteral Hills, Bordighera Point in Italy and the Maritime Alps. Below it, a swimming pool has been hollowed from the rocks. One final interesting spot is Point St Hospice, the finger of land that pokes out eastwards from the main peninsula. The tip of this finger is rounded by a very pleasant walk, with fine views to Eze and Monaco.

Back on the main Lower Corniche, **Beaulieu** is the next town reached. Beaulieu is a fashionable, though much less hectic, resort than those to the west. Take a stroll through the gardens beside Boulevard Alsace-Lorraine or relax in the sheltered Baie des Fourmis. On the bay's eastern tip is Villa Kerylos, a faithfully reproduced ancient Greek house built by Theodore Reinach, a Hellenistic scholar, during the 1900s. The frescoes and murals are copies, or variations, of originals and the materials — marble, alabaster, wood, leather etc — are, as far as possible, authentic. Some of the artwork is original and though most of the furniture is from the time of building, Greek ideas on design have been followed. The villa's name means 'sea swallow' in Greek.

Eastward on the Lower Corniche the visitor now passes below Eze to reach Monaco.

The **Principality of Monaco**, covering an area of under 200 hectares and with a population of only 25,000, is a sovereign state enclave surrounded by the *département* of Alpes-Maritimes. However, there are no frontier formalities even though the police uniform is different and distinctive.

The state consists of the capital

town, Monaco, from whose Royal Palace it is administered, the resort of Monte-Carlo, and the commercial centre of La Condamine — not that much open space is available to separate one from another. So precious is land that, in 30 years, the principality has transformed itself into tier upon tier of skyscrapers, and reclaimed strips of land from the sea to create imported sand beaches.

Monaco's name derives from a temple to *Monoïkos* (Hercules) erected on the rock by Phoenicians. In 1308, the Grimaldis acquired Monaco from the Genoese and have ruled ever since. Their fidelity to France won them other territories along the coast. A turbulent history has seen the principality occupied by Spaniards and French or protected by the Kingdom of Sardinia. It was incorporated into the County of Nice (roughly, the Alpes-Maritimes) in 1793, when the Revolutionaries renamed it Fort Hercule.

Independence returned at the end of the Napoleonic Wars. The rest of the Alpes-Maritimes were ceded to Italy, to return to France by the plebiscite of 1860. Later, Monaco was on the verge of bankruptcy and Menton and Roquebrune were sold off to France by Charles III Grimaldi. He struck on the lucrative idea of catering for Europe's gamblers and the casino was built on the rock named after him (Monte-Carlo). This first venture failed, but in 1862 the prince brought in François Blanc, the director of a German Casino. Blanc's casino was so successful that Monaco's wealth was drawn from it until the end of World War II.

Today, Monaco is a highly efficient centre of business and commerce. It comes as a surprise to many to learn that gambling yields less than 5 per cent of the state's revenue. The legend of glamour is still cultivated through the image of lavish, year-round programmes of entertainment, of galas, operas, Grand Prix (in May), and opulent yachts in the harbour. Such events are financed out of VAT as there is no personal taxation for Monégasques.

Still wearing its Second Empire pride, the sumptuous casino (and its gardens) sees tourists gamble in a modest way. To gamble you need to show your passport.

The casino is in Monte Carlo where parking is a bit easier (though never easy) than in Monaco. To the front of the building the terraced gardens, linked by broad steps, are an outdoor art gallery of contemporary sculpture. At the rear, the gardens are equally good and offer tremendous views over the harbour — crowded with expensive yachts — and Monaco. North of the casino, beyond the famous Loews hairpin is the National Museum, housed in a delightful villa. The museum houses the Galea collection of dolls and automatons, one of the best of its kind in Europe and a must for enthusiasts. There are also annual exhibitions in keeping with the collection — teddy bears for example.

From the casino, wide pavements and steps take the visitor over the tunnel used by the Grand Prix to the quayside. To the right as you walk

The Casino, Monte Carlo

Fontvieille harbour, Monaco

Palais du Prince, Monaco

Guards at the Palais du Prince

Menton

along is La Condamine, packed with shops catering for everyone from the casual visitor to the seriously rich. Ahead, a pleasant, if steep, path leads up the side of Monaco's Rock to the Place du Palais. The palace itself can be visited and is worthwhile for its elegant decoration and for the Napoleon Museum. The Princes of Monaco are distant relatives of the old emperor and have amassed an interesting collection of memorabilia. The museum also houses an archive collection on the history of the principality, with stamps, coins and medals as well as documents.

On the other side of the Place du Palais there is a fine viewpoint of the harbour and Monte Carlo. Nearby is the Museum of the History of Princes of Monaco where scenes from the principality's past are enacted in dioramas with full-size wax models. Within the main 'town' of Monaco on the rock is the cathedral, built in the late nineteenth century in neo-Romanesque style, and the Oceanography Museum, one of the foremost of its kind in the world. The museum was founded by Prince Albert I, an enthusiast, in 1910. In its basement is an aquarium of over 4,000 Mediterranean fish (some fifty species in all), probably the best in Europe and certainly the most complete collection of Mediterranean species. The ground floor has a collection illustrating the development of underwater exploration and the skeletons of sea creatures, including a narwhal. The first floor illustrates Prince Albert's own voyages, marine phenomena (waves, tides etc) and has a collection of shells. There is also a model of a giant squid. From the museum's terrace, or from the nearby St Martin's Garden (on the west side, towards the palace) the view along the coast extends to the Esterel Hills and the Italian Riviera.

On the western side of the palace, but not accessible from the Place du Palais, is Monaco Zoo, with collections of mammals, birds and reptiles. From it there is a good view of the harbour of Fontvieille. In this suburb are three museums and a fine park. The Naval Museum has about 150 model ships from all ages, including the battleship *Potemkin*. Prince Rainier's car collection, the second museum, includes a De Dion Bouton from 1903 and other very early European and American cars. The last of the three, the Stamp and Coin Museum, has collections covering Monaco's history. Fontvieille Park includes Princess Grace's Rose Garden with almost 4,000 varieties and a statue of the princess by Kees Verkade in 1983.

Beyond Monaco Zoo is the splendid Jardin Exotique with a collection of over 5,000 cacti and succulents from all the world's desert and sub-desert areas. Within the garden is the interesting Observatory Cave with good formations. The cave was inhabited some 200,000 years ago, the excavated finds, and others from the Riviera region, being display in the Prehistoric Anthropology Museum, also in the garden.

North of Monaco the corniche roads converge at **Roquebrunne**, a skillfully restored hill-village. Medieval houses and steep, arched-over alleys lead up to the tenth-century castle, one of the oldest in France. It is a fine sight when floodlit at night and deserves to be visited for the furnished apartments and primitive kitchen on the third floor. Above is a terrace from which Cap Martin can be seen, 300m (985ft) below.

On the afternoon of August 5, the visitor to Roquebrune can witness scenes from the Passion enacted between the village and the chapel of La Pausa. It is a 500-year-old tradition, fulfilling a vow made in 1467 by villagers who survived the plague.

A second traditional procession takes place on the evening of Good Friday, when some villagers dress as Roman soldiers, with others dressed as disciples and carrying a statue of Christ. The windows of Roquebrune are decorated with flowers and upturned empty snail shells holding lighted wicks. The procession is known in Provençal as Proucessioun dei Limassa (the Procession of the Snails); its religious name is Procession of the Entombment of Christ. Some say the ritual dates back to 1316, the snails being a Christian symbol of resurrection.

The newly opened Espace Ananke holds exhibitions of contemporary art, while those with an interest in twentieth-century architecture can visit Le Corbusier's Bungalow, designed as a model for minimal, modular living. Le Corbusier did actually live in the bungalow, and is buried in the village cemetery.

Finally, on the Menton road, 200m (220yd) beyond Roquebrune, is an olive tree thought to be 1,000 years old.

Although many modern buildings have been built outside the Old Town, **Menton** remains a picture-postcard, Italianate town. Tall, honey-coloured houses rise gracefully from near the sea to the church of St Michel. Outside the church, a prestigious chamber-music festival is held under floodlights during the first half of August.

Menton's setting is idyllic. The mountains stand well back, respectfully, yet give the town its enviable winter climate which allows lemon crops to ripen. A local legend states that when God expelled Adam and Eve from the Garden of Eden, Eve took a lemon with her. When the pair found the site on which Menton now stands, Eve decided it was an earthly paradise and planted the seeds from her lemon. All local lemon trees are said to stem from those seeds. For centuries Menton's prosperity was based on lemons: it is said that when Roquebrune and Menton were sold by Monaco to France it was due not only to the Monaco Prince's poverty but also to agitation from local lemon growers who knew that France was a better market than Italy for their crop. It is also said that when the British ambassador heard the price France was paying he shook his head and said it was an awful lot of money for a few lemons. Today, the lemon's part in the town's history is celebrated at the annual lemon festival is held in February.

Queen Victoria's early visits to the Riviera were to Menton — the grateful town raised a statue to her — and she was followed by other members of the European aristocracy, and then by the great names of literature. Despite the stardom, compared with other resorts along the coast, Menton retains a more leisurely atmosphere.

Start your exploration on the Promenade du Soleil, the sea front road which leads to Quai Napoleon III. In a bastion, built into the harbour wall, is the Cocteau Museum, an important collection of the artist's work. From the Quai the view of the town falling down the hill towards the sea is breathtaking. Quai Napoleon ends at a lighthouse, the other retaining arm finishing at Volti's statue of St Michael. Follow the sea front past that quay (Jetée Impératrice-Eugénie) to reach, to the left, a surprising set of steps which lead to Parvis St-Michel, a distinctly Italian square overlooked by the town church. The old town lies to the north (turn right from the square). Especially good are Rue Longue — which intersects the steps at about half-way — and Rue Vieux-Château. The latter leads to the old cemetery, interesting for its well-known English names, Menton having first been used as a health resort for the treatment of tuberculosis on the initiative of the English specialist, Dr Henry Bennet, in the 1860s.

From the church, descend the steps on its right side and follow Rue St Michel through the shopping heart of the town. To the right after about 500m (600yd) a short walk leads to the town hall and Cocteau's marriage hall. All marriage ceremonies in France must have a civil component to be legal and all those in Menton are performed here. The hall was entirely decorated by Cocteau — heavy black doors, Spanish seats and a series of allegorical paintings. Behind the stage a local boy and girl exchange loving glances. He has a fish for an eye, an old legend claiming that the truth of anyone's life is in their eyes — and he is a fisherman. The hall's main reception (used only for ceremonies) has mirrors set on a curve to give an illusion of infinity. There is also a portrait of Marianne, the mythical French heroine whose image adorns the coinage and whose portrait must hang in all marriage halls.

Continuing along the main street the visitor reaches Jardin Biovès, beautiful gardens surrounded by palm and lemon trees. The statues are by Volti. To the north of Biovès is the Palais Carnoles, an Italian style eighteenth-century mansion that was formerly the summer palace of the Monacan Princes. It now houses the town's Fine Arts Museum with contemporary work on the ground floor and work of the sixteenth to eighteenth centuries on the first floor.

Elsewhere in the town the Palais de l'Europe, in Avenue Boyer, houses a continuous cycle of exhibitions of contemporary art, while the Museum of Local Prehistory, north of the town hall, has collections from local sites, including the skull of

Menton Man who lived here several hundred thousand years ago.

Finally, follow the coast road northwards out of Menton to reach the Jardin Botanique Exotique, a garden of Mediterrenean and tropical species grouped around the Villa Val Rameh.

North of Menton the visitor can explore the Upper Roya Valley and the eastern section of the Mercantour National Park. The quickest approach is to cross into Italy, heading north from the A8's 'Ventimiglia' turn off. This road, the S20, soon crosses the border again, reaching **Breil-sur-Roya**, a pleasant village, its old section still dotted with the remnants of gateways and defensive walls. Breil can also be reached by a route that stays in France, heading north on the D2566 from Menton to **Sospel** another excellent village, its 'eleventh-century' bridge a copy of the original which was destroyed in World War II. Close to the village, on Col St-Jean along the road to Nice, Fort Suchet (also called Le Barbonnet) houses the Museum of the Alpine Army, a tribute to men who survived cold and natural dangers as well as the more obvious threats of warfare.

North of Breil the Roya valley tightens at the Saorge Gorge, the village of **Saorge** hanging above the river in an almost surreal way. The village's steep, sometimes stepped and arched, streets meander about the hillside in enchanting fashion: from the southern end the fine Romanesque church of Madonna del Poggio can be reached by a short walk, worthwhile for the fine Italian-style campanile and the excellent fifteenth-century artwork.

North again the valley is increasingly tight and picturesque. At **St Dalmas-de-Tende**, a right turn should be made, going through La Brigue to visit the extraordinary chapel of Notre-Dame des Fontaines. In the fourteenth century seven springs (*fontaines*) watered the valley at this point but an earthquake sealed them off. The valley dwellers prayed to the Virgin for salvation and the springs miraculously began to flow again. In thanks they built a chapel which soon became an important pilgrimage centre. As befitted its status, the chapel walls were frescoed, the chancel by the local Gothic master Jean Baleison, the nave by a genius of the primitive Renaissance school, Giovanni Canavesio.

Baleison's works have not been well-served by time, but Canavesio's panels, telling the story of Jesus' life, are almost perfect, displaying an exuberance and enthusiasm that is stunning. There is no compromise in the scenes, that of the hanging Judas being quite gruesome, the Crucifixion being unflinchingly painful and the Last Judgement, on the end wall, remorseless. It seems almost that Canavesio wanted to instruct the viewer — do not tread from the Christian path or this will be your fate. The effect of the panels on the superstitious medieval valley folk can well be imagined: after the service, they were confronted with the

Last Judgement as they left, just to press the message home.

Back in the main valley, as you drive towards Tende note that the Roya Valley has been French only since 1947. At the time of the transfer of Nice and its hinterland to France in 1860, the logical border — following the ridge of the Maritime Alps — was ignored because the Italian king wished to preserve his favourite hunting ground!

Tende is the capital of the upper valley, an Italianate village of interesting narrow streets. The fifteenth-century town church is the best example of the Italian Gothic style in the Maritime Alps. Tende is a centre for exploration of the Mercantour National Park. The park was created in 1979, adjoining Italy's Argentera National Park, to protect the vegetation — which includes both alpine and Mediterranean species — and wildlife. Half of France's wild flower species grow here, over forty of which bloom nowhere else in the country. The wildlife includes several rare species of butterfly, as well as marmot, ibex and chamois. Birds includes golden eagles and Tengmalm's owl. The chief interest, however, lies in the rock engravings of the Vallée des Merveilles (the Valley of Marvels) surrounding Mont Bégo. On rocks surrounding the peak some 100,000 engravings have been found, each produced from dots made by striking a sharp point (an antler for instance) against the rock. The engravings are of limited patterns — oxen pulling a plough, fields and houses represented as squares,

daggers — but there are a small number of strange shapes. Of these a Christ-like head and a curious figure with feet turned in — the so-called Chief of the Tribe — are the most interesting.

Specialists favour a Bronze Age date for the engravings, suggesting a religious significance. Mont Bégo is set where cold dry alpine air meets warm, moist Mediterranean air, and so sees many thunderstorms. It is also a ferritic mountain and so is frequently struck by lightning. It is thought that the early dwellers of the Mercantour noticed this and believed that gods lived in the peak, talking to the gods of the sky by means of lightning. They therefore completed their engravings (offerings to the gods) while looking at the peak: all the engravings are on rocks worn smooth by glaciers and face away from Mont Bégo.

To see the engravings, particularly the most interesting ones, it is essential to have a guide: the Marveilles is huge and there are countless rocks. It is also necessary to be prepared for a long hard day — the walk up to the valley takes several hours, although jeep transport can be arranged in Tende and St Dalmas. There are a few engravings in the Fontanable Valley which can be reached by car, but they are not easy to find. An alternative is the soon-to-be-opened Musée des Merveilles in Tende. For information on guides, jeeps and the museum's opening times, ask at Tende's Information Centre.

North of Tende the main road

uses a tunnel to cross into Italy, though the adventurous can use a multi-hairpin road to reach the Col de Tende, a fine viewpoint. From it, a short walk visits Fort Central, one of a line of forts built in about 1882 at a time of tension between France and Italy. The fort cannot be visited, except by the intrepid visitor, but is still a worthwhile destination. Those that do venture inside will be astonished at the size of the gun emplacements. The field of view meant that any army advancing up the Roya Valley would have found taking the col very difficult.

From the Col with its view of high mountains, it is a drive of little more than an hour to Menton or Nice, where the visitor can watch the sun go down into the azure sea.

ADDITIONAL INFORMATION

PLACES TO VISIT

Antibes

Musée d'Archéologie
Bastion St André
Open: all year except November, Monday to Friday 9am-12noon, 2-6pm
☎ 92 90 5435

Musée Picasso
Château Grimaldi
Open: June to September daily except Monday 10am-6pm; October, December to May daily except Monday 10am-12noon, 2-6pm. Closed on official holidays
☎ 92 90 54 20

Musée Naval et Napoléonien
Batterie du Grillon
Avenue John Kennedy
Cap d'Antibes
Open: all year except October, Monday to Friday 9.30am-12noon, 2.15-6pm, Saturday 9.30am-12noon
☎ 93 61 45 32

Musée Peynet
Place Nationale
Open: all year except November, daily except Monday 10am-12noon, 2-6pm
☎ 92 90 54 30

Musée de la Tour
Cours Masséna
Open: April to September Wednesday, Thursday and Saturday 4-7pm; October to March Wednesday, Thursday and Saturday 3-5pm
☎ 93 34 50 91

Jardin Thuret
Cap d'Antibes
Open: all year, Monday to Friday 8am-5.30pm. Closed on official holidays

Marineland
On the N7 4km north of Antibes
Open: all year daily 10am-6pm (7pm from June to September)
☎ 93 33 49 49

Beaulieu-sur-Mer

Villa Kerylos
(Fondation Théodore Reinach)
Avenue Gustave Eiffel
Open: Mid-March to June and October daily 10.30-11.30am, 2-6pm; July and August daily 10am-7pm; September daily 10am-6pm; December to mid-March Tuesday to Friday 2-5.30pm
☎ 93 01 01 44

Biot

Musée National Fernand Léger
Signposted off the D4 south-east of
the village
Open: daily except Tuesday, April to
September 10am-12noon, 2-6pm; November to March 10am-12noon, 2-5pm
☎ 93 65 63 49/93 65 63 61

Musée d'Histoire Locale
6 Place de la Chapelle
Open: April to September daily except
Monday 2.30-6pm; November to
March Thursday, Saturday and
Sunday 2.30-6pm
☎ 93 65 54 54

La Verrerie de Biot
Chemin des Combes
Open: all year Monday to Saturday
9am-6pm (8am-8pm in July and
August); Sunday 2.30-6.30pm
☎ 93 65 03 00

Cagnes-sur-Mer

Château Musée
Haut-de-Cagnes
Place Grimaldi
Open: July to September daily 10am-
12noon, 2.30-7pm, rest of year (except
mid-October to mid-November when
closed) daily except Tuesday 10am-
12noon, 2-5pm
☎ 93 20 85 57

Musée Renoir
La Maison de Renoir
'Les Collettes'
Avenue des Collettes
Open: daily except Tuesday, June to
mid-October 10am-12noon, 2-6pm;
mid-November to May 2-5pm (gardens
10am-5pm). Closed official holidays
☎ 93 20 61 07

Cannes

Musée de la Castre
Château da la Castre
Le Suquet
Open: daily except Tuesday, April to

June 10am-12noon, 2-6pm; July to
September 10am-12noon, 3-7pm;
October to March 10am-12noon, 2-
5pm
☎ 93 38 55 26

La Californie
Super Cannes
Open: all year daily 2-6pm
☎ 93 39 15 55

Confiserie Blachère
6 Rue Pasteur
Open: May to mid-October daily
9.30am-7pm; mid-October to April
daily 9.30am-12noon, 2-6pm
☎ 93 94 57 59

La Malmaison
47 Boulevard de la Croisette
Open: all year, opening times depend
upon exhibition but are generally
daily except Tuesday 10am-5pm
☎ 93 99 04 04

Chapelle St Sauveur-Tobiasse
74 Rue St Saveur
Le Cannet
Open: all year Monday-Friday 8.30-
11.30am, 1.30-4.30pm, Saturday and
Sunday 9.30am-12noon, 3-6pm
☎ 93 46 68 79

Chapelle Bellini
Parc Fiorentina
67 bis Avenue de Vallauris
Open: all year Monday to Friday 2-5pm
☎ 93 39 15 55/93 38 61 80

Monastère de St Honorat
Ile de St Honorat
Open: June to September 10.15am-
12noon,2-5.30pm; October to May
9.30am-5.30pm. Closed Good Friday
☎ 93 48 68 68

Musée de la Mer
Ile Ste Marguerite (in the enclosure of
the Royal Fortress)
Open: daily, July to September
10.30am-12noon; April to June
10.30am-12noon, 2-5.30pm; October
to March 10.30am-12noon, 2-4.30pm
☎ 93 43 18 17

Eze

Jardin Exotique
Open: June to October daily 8am-7pm (8pm in July and August); November to May daily 9am-12noon, 2-6pm (7pm April to June)
☎ 93 41 03 03

Parfumerie Fragonard
Open: May to September daily 9.30am-7pm; October to April daily 9.30am-12noon, 2-6pm
☎ 93 36 44 65

Parfumerie Galimard
Open: May to mid-October daily 9.30am-7pm; mid-October to April daily 9.30am-12noon, 2-6pm
☎ 93 41 10 70

Grasse

Musée d'Art et d'Histoire de Provence
2 rue Mirabeau
Open: June to September daily10am-1pm, 2-7pm; October, December to May Wednesday to Sunday 10am-12noon, 2-5pm; Closed official holidays
☎ 93 36 01 61

Musée de la Marine
2 boulevard Jeu de Ballon
Open: all year except first two weeks of November; Monday to Saturday 10am-12noon, 2-6pm. Closed holidays
☎ 93 09 10 71

Musée Fragonard
20 Boulevard Fragonard
Open: June to September daily 10am-7pm; October, December to May Wednesday to Sunday 10am-12noon, 2-5pm. Closed official holidays
☎ 93 36 44 65

Musée International de la Parfumerie
8 place du Cours
Open: June to September daily 10am-7pm; October, December to May Wednesday to Sunday 10am-12noon, 2-5pm. Closed on official holidays
☎ 93 36 80 20

Parfumerie Fragonard
Route de Cannes
Open: April to October daily 9am-6.30pm; November to March daily 9am-12.30pm, 2-6pm
☎ 93 36 44 65

Parfumerie Galimard
Route de Cannes
Open: April to October daily 9am-6.30pm; November to March Monday to Saturday 9am-6pm; Sunday 9am-12noon, 2-6pm
☎ 93 09 20 00

Parfumerie Molinard
60 Boulevard Victor Hugo
Open: May to September daily except Sunday 9am-6pm; October to April daily 9am-12.30pm, 2-6pm
☎ 93 36 01 62

Les Grottes de St Cézaire
On the D613 north of St Cézaire-sur-Siagne, to the west of Grasse
Open: July and August daily 10.30am-6.30pm; June and September daily 10.30am-12noon, 2.30-6pm; October, April and May daily 2.30-5pm; November to March Sundays 2.30-5pm
☎ 93 60 22 35/93 60 22 87

Model Railway Exhibition
4km south of Grasse on the N85
Open: all year daily 9.30am-6.30pm
☎ 93 77 97 97

Château de Mouans
Mouans-Sartoux
Open: June to September daily except Tuesday 11am-7pm; October to May Thursday to Sunday 11am-6pm
☎ 93 75 71 50

Musée des Arts et Traditions Populaires
Place de l'Église
Valbonne
7 km south-east of Grasse on the D5
Open: July to September daily except Monday 3-7pm; October to June Saturdays and Sundays 2-6pm
☎ 93 12 96 54

Audides Caves/Prehistoric Park
(Open Air Museum)
Domaine des Audides
Route de Cabris (D4)
St Vallier de Thiey, 8km north-west of
Grasse on the D4 off the N85
Open: July and August daily 10am-
6pm; May, June and September
Wednesday to Sunday 10am-6pm;
October to April Wednesday to
Saturday 10am-3.30pm, Sunday 2-
4.30pm
☎ 93 42 64 15

Laghet

Madonne-de-Laghet
Sanctuaire de Laghet
La Trinité (Reached from La Turbie or
the A8 exit at La Turbie)
Open: all year daily 3-5pm
☎ 93 41 09 60

Levens

Musée Educatif d'Entomologie
(Insect Museum)
Quartier Les Traverses
20 km north of Nice on the D19, off
the D2565
Open: all year by appointment only.
Guided tours (in French) by request.
☎ 93 79 70 12

Maison du Portal
Place du Portal
Open: July and August daily 2.30-
5.30pm; September to June Saturday,
Sunday and holidays 2.30-5.30pm
☎ 93 79 85 84

Mandelieu-La-Napoule

Fondation Henry Clews
Château de la Napoule
Boulevard Henry Clews
Open: February to October daily
except Tuesday 3-5pm (6pm in July
and August)
☎ 93 49 95 05

Menton

Musée Cocteau
Bastion du Vieux Port
2 Quai Napoléon III
Open: daily except Tuesday, mid-
June to mid-September 10am-
12noon, 3-7pm; mid-September to
mid-June10am-12noon, 2-6pm.
Closed on official holidays
☎ 93 57 72 30

Cocteau's 'Salles des Mariages'
Mairie (town hall), Place Ardoïno
Rue de la République
Open: all year Monday to Friday
8.30am-12.30pm, 1.30-5pm. Closed
on official holidays.
☎ 93 57 87 87

Musée du Palais Carnolès
3 avenue de la Madone
Open: mid-June to mid-September
daily except Tuesday 10am-12noon,
3-7pm; mid-September to mid-June
daily except Tuesday 10am-12noon,
2-6pm. Closed on official holidays.
☎ 93 35 49 71

Musée de Prehistoire Régionale
Avenue Lorédan Larchey
Open: mid-June to mid-September
daily except Tuesday 10am-12noon,
3-7pm; mid-September to mid-June
daily except Tuesday 10am-12noon,
2-6pm. Closed on official holidays.
☎ 93 35 84 64

Palais de l'Europe
Avenue Boyer
Open: mid-June to mid-September
Tuesday to Saturday 10am-12noon,
3-7pm; mid-September to mid-June
Tuesday to Saturday 10am-12noon,
2-6pm. Closed on official holidays.
☎ 93 57 57 00

Le Jardin Botanique Exotique
Avenue St Jacques
Garavan, near Menton
Open: all year daily except Tuesday
10am-12noon, 3-6pm or dusk.
☎ 93 35 86 72

Monaco

Jardin Exotique, Musée d'Anthropologie Préhistorique & Grotte de l'Observatoire
55 bis Boulevard du Jardin Exotique
Monaco
Open: May to September 9am-7pm;
October to April 9am-6pm
☎ 93 15 80 06

Zoo
Boulevard Charles III
Monaco
Open: daily, June to September 9am-12noon, 2-7pm (8pm in July and August); October to May 10am-12noon, 2-5pm (6pm from March to May)
☎ 93 25 18 31

Musée Océanographique
Avenue St Martin
Monaco
Open: daily July and August 9am-8pm; April-June, September 9am-7pm; October and March 9.30am-7pm; November to February 10am-6pm. Closes 12.30pm on Grand Prix day
☎ 93 15 36 00

Historical des Princes de Monaco/ Musée de Cires (Waxworks)
27 rue Basse
Monaco
Open: daily April to October 9.30am-7pm; November-March 10.30am-5pm
☎ 93 30 39 05

Le Palais Princier
Place du Palais, Monaco
Open: June to September daily 9.30am-6.30pm; October daily 10am-5pm. Guided tours (in English) available.
☎ 93 25 1831

Musée du Souvenir Napoléonien et Archives du Palais Princier
Place du Palais, Monaco
Open: June-September daily 9.30am-6.30pm; October daily 10am-5pm; December-May daily except Monday 10.30am-12.30pm, 2-5pm
☎ 93 25 18 31

Musée National de Monaco (Collection de Galea)
17 Boulevard Princesse Grace
Monte-Carlo
Open: Easter to September daily 10am-6.30pm; October to Easter daily 10am-12.15pm, 2.30-6.30pm
☎ 93 30 91 26

Musée Naval
Centre Commercial de Fontvieille
Open: all year except November daily except Friday 10am-6pm
☎ 92 05 28 48

Fontvielle Park
Avenue des Papalins
Fontveille
Open: April to September daily 9am-7pm (8pm in July and August); October to March daily 9am-5pm
☎ 92 16 61 16 for information

Prince Rainier's Vintage Car Collection
Les Terraces de Fontvieille
Open: all year except November daily 10am-6pm
☎ 92 05 28 56

Stamp & Coin Museum
Les Terrasses de Fontvieille
Open: all year daily 10.30am-5.30pm
☎ 92 16 61 16 for information

Mougins

Musée de l'Automobiliste
(Autoroute A8 Nice-Cannes, Aire de Bréguierès)
Les Hautes Bréguirès
772 Chemin de Font-de-Currault
Open: daily, April to September 10am-7pm; October to March 10am-6pm
☎ 93 69 27 80

Musée de la Photographie
Porte Sarrazine
Mougins-Village
Open: July and August daily 2-11pm; other months Wednesday to Sunday, 1-7pm; closed November
☎ 93 75 8567

Nice

Musée des Beaux Arts
33 avenue des Baumettes
Open: May to September daily except
Monday 10am -12noon, 3-6pm;
October to April daily except Monday
10am -12noon, 2-5pm. Closed on
official holidays.
☎ 93 44 50 72

Musée d'Art Naïf Anatole Jakovsky
Château Ste Hélène
Avenue Val Marie
Open: May to September daily except
Tuesday 10am-12noon, 2-6pm;
October to April daily except Tuesday
10am-12noon, 2-5pm. Closed on
official holidays.
☎ 93 71 78 33

Musée National Message Biblique Marc Chagall
Avenue du Docteur Ménard
Open: July to September daily except
Tuesday 10am-7pm; October to June
daily except Tuesday 10am-12noon,
2-5.30pm
☎ 93 81 75 75

Musée Barla (Musée d'Histoire Naturelle)
60 bis Boulevard Risso
Open: all year except mid-August to
mid-September daily except Tuesday
9am-12noon, 2-6pm. Closed on
official holidays.
☎ 93 55 15 24

Musée International de Malacologie
3 Cours Saleya
Open: all year except November,
Tuesday to Saturday 10.30am-1pm,
2-6pm. Closed on official holidays.
☎ 93 85 18 44

Musée Naval
Tour Bellanda
Parc du Château
Open: June to September daily
Wednesday to Sunday 10am-12noon,
2-7pm; October to May Wednesday

to Sunday 10am-12noon, 2-5pm.
Closed mid-November to mid-
December and on official holidays.
☎ 93 80 4761

Musée Matisse
164 Avenue des Arènes de Cimiez
Open: April to September daily except
Tuesday 11am-7pm; October to
March daily except Tuesday 10am-5pm
☎ 93 81 08 08

Musée d'Archéologie
160 Avenue des Arènes de Cimiez
Open: May to September Tuesday to
Saturday 10am-12noon, 2-6pm;
Sunday 2-6pm; October, December
to April Tuesday to Saturday 10am-
12noon, 2-5pm; Sunday 2-5pm.
Closed November. The archaeological site is also open on Mondays,
times as weekdays above.
☎ 93 81 59 57

Musée Masséna
Palais Masséna
65 Rue de France and 35 Promenade
des Anglais
Open: May to September daily except
Monday 10am-12noon, 3-6pm;
October to April daily except Monday
10am-12noon, 2-5pm. Closed on
official holidays.
☎ 93 88 11 34/93 88 06 22

Palais Lascaris
15 Rue Droite
Open: all year except November
daily except Monday 9.30am-12noon,
2.30-6pm
☎ 93 62 05 54

Musée de Paleontotologie Humaine de Terra Amata
25 Boulevard Carnot
Open: all year except first two weeks
of September, daily except Monday
9am-12noon, 2-6pm
☎ 93 55 59 93

Musée Franciscain et Monastére de Cimiez
Place du Monastère
Open: all year, daily except Sunday 8am-12.30pm, 2.30-7pm. Closed on official holidays.
☎ 93 81 00 04

Musée d'Art Moderne et d'Art Contemporaire
Promenade des Arts
Open: all year daily except Tuesday 11am-6pm (open until 10pm on Fridays). Closed on official holidays.
☎ 93 62 61 62

Prieuré du Vieux Logis
59 Avenue Barthelemy
Open: all year Wednesday, Thursday, Saturday and first Sunday of the month 3-5pm. At other times by prior appointment.
☎ 93 88 44 74

Gallery-Museum Massa
59 Quai des Etats-Unis
Open: all year Tuesday to Saturday 10.30am-12noon, 2-6pm; Sunday 2-6pm
☎ 93 62 37 11

Gallery-Museum Raoul Dufy
77 Quai des Etats-Unis
Open: all year Tuesday to Saturday 10am-12noon, 2-6pm; Sunday 2-6pm
☎ 93 62 31 24

Parc des Miniatures Côte d'Azur
Boulevard Impératrice Eugénie
Open: all year Wednesday, Saturday, Sunday and official holidays 9am-7pm (5pm for October to May)
☎ 93 44 67 74

Musée des Trains Miniatures
Boulevard Impératrice Eugénie
Open: all year daily 9am-6pm
☎ 93 97 41 40

Phoenix Parc Floral
Promenade des Anglais
Open: April to September daily 9am-7pm; October to March daily 9am-5pm
☎ 93 18 03 33

Roquebrune-Cap Martin

Château Musée
Roquebrune Village
Open: May to September daily 10am-12noon, 2-7pm; October to mid-November, mid-December to April daily except Friday 10am-12noon, 2-5pm
☎ 93 35 07 22

Espace Ananka
1&3 Place de la Sariette
Open: all year Tuesday to Saturday 10.30am-12.30pm, 2-6pm
☎ 93.289766

Le Corbusier's Bungalow
Promenade Le Corbusier
Open: all year by appointment only, at 9.30am on Tuesdays
☎ 93 35 62 87 to add your name to the invitation list.

Roya Valley

Vallée des Merveilles
Information on guides and transport is available at the Tourist Office in Tende
☎ 93 04 73 71

Musée des Merveille
Avenue 16 Septembre 1947
For the opening hours of this new museum ☎ 93 04 61 13 or ask at the Tourist Information Office
☎ 93 04 73 71

Mercantour National Park
Local information office for the park is at the station in St Dalmas de Tende
☎ 93 04 67 00
From June to September there is also an office in Maison de la Minière, l'Authion and at Chalet de Castérino at the head of the road to Fontanable Valley
☎ 93 04 6866

Musée Armée des Alpes
Fort Suchet (Le Barbonnet)
Col St Jean, Sospel
on the D2201 about 15km west of the Roya Valley

Open: July and August Saturday and Sunday 3.30-5.30pm
☎ 93 15 32 57/93 04 15 80

St Jean-Cap-Ferrat

Villa et Jardins Ephrussi de Rothschild
Open: mid-February to November daily 10am-6pm (7pm in July and August); November to mid-Febrary Monday to Friday 2-6pm Saturday and Sunday 10am-6pm
☎ 93 01 33 09

Parc Zoologique
Open: May to September daily 9.30am-7pm (11pm in July and August); October to April daily 9.30am-5pm
☎ 93 76 04 98

Cap Ferrat Lighthouse
Open: daily April to October 9.30am-12noon, 3-6pm; November to March 9.30am-12noon, 3-4.30pm. Lighthouse occasionally closed in bad weather.
☎ 93 76 08 36

St Paul-de-Vence

Fondation Maeght
Route Passe-Prest
St Paul
Open: July to September daily 10am-7pm; October to June daily 10am-12.30pm, 2.30-6pm
☎ 93 32 81 63

Musee d'Historie
Place de la Castre (beside the church and town hall)
Open: all year except mid-November to mid-December, daily 10am-5.30pm (7pm in July and August)
☎ 93 32 53 09

Chapelle du Rosaire
Avenue Henri Matisse
Vence
Open: all year except November to mid-December; Tuesday and Thursday 10-11.30am, 2.30-5.30pm. At other times by prior appointment.
☎ 93 58 03 26

Fondation Emile Hugues
Château des Villeneuve
Place du Frêne
Vence
Open: July to October daily 10am-7pm; December to June daily except Monday 2-6pm. Closed November
☎ 93 58 15 78/93 58 75 75

Musée du Parfum et de la Liqueur
Château Notre-Dame des Fleurs
Route de Grasse
Vence
Open: all year Monday to Saturday 10am-12.30pm, 2-5.30pm (6.30 from March to October); Sunday 2-5.30pm
☎ 93 58 06 00

Musée d'Art Naïf et Medieval
Château de Gourdon
Gourdon
In the Loup Valley, 20km west of Vence on the D3
Open: June to September daily 11am-1pm, 2-7pm; October to May daily except Tuesday 2-6pm
☎ 93 09 68 02

La Turbie

Le Trophée des Alpes
Open: all year daily 9am-12noon, 2-5pm. Closed on official holidays
☎ 93 41 10 11

Vallauris

Musée National Picasso
Place de la Libération
Open: April to September daily except Tuesday 10am-12noon, 2-5pm; October to March daily except Tuesday 2-6pm. Closed on official holidays.
☎ 93 64 18 05

Municipal Museum of Modern Art
Place de la Libération
Open: all year daily except Tuesday 10am-12noon, 2-6pm
☎ 93 64 16 05

Musée de la Poterie
(Pottery Museum)
Rue Sicard
Open: May to September daily 9am-7pm; October to December, February to April daily 10am-12noon, 2-6pm
☎ 93 64 66 51

Villefranche-sur-Mer
Fondation Volti
La Citadelle
Open: July and August Monday, Wednesday-Saturday 10am-12noon, 3-7pm, Sunday 3-7pm; June and September Monday, Wednesday-Saturday 9am-12noon, 3-6pm, Sunday 3-6pm; October, December to May Monday, Wednesday-Saturday 10am-12noon, 2-5pm, Sunday 2-5pm
☎ 93 76 33 27

Musée Goetz-Boumeester
La Citadelle
Open: July and August Monday, Wednesday-Saturday 10am-12noon, 3-7pm, Sunday 3-7pm; June and September Monday, Wednesday-Saturday 9am-12noon, 3-6pm, Sunday 3-6pm; October, December to May Monday, Wednesday-Saturday 10am-12noon, 2-5pm, Sunday 2-5pm
☎ 93 76 33 44

Musée Roux
La Citadelle
Open: June to September Monday, Wednesday-Friday 2.30-6pm; October to May Monday, Wednesday-Friday 2-5pm
☎ 93 76 33 33

Chapelle St Pierre
Port de Villefranche
Open: July to September daily 9am-12noon, 4-8.30pm; October to November daily 9.30am-12noon, 2-6pm; mid-December to March daily 9.30am-12noon, 2-5pm; April to June daily except Friday 9.30am-12noon, 3-7pm
☎ 93 76 90 70

Villeneuve-Loubet
Musée d'Art Culinaire
(Fondation Auguste Escoffier)
3 Rue Escoffier
Open: all year except November daily except Monday 2-6pm (7pm in July and August). Closed on official holidays.
☎ 93 20 80 51

Musée Militaire
Place de Verdun
Open: all year daily except Monday 10am-12noon, 2-5pm. Closed on official holidays
☎ 93 22 01 56

FACTS FOR VISITORS

ACCOMMODATION

* = inexpensive
** = moderate
*** = expensive

Aix-en-Provence
Château de la Pioline***
Les Milles
☎ 42 20 07 81
Fax: 42 59 96 12

Antibes/Juan-les-Pins
Château Fleuri**
Boulevard du Cap
☎ 93 61 38 66
Fax: 93 67 39 22

Arles
Hôtel Nord Pinus***
14 Place du Forum
☎ 90 93 44 44
Fax: 90 93 34 00

Avignon
Hôtel de la Mirande***
Place de l'Amirande
☎ 90 85 93 93
Fax: 90 86 26 85

Barjols
Hôtel Le Pont d'Or*
Rue Eugéne Payan
☎ 94 77 05 23

Baux-de-Provence, Les
Hôtel Bautezar et Musée**
Grand Rue
☎ 90 54 32 09

Beaulieu-sur-Mer
Hôtel Bellevue*
6 Boulevard Paul Déroulède
☎ 93 01 01 70
Fax: 93 01 11 99

Bonnieux
Hôtel de l'Aiguebrun**
Relais de la Combe
☎ 90 74 04 14

Bormes-les-Mimosas
Hôtel Les Palmiers**
Village Cabasson
240 Chemin deu Petit Fort
☎ 94 64 81 94
Fax: 94 64 93 61

Brignoles
Château Brignoles en Provence*
Avenue Dréo
☎ 94 69 06 88

Cannes
Carlton InterContinental***
58 Boulevard de la Croisette
☎ 93 43 44 45
Fax: 93 38 20 90

Cassis
Hôtel Jardins du Campanile**
Rue Auguste Favier
☎ 42 01 84 85
Fax: 42 01 32 38

Châteauneuf du Pape
Château des Fines Roches***
Route d'Avignon
☎ 90 83 70 23
Fax: 90 83 78 42

Cogolin
Coq Hôtel*
Place de la Mairie
☎ 94 54 63 14
Fax: 94 54 03 06

Draguignan

Hôtel Les Etoiles de l'Ange**
Route de Lorgues
☎ 94 68 23 01
Fax: 94 68 13 30

Gordes

Auberge de Carcarille*
Les Gervais
☎ 90 72 02 63

Grasse

Hôtel Palmiers*
17 Boulevard Beaudouin
☎ 93 36 07 24

Lavandou, Le

Hôtel La Petite Bohéme*
5 Avenue F Roosevelt
☎ 94 71 10 30
Fax: 94 64 73 92

Lourmarin

Le Moulin de Lourmarin***
Rue du Temple
☎ 90 68 06 69
Fax: 90 68 31 76

Marseille

Hôtel Concorde Prado***
11 Avenue de Mazargues
☎ 91 76 51 11
Fax: 91 77 95 10

Malaucéne

Hôtel L'Origan*
Cours des Isnards
☎ 90 65 27 08
Fax: 90 65 13 51

Manosque

Hôtel des Quintrands**
Route de Sisteron
☎ 92 72 08 86
Fax: 92 72 80 53

Menton

Hôtel Princess et Richmond**
617 Promenade du Soleil
☎ 93 35 80 20
Fax: 93 57 40 20

Nans-les-Pins

Domaine de Châteauneuf***
☎ 94 78 90 06
Fax: 94 78 63 30

Nice

Hôtel Negresco***
37 Promenade des Anglais
☎ 93 88 39 51
Fax: 93 88 35 68

Nîmes

Le Cheval Blanc***
Place Arènes
☎ 66 76 32 32
Fax: 66 76 32 33

Orange

Hôtel Arène**
Place de Langes
☎ 90 34 10 95
Fax: 90 34 91 62

Salon de Provence

Hôtel Provence*
450 Boulevard Maréchal Foch
☎ 90 56 27 04

Sisteron

Hôtel du Rocher*
7 Rue du Cdt Willmart
☎ 92 61 12 56
Fax: 92 62 65 59

Stes-Maries-de-la-Mer

Hôtel Plage*
95 Boulevard de la République
☎ 90 97 85 09
Fax: 90 28 10 20

St Maximin-la-Ste-Baume

Hôtel de France**
Avenue Albert 1er
☎ 94 78 00 14
Fax: 94 59 83 80

St Rémy-de-Provence

Hôtel Van Gogh**
1 Avenue Jean Moulin
☎ 90 92 14 02
Fax: 90 92 09 05

St Tropez

Hôtel Le Byblos***
Avenue Paul Signac
☎ 94 97 00 04
Fax: 94 97 40 52

Vaison la Romaine

Hôtel Le Beffroi**
Rue de l'Evêché
Haute Ville
☎ 90 36 04 71
Fax: 90 36 24 78

Valensole

Hôtel La Fuste***
☎ 92 72 05 95
Fax: 92 72 92 93

Valréas

Hôtel La Camargue*
49 Cours Jean Jaures
☎ 90 35 01 51
Fax: 90 2810 20

ANNUAL EVENTS

Only the main events are given here. It is worth checking with local Tourist Offices as new events are constantly being added to the programmes of the major, and many minor, resorts.

Aix-en-Provence

Mid-July to mid-August, music festival.

Antibes

Sunday after 29 June, Festival of St Peter, procession to Harbour.

Apt

Whit Sunday and Monday, cavalcade, music festival.
Last week in July, pilgrimage of Ste Anne.

Arles

Easter Friday to Monday, bullfight festival.
Last Sunday in April, *Fête des Gardians*.
July, international festival of music, dance and drama in Roman theatre.
July, international photography festival.
Mid-December to mid-January, *santons* trade fair.

Avignon

Last 3 weeks of July, international drama festival, mainly in Great Courtyard of Palais de Papes.
14 July, fireworks display.
15 July, jousting on Rhône.

Barjols

16 January every 4 years, Fête du St Marcel.

Les Baux

24 December, midnight mass in St Vincent church and pageant of Nativity.

Beaucaire

End July to early August, *fête* to commemorate medieval fair.

Bollène

Last Saturday in June, Fête du Papagaî.

Cannes

February, mimosa festival.

March, photography and amateur cinema festival.

May, international film festival.

July-August, *Nuits des Lérins*.

August, fireworks festival.

September, international yachting festival; royal regattas.

September, festival of vintage cars.

October-November, international golf championships.

Carpentras

July, festival of Notre-Dame de Santé.

Cavaillon

First Monday in September, traditional festival.

Châteaunauf-du-Pape

24 and 25 April, festival of St Marc.

1 May, lily of the valley festival.

Cucuron

Saturday after 21 May, procession with poplar tree in honour of Ste Tulle.

Digne

First Sunday in August, lavender festival.

Entrevaux

Weekend nearest 24 January, festival of St John the Baptist.

Two weeks in August, sixteenth-and seventeenth-century music festival.

Fontaine-de-Vaucluse

Mid-June to mid-September, *son-et-lumière*.

July, *Festival de la Sorgue*.

Fréjus

Third Sunday after Easter, *bravade* costume procession.

Grasse

Last two weeks of July, international amateur music, folk and drama festival.

Graveson

Last Sunday in July, festival of St Eloi.

Ile Ste Marguerite

1 June to 15 September, *son-et-lumière* at fort.

Istres

First Sunday in August, *Fête de St Pierre*, jousting, bullfighting.

Lagnes

Mardi Gras, *Fête du Caramentran*.

Marseille

Two weeks from first Sunday in November, *santons* fair on La Canebière.

Martigues

First Saturday in July, nocturnal cavalcade of jousting boats.

Menton

Week before Shrove Tuesday, lemon festival.

First two weeks of August, international festival of chamber music in floodlit Place de l'Eglise.

Monaco

January, Monte-Carlo motor rally.

27 January, festival of Ste Dévote.

February, international TV festival.

April, international tennis championships.

May, Monaco Grand Prix.

July to August, international fireworks festival.

August to September, world amateur theatre festival.

November, Monégasque National Festival.

December, international circus festival.

Nice

Two weeks before Lent, Carnival, fireworks display (Shrove Tuesday), Battle of Flowers (day after Ash Wednesday).

April, international dog show.

Each Sunday in May, *Fête des Maïs* in Cimiez Gardens.

May, spring music festival.

July, grand jazz parade in Cimiez Gardens.

July, international folklore festival.

August, wine festival in Cimiez Gardens.

October, autumn music festival.

Orange

Last two weeks in July, international music festival in Roman theatre.

Pernes-les-Fontaines

May, international moto-cross.

Roquebrune-Cap Martin

Good Friday evening, procession of the Entombment of Christ.

Afternoon of 5 August, procession of the Passion.

St Paul-de-Vence

Second fortnight in July, *Nuits de la Fondation Maeght*.

St Tropez

16-18 May, *Bravade de St Torpes*.

15 June, *Fête des Espagnols*, the Spanish *bravade*.

Once a month in July and August, classical concerts in Citadel.

La Ste Baume

21-2 July, festival of Mary Magdalene and midnight mass.

Les Ste Maries-de-la-Mer

24-5 May, *Pèlerinage des Gitanes*, gipsy celebrations.

Sunday nearest 24 July, *Fête Virginenco*.

Weekend nearest 22 October, gipsy pilgrimage.

Séguret

April to September, ethnological exhibition.

Second fortnight in August, Provençal festival.

July to August, and December to January, exhibition of *santons* (clay figurines).

Third Sunday in August, *bravade*.

24 December, mystery play.

Sisteron

Mid-July and mid-August, festival of drama, music and dance.

Tarascon

Last Sunday in June, Fête de la Tarasque.

Toulon

April, flower festival.

July to August, festival of circus artistes.

November, *santons* fair.

Vaison-la-Romaine

Early July, international folklore festival.

Mid-July to mid-August, theatre and music festival in Roman theatre.

First Sunday after 15 August, Provençal mystery play.

Valréas

23 June at 10.15pm, nocturnal procession of 'Petit St Jean' (500 years old).

July and August, musical evenings, theatre.

First Sunday and Monday in August, lavender fair.

Christmas to January, *santons* cribs.

Vence

Easter Sunday and Monday, Battle of Flowers, Provençal dancing.

Villeneuve-lès-Avignon

End April, festival of St Marc. July, international summer festival of music, dancing, theatre, poetry, art and cultural exhibitions, workshops.

CONSULATES-GENERAL

Great Britain
24 Avenue du Prado
Marseille
☎ 91 53 43 32

United States of America
9 Rue Armeny
Marseille
☎ 91 54 92 00

1 Rue du Maréchal-Joffre
Nice
☎ 93 88 89 55

Canada
24 Avenue du Prado
Marseille
☎ 91 37 19 37/37 19 40

CUSTOMS REGULATIONS

Normal European Union customs regulations apply for those travelling from Britain. Normal European regulations apply for those travelling from North America.

DISABLED VISITORS

Not all the sites listed in this guide are accessible to disabled visitors. A list of those that are, not only in Provence/Côte d'Azure but in the whole of France, can be found in the publication *Touristes quand même! Promenades en France*

pour les voyageurs handicapés. This excellent guide can be obtained from:
Comité National Français de Liaison pour la Réadaptiondes Handicapés
38 Boulevard Raspail
75007 Paris
It will be of interest not only to those with a physical handicap, but to the visually handicapped and visitors with a hearing difficulty.

ELECTRICITY

220V AC, 50 Hertz (cycles/sec) in most places. Some small areas are still at 110V AC. Adaptors will be needed by those who do not use continental two-pin plugs at home.

ENTRY INTO FRANCE

No visa is required for holders of British, American and Canadian passports.

HEALTH CARE

British travellers have a right to claim health services in France by virtue of EU regulations. Form E111 — available from the Department of Health and Social Security — should be obtained to avoid complications.

American and Canadian visitors will need to check the validity of their personal health insurances to guarantee they are adequately covered. For emergency assistance, dial 19 in all towns. In country areas it may be necessary to phone the local *gendarmerie* (police).

Pharmacies, clearly marked with a green cross, can usually deal with minor ailments or advise people where to go if any additional help is needed.

Measurements

France uses the metric system. Conversions are:
1 kilogram (1,000 grams) = 2.2lb
1 litre = 1¾ pints
4.5 litres = 1 gallon
1.6km = 1 mile
1 hectare = 2½ acres (approx)

Money

The French unit of currency is the French franc. There are no restrictions on the import of French or foreign currency but amounts must be declared if bank notes worth in excess of 5,000 French francs are likely to be exported.

All major credit cards (Visa, MasterCard, Access, American Express etc) are accepted at most large restaurants, hotels, shops and garages. Eurocheques and traveller's cheques are also accepted.

Banks are normally open 9am-12noon, 2-4.30pm, Monday to Friday only. They close early on the day before a Bank Holiday.

National Holidays

France has the following national holidays:
New Year's Day
Easter Monday
May Day
Ascension Day
VE Day — 8 May
Whit Monday
Bastille Day — 14 July
Assumption Day — 15 August
All Saints' Day — 1 November
Armistice Day — 11 November
Christmas Day

Post & Telephone Services

Stamps (*timbres*) are available from post offices, which are normally open 8am-7pm Monday to Friday and 8am-12noon on Saturday. In some smaller towns and villages, the post office may be shut for lunch, both the timing and the duration of the break being a local custom.

Telephones in France take coins rather than tokens. The dial codes from France are:

Great Britain	19	44
Canada	19	1
USA	19	1

Remember to leave out the first zero of your home country number — eg to dial the French Government Tourist Office in London (071 491 7622) from France, dial 19 44 17 491 7622. Many telephone booths now take phonecards; buy the *télécarte* from post offices and where advertised on telephone booths. Calls can be received at phone boxes with a blue bell.

RESTAURANTS

   * = inexpensive
   ** = moderate
   *** = expensive

Aix-en-Provence
L'Abbaye des Cordeliers***
21 Rue Lieutaud
☎ 42 27 29 47

Le Clos de la Violette***
10 Avenue de la Violette
☎ 42 23 30 71

Antibes
Le Bacon***
Boulevard de Bacon
Cap d'Antibes
☎ 93 61 50 02

Apt
Auberge du Luberon**
17 Quai Léon Sagy
☎ 90 04 79 49

Arles
Le Vaccarès**
11 Rue Favorin
☎ 90 96 06 17

Avignon
Christian Etienne**
10 Rue de Mons
☎ 90 86 16 50

Hiély-Lucullus***
5 Rue de la République
☎ 90 86 17 07

Baux-de-Provence, Les-
L'Oustau de Baumanière***
Le Vallon ☎ 90 54 33 07

Brignoles
Le Mas la Cascade**
La Celle (near Brignoles)
☎ 94 69 01 49

Cannes
Au Bec Fin*
12 Rue du 24-Août
☎ 93 38 35 86

Carpentras
L'Orangerie*
26 Rue Duplessis ☎ 90 67 27 23

Cassis
El Sol**
23 Quai des Baux
☎ 42 01 76 10

Castellane
Ma Petite Auberge*
8 Boulevard de la République
☎ 92 83 62 06

Comps-sur-Artuby
Grand Hôtel Bain**
☎ 94 76 90 06

Cavaillon
Le Prévôt***
353 Avenue de Verdun
☎ 90 71 32 43

Gordes
Comptoir du Victualler**
Place du Château
☎ 90 72 01 31

Fonatine-de-Vaucluse
Hostellerie du Château*
Quartier Petit Prince
☎ 90 20 31 54

Garde-Freinet, La
Faücado*
31 Boulevard de l'Esplanade
☎ 94 43 60 41

Grimaud
La Bretonnière***
Place des Pénitents
☎ 94 43 25 26

Hyéres
Chez Marius*
Place Massillon
☎ 94 35 83 13

Marseille
Chez Fonfon***
140 Rue du Vallon des Auffes
☎ 91 52 14 38

Ménerbes
Hostellerie Le Roy Soleil***
Route des Beaumettes
☎ 90 72 25 61

Monte Carlo
Maison de Caviar**
1 Avenue St-Charles
☎ 93 30 80 06

Nice
Ane Rouge***
7 Quai des Deux-Emmanuel
☎ 93 89 49 63

Queenie**
19 Promenade des Anglais
☎ 93 88 52 50

Nîmes
Le Magister***
5 Rue Nationale
☎ 66 76 11 00

Tarterie Delices*
Place aux Herbes
☎ 66 36 33 16

Pont de Gau (Camargue)
Restaurant Pont de Gau*
☎ 90 97 81 53

Orange
Le Pigraillet***
Colline St Eutrope
☎ 90 34 44 25

Remoulins
Le Vieux Mouin*
☎ 66 37 14 35

Roquebrune-Cap-Martin
Les Lucioles*
12 Avenue Poincaré
☎ 93 35 02 19

Roussillon
Le David*
Place de la Poste
☎ 90 05 60 13

Séguret
La Table du Comtat**
☎ 90 46 91 49

St-Maximin-la-Ste-Baume
Chez Nous*
3 Boulevard Jean-Jaurés
☎ 94 78 02 57

St Rémy-de-Provence
Des Arts**
30 Boulevard Victor Hugo
☎ 90 92 08 50

St Tropez
Le Mas de Chastelas**
Route de Gassin
☎ 94 56 09 11

SPORT

The South of France has one of the highest concentrations of sporting facilities in Europe, covering the whole spectrum of sport and more are being added all the time. They range from watersports

— at their best here in the warm waters of the Mediterranean — to hang gliding, rock climbing, and skiing in the mountains of the pre-Alps.

It would be impossible to provide a comprehensive glossary of the sports available in the area. However, two facilities do bear special mention. The first is golf, the area having seen an increase in both the number and quality of courses in recent years.

The second is walking on the superb French system of way-marked footpaths, the Sentiers de *Grande Randonnée*. Five routes (GRs 4, 5, 6, 9 and 52) of varying difficulty cross some of the region's most striking scenery. They are part of a network covering the whole country, and their Provençal sections are marked on Michelin maps 81 and 84 (1:200,000) by broken lines together with their identification numbers (GR4, GR5 etc).

Detailed illustrated guides, known as *Topo-guides*, can be bought at local bookshops. More information can be obtained from Fédération Français de la Randonnée Pédestre, 64 rue de Gerovie, 75014 Paris.
☎ 45 45 31 02

TIPPING

Tips (*pourboires*) are given as in your home country but in France they also apply to guides at both *châteaux* and museums.

TOURIST INFORMATION OFFICES

French Government Tourist Offices
Great Britain
178 Piccadily
London W1V 0AL
☎ 071 491 7622

United States of America
610 Fifth Avenue Suite 222
New York
NY 10020-2452
☎ 212 757 1683

Canada
1981 Avenue McGill College
Tour Esso Suite 490
Montreal
Quebec H3A 2W9
☎ 514 288 4264

Tourist Offices in France
Almost all towns and many villages have their own *Syndicats d'Initiative* and these will supply local information and maps.
The main offices are listed below.

Aix-en-Provence
2 Place du Général de Gaulle
☎ 42 26 11 61

Arles
Esplanade Charles de Gaulle
☎ 90 18 41 20

Avignon
41 Cours Jean-Jaurès
☎ 90 82 65 11

Cannes
Palais des Festivals
Esplanade President-Georges-Pompidou
☎ 93 39 24 53

Marseille
4 Le Canebière
☎ 91 54 91 11

Monaco
2A Boulevard des Moulins
☎ 92 16 61 16

Nice
Gare SNCF
Avenue Thiers
☎ 93 87 07 07

Toulon
8 Avenue Colbert
☎ 94 22 08 22

TRAVEL

By Air

Provence is served by the international airport of Marseille-Provence, situated to the north-west of the city on the shore of the Etang de Berre, north of the town of Marignane. There is an excellent, direct road connection with the A7 autoroute.

The Côte d'Azur is served by the international airport of Nice-Côte d'Azur, situated above the Mediterranean at the south-western end of the town. It, too, is well connected to the *autoroute* system.

Both airports are served by international flights and also have regular services to Paris.

There is an airport served by domestic flights to the south-east of Hyères. There are also smaller airports served by more infrequent flights at Nîmes and Fréjus-St Raphaël.

Finally, there is a helicopter link between Nice-Côte d'Azur airport and Monaco.

Rail

The French national railway company, SNCF (Systéme National de Chemin-de-Fer), has both fast and express trains linking Provence and the Côte d'Azur with other parts of France and the Channel ports. Of particular interest to the traveller keen to cut down on travel time is the TGV (pronounced Tay-Jay-Vay) service, a very fast 250kph (155mph) bullet-shaped train that speeds between Paris and the South. The TGV offers only first-class accommodation but does cut journey time considerably.

SNCF also offer motorail services to those not wishing to spend a part of their holiday gazing at the ribbon of the Autoroute du Soleil. These services are available from the Channel ports, but not to Marseille, the most desirable destination for the traveller who has just crossed to France. To use the service to reach Marseille — or to reach Avignon, Toulon, Fréjus-St Raphaël or Nice — the traveller must first reach Paris. The service is not cheap but the journey is overnight, which does have the advantage of extending the holiday by a day if travelling is not considered to be part of the holiday. Night-time accommodation is in a couchette — six berths, in three tiers, to a compartment, with blanket and pillow supplied — or in T1, T2 or T3 cabins. As the names imply, these offer one (first class ticket only), two or three berths. Breakfast at the destination is included in the price of the ticket.

Road

Coaches & Buses

France has an extensive, long-distance coach system and good local bus services. Not surprisingly, the majority of long-distance coach services head for Paris.

Cars

France has an excellent network of autoroutes backed up by a good system of 'ordinary' routes. The south of the country is served by the Autoroute du Soleil, the A7, that links it with Paris and the Channel ports. The A7 follows the Rhône Valley to Orange, where the A9 leaves it to reach Nîmes, continuing to Avignon and Salon-de-Provence. To the south of Salon, the A8 heads off east to Cannes and Nice, while the A7 continues south to Marseille and Toulon. French *autoroutes* are toll roads but they do offer a much quicker and, for those not used to driving on the right, safer way to travel. Quicker they may be, but it is still over 1,100km (700 miles) from the Channel to the South, so several days should be taken over the journey.

Car Hire

Car hire is available from many companies, including all the well-known major European ones, and from all the big towns, the airports and all large railway stations.

Speed Limits & Driving Regulations

The speed limits currently applied to French roads are:

	In dry conditions	In the wet
Autoroutes	130kph (81mph)	110kph (68mph)
National (N) roads	110kph (68mph)	90kph (56mph)
Other roads	90kph (56mph)	80kph (50mph)
In towns	50kph (31mph)	65kph (40mph)

Note that there are new speed limits on *autoroutes* : a minimum of 80kph (50mph) for the outside lane during daylight, on level ground and with good visibility; and a maximum of 50kph (31mph) if the visibility is less than 50m.

No driving is permitted on a provisional licence and the minimum age to drive is 18. Stop signs mean that vehicles **must** come to a complete halt.

It is compulsory for front seat passengers to wear seat belts and children below the age of 10 are not allowed to travel in the front seats. All vehicles must carry a red warning triangle and a spare headlamp bulb.

There are strict — and very strictly interpreted — laws on speeding and drink-driving. The former will usually result in an on-the-spot fine, while the latter will usually result in confiscation of the car.

In built-up areas motorists must give way to anybody coming out of a side-turning on the right. This is indicated by the sign, *priorité à droite*. However, this rule no longer applies at roundabouts which means vehicles already on the roundabout have right of way (*passage protégé*). All roads of any significance outside built-up areas have right of way.

Car Parking

Car parking is no easier in French towns than it is in most other large European cities. The by-laws vary from town to town and, occasionally, from day to day. To be safe it is best to use car parks. Check before leaving your parked car: it is common practice to take your ticket with you, to pay as you return and to use the stamped ticket or token to raise the exit barrier. If you drive to an exit and then discover this rule, it is likely that you will have a queue of cars behind you when you are trying to work out what has gone wrong or are trying to reverse. Since tokens are time-limited, the queue is unlikely to be sympathetic.

Index

Visitor's Guides

Let us guide you again! If you have enjoyed this book then we have many more in this series to choose from

MPC

Austria:
Austria
Austria: Tyrol &
Vorarlberg

Britain:
Cornwall & Isles of
Scilly
Cotswolds
Devon
East Anglia
Guernsey, Alderney,
Herm & Sark
Hampshire & Isle of
Wight
Jersey
Kent
Lake District
Scotland
Somerset, Dorset &
Wiltshire
North Wales &
Snowdonia
North York Moors,
York & Coast
Northern Ireland
Peak District
Yorkshire Dales &
North Pennines

Belgium:
Belgium & Luxem-
bourg
Bruges

Canada
Cuba
Cyprus
Czech & Slovak
Republics
Prague
Denmark
Egypt

France:
France
Alps & Jura

Brittany
Burgundy &
Beaujolais
Champagne &
Alsace-Lorraine
Corsica
Dordogne
Gascony & Midi
Pyrenees
Loire
Massif Central
Normandy
Normandy Landing
Beaches
Provence & Côte
d'Azur
Vendee & Poitou-
Charentes

Germany:
Bavaria
Black Forest
Rhine & Mosel
Southern Germany

Greece:
Greece (mainland)
Athens & Pelopon-
nese
Crete
Rhodes

Holland
Hungary
Iceland & Greenland

India:
Delhi, Agra &
Rajasthan
Goa
Kerola

Italy:
Florence & Tuscany
Italian Lakes
Northern Italy
Sardinia
Southern Italy

Jamaica
Malta & Gozo
Mauritius, Rodrigues
& Reunion
Windward Islands
New Zealand
Norway

Portugal:
Portugal
Madeira

Seychelles

Spain:
Costa Brava
& Costa Blanca
Gran Canaria
Mallorca, Menorca,
Ibiza & Formentera
Northern & Central
Spain
Southern Spain
& Costa del Sol
Tenerife

South Africa
Sri Lanka
Sweden
Switzerland
Thailand
Turkey

USA:
California
Florida
Massachusetts,
Rhode Island &
Connecticut
Orlando & Central
Florida
South West National
Parks
USA
Vermont, New
Hampshire &
Maine

We also have many other guides. Send for your free catalogue for the full listing from: Moorland Publishing Co Ltd, Moor Farm Road, Ashbourne, Derbys DE6 1HD, UK ☎ 01335 344486
or Hunter Publishing Inc, 300 Raritan Center Parkway, Edison, NJ 08818, USA

Published by: Moorland Publishing Co Ltd,
Moor Farm Road West, Ashbourne, Derbyshire DE6 1HD England

Published in the USA by: Hunter Publishing Inc,
300 Raritan Center Parkway, CN94, Edison, NJ 08818

ISBN 0 86190 625 X

1st edition 1984,
2nd revised edition 1990
3rd rewritten and redesigned edition 1996

British Library Cataloguing in Publication Data:
A catalogue record for this book is available from the British Library

Colour origination by: GA Graphics, Stamford
Printed in Honk Kong by: South China Printing Co (1988) Ltd

Front cover: Menton *(Richard Sale)*
Title page: Jardin Exotique at Eze on the Côte d'Azur *(Richard Sale)*

Illustrations have been supplied by: Comité Regionale du Tourisme Côte d'Azur
pages 19, 35 top; Comité Regionale du Tourisme Longuedoc-Roussillon page 99,
102 top, Comité Regionale du Tourisme Provence page 154 lower right. All the
remaining photographs have been taken by the author.

Acknowledgements

The author would like to thank Elizabeth Powell of the French Government
Tourist Office in London for her assistance during the preparation of this book.
    He would also like to thank those people in Tourist Offices in the South of
France who assisted him for their help and kindness. There are many such people,
but it would be unfair not to thank Martine Duffaud and Veronique Seban of the
Nice office, and Sylvie Keuillan of the Marseille office, personally for their help.